Thomas Ken

Christian Year

Hymns and poems for the holy days and festivals of the church

Thomas Ken

Christian Year
Hymns and poems for the holy days and festivals of the church

ISBN/EAN: 9783337082987

Printed in Europe, USA, Canada, Australia, Japan

Cover: Foto ©Lupo / pixelio.de

More available books at **www.hansebooks.com**

BISHOP KEN'S

Christian Year

OR HYMNS AND POEMS FOR THE HOLY

DAYS AND FESTIVALS OF

THE CHURCH

LONDON

BASIL MONTAGU PICKERING

196 PICCADILLY

1868

PREFACE.

FOR more than a century and a half the name of Bishop Ken has been associated with the three opening Hymns of this Collection, which since their first publication in 1700, at the end of a Manual of Prayers which he compiled for the use of the scholars of Winchester College, have perhaps enjoyed more popularity, and been more sung in our churches, than any similar compositions in the language. In the meantime, the equally fine Hymns on the Christian Festivals, published posthumously in 1721, have been undeservedly neglected, though they have been highly praised by the late John Keble, who was probably indebted to them for the idea of his own " Christian Year."

Many, therefore, who reverence the name of Ken and love to linger on the details of his holy and self-denying career—who look up to him as the model of a Christian bishop—will now learn for the first time what a rich legacy of sacred verse he left behind him, and what a new claim he has to their admiration and love.

Poetical blood flowed in his veins; for he was descended on his mother's side from John Chalkhill, the author of " Thealma and Clearchus." Left an orphan in 1651, at the early age of fourteen, he had the advantage of being nurtured in the love of all that is beautiful and pure by one of the gentlest and tenderest spirits of the seventeenth century—Izaak Walton, who had married his elder sister Ann in 1646. Having spent so many years in familiar intercourse with such a mind, it is no wonder that he became a poet.

The tale of his saintly and devoted life has been told so often and so well, that there is no need to dwell on it here. It is only necessary to refer the reader to the narratives of Hawkins, Bowles, and Markland, and last but not least to the exhaustive " Life of Bishop Ken by a Layman," published by the late William Pickering in 1848.

These hymns were the one consoling occupation of his declining years, when, deprived of his wealth and honours for conscience' sake and suffering the direst tortures of physical pain, he was looking forward with longing eyes to that "rest prepared for the people of God," to which he had spent his life in showing the way.

The reader must not expect to find in his verse the mellifluous smoothness of a later age. With Cowley and the "metaphysical school" as models, his diction is necessarily somewhat obsolete and his style diffuse, and he indulges sometimes in a vein of conceit that has long been out of fashion. This will not invalidate his claim to a high place among our earlier sacred poets—for Herbert, Crashaw and Quarles, Vaughan and Wither, if they shared with him in his excellencies, shared with him also in his most characteristic faults. The hallowed atmosphere of devotion that impregnates every line will endear him to all good churchmen of the olden type: his lips seem for ever touched with a live coal from off the Altar. Occafional quaintnefs will be condoned for the fake of the holy thoughts and afpirations which abound in the poetry of Thomas Ken.

CONTENTS.

	PAGE
A MORNING Hymn	1
An Evening Hymn	3
A Midnight Hymn	5
Advent Sunday. *Days Numbered*	7
Second Sunday in Advent. *Judgment*	11
Third Sunday in Advent. *Resurrection*	13
Fourth Sunday in Advent	16
Christmas Day	17
St. Stephen's Day	22
St. John the Evangelist's Day	28
The Holy Innocents	34
First Sunday after Christmas. *God a Father*	39
The Circumcision	43
Second Sunday after Christmas. *On the Nativity*	47
The Epiphany	53
First Sunday after Epiphany	58
Second Sunday after Epiphany. *Christ-like Love*	65
Third Sunday after Epiphany. *The Saints with Jesus*	67
Fourth Sunday after Epiphany. *Omnipotence*	69
Fifth Sunday after Epiphany	73
Sixth Sunday after Epiphany. *The Trumpet*	75
Septuagesima Sunday. *Justice*	78
Sexagesima Sunday	82

CONTENTS.

	PAGE
Quinquagesima Sunday	83
Ash Wednesday	86
First Sunday in Lent. *The Temptation*	92
Second Sunday in Lent	99
Third Sunday in Lent	101
Fourth Sunday in Lent. *The Life of Jesus*	104
Fifth Sunday in Lent. *God's Attributes*	112
Sunday next before Easter. *Name of Jesus*	117
Monday before Easter. *On the Agony*	120
Tuesday before Easter. *The Arraignment of Jesus*	127
Wednesday before Easter. *The Passion*	138
Thursday before Easter	149
Good Friday	152
Easter-Eve	163
Easter Day	165
Monday in Easter Week	173
Tuesday in Easter Week. *The Resurrection*	179
First Sunday after Easter. *Jesus on Tabor*	188
Second Sunday after Easter	191
Third Sunday after Easter	194
Fourth Sunday after Easter	195
Fifth Sunday after Easter	198
Ascension Day, or Holy Thursday	199
Sunday after Ascension Day. *Jesus Present*	208
Whit Sunday	211
Monday in Whitsun Week. *All Blessings by Jesus*	218
Tuesday in Whitsun Week	222
Trinity Sunday	227
First Sunday after Trinity	233
Second Sunday after Trinity. *God is Love*	237
Third Sunday after Trinity	242
Fourth Sunday after Trinity	244
Fifth Sunday after Trinity. *Life*	247
Sixth Sunday after Trinity. *Jesus our All in All*	251
Seventh Sunday after Trinity	254
Eighth Sunday after Trinity	257

CONTENTS.

	PAGE
Ninth Sunday after Trinity	259
Tenth Sunday after Trinity. *Jesus' Love preserved*	264
Eleventh Sunday after Trinity. *Jesus our Priest*	267
Twelfth Sunday after Trinity. *Likeness to Jesus*	271
Thirteenth Sunday after Trinity	274
Fourteenth Sunday after Trinity	276
Fifteenth Sunday after Trinity. *The Sermon on the Mount*	279
Sixteenth Sunday after Trinity. *Love taught by Jesus*	287
Seventeenth Sunday after Trinity. *Unity*	291
Eighteenth Sunday after Trinity	295
Nineteenth Sunday after Trinity	297
Twentieth Sunday after Trinity	299
Twenty-first Sunday after Trinity	303
Twenty-second Sunday after Trinity. *Prayer for Love*	305
Twenty-third Sunday after Trinity. *Heaven first sought*	308
Twenty-fourth Sunday after Trinity. *Heaven*	311
Twenty-fifth Sunday after Trinity. *Jesus our King*	314
St. Andrew's Day	318
St. Thomas the Apostle	322
Conversion of St. Paul	326
Purification of St. Mary the Virgin	334
St. Matthias' Day	339
Annunciation of the Blessed Virgin Mary	345
St. Mark's Day	352
St. Philip and St. James's Day	357
St. Barnabas the Apostle	362
St. John Baptist's Day	369
St. Peter's Day	374
St. James the Apostle	382
St. Bartholomew the Apostle	387
St. Matthew the Apostle	394
St. Michael and all Angels	400

CONTENTS.

	PAGE
St. Luke the Evangelist	405
St. Simon and St. Jude, Apostles	411
All Saints' Day	418

Holy Baptism	425
Confirmation	427
The Holy Eucharist	429
Absolution	432
The Visitation of the Sick	439
Holy Order	444
Matrimony	451

APPENDIX—
    First Version of the Three Hymns printed in the Manual of Prayers for the Scholars of Winchester College 455

A MORNING HYMN.

WAKE, my soul, and with the sun
Thy daily stage of duty run,
Shake off dull sloth, and joyful rise,
To pay thy morning sacrifice.

Thy precious time misspent, redeem,
Each present day thy last esteem,
Improve thy talent with due care,
For the Great Day thyself prepare.

In conversation be sincere,
Keep conscience as the noon-tide clear,
Think how All-seeing God thy ways,
And all thy secret thoughts surveys.

By influence of the Light Divine,
Let thy own light to others shine,
Reflect all Heaven's propitious rays,
In ardent love, and cheerful praise.

'Wake, and lift up thyself, my heart,
And with the angels bear thy part,

Who all night long unwearied sing,
High praise to the Eternal King.

I wake, I wake, ye Heavenly Choir,
May your devotion me inspire,
That I like you my age may spend,
Like you may on my God attend.

May I like you in God delight,
Have all day long my God in sight,
Perform like you my Maker's Will,
O may I never more do ill.

Had I your wings to Heaven I'd fly,
But God shall that defect supply,
And my soul wing'd with warm desire,
Shall all day long to Heaven aspire.

All praise to Thee, Who safe hast kept,
And hast refresh'd me whilst I slept,
Grant, Lord, when I from death shall wake,
I may of endless Light partake.

I would not wake, nor rise again,
Ev'n Heaven itself I would disdain,
Wert not Thou there to be enjoy'd,
And I in hymns to be employ'd.

Heaven is, dear Lord, where'er Thou art,
O never then from me depart:
For to my soul, 'tis hell to be
But for one moment void of Thee.

Lord, I my vows to Thee renew,
Disperse my sins as morning dew,
Guard my first springs of thought and will,
And with Thyself my spirit fill.

Direct, control, suggest, this day,
All I design, or do, or say,
That all my powers, with all their might,
In Thy sole glory may unite.

Praise God, from Whom all blessings flow,
Praise Him, all creatures here below;
Praise Him above, ye Heavenly Host;
Praise Father, Son, and Holy Ghost.

AN EVENING HYMN.

ALL praise to Thee, my God, this night,
For all the blessings of the light;
Keep me, O keep me, King of kings,
Beneath Thy own Almighty Wings.

Forgive me, Lord, for Thy dear Son,
The ill that I this day have done;
That with the world, myself and Thee,
I, ere I sleep, at peace may be.

Teach me to live, that I may dread
The grave as little as my bed;

To die, that this vile body may
Rise glorious at the awful day.

O! may my soul on Thee repose,
And may sweet sleep my eyelids close;
Sleep that may me more vigorous make,
To serve my God when I awake.

When in the night I sleepless lie,
My soul with heavenly thoughts supply;
Let no ill dreams disturb my rest,
No powers of darkness me molest.

Dull sleep of sense me to deprive,
I am but half my time alive,
Thy faithful lovers, Lord, are grieved
To lie so long of Thee bereaved.

But tho' sleep o'er my frailty reigns,
Let it not hold me long in chains;
And now and then let loose my heart,
Till it an Hallelujah dart.

The faster sleep the senses binds,
The more unfetter'd are our minds,
O may my soul, from matter free,
Thy loveliness unclouded see!

O when shall I in endless Day,
For ever chase dark sleep away;
And hymns with the Supernal Choir,
Incessant sing, and never tire!

O may my guardian while I sleep,
Close to my bed his vigils keep;
His love angelical instil;
Stop all the avenues of ill.

May he celestial joy rehearse,
And thought to thought with me converse,
Or in my stead, all the night long,
Sing to my God a grateful song.

Praise God, from Whom all blessings flow,
Praise Him, all creatures here below;
Praise Him above, ye Heavenly Host;
Praise Father, Son, and Holy Ghost.

A MIDNIGHT HYMN.

MY God, now I from sleep awake,
The sole possession of me take,
From midnight terrors me secure,
And guard my heart from thoughts impure.

Bless'd Angels! while we silent lie,
You Hallelujahs sing on high,
You joyful hymn the Ever-Bless'd,
Before the Throne and never rest.

I with your choir celestial join,
In offering up a hymn divine,
With you in Heaven I hope to dwell,
And bid the night and world farewell.

My soul, when I shake off this dust,
Lord, in Thy Arms I will intrust:
O make me Thy peculiar care,
Some mansion for my soul prepare.

Give me a place at Thy saints' feet,
Or some fall'n angel's vacant seat;
I'll strive to sing as loud as they
Who sit above in brighter day.

O may I always ready stand,
With my lamp burning in my hand;
May I in sight of Heaven rejoice,
Whene'er I hear the Bridegroom's voice.

All praise to Thee in light array'd,
Who light Thy dwelling-place hast made,
A boundless ocean of bright beams
From Thy all-glorious God-head streams.

The sun in its meridian height
Is very darkness in Thy sight!
My soul, O lighten and enflame,
With thought and love of Thy Great Name.

Bless'd Jesu, Thou on Heaven intent,
Whole nights hast in devotion spent;
But I, frail creature, soon am tired,
And all my zeal is soon expired.

My soul, how canst thou weary grow
Of antedating bliss below,

In facred hymns, and heavenly love,
Which will eternal be above.

Shine on me, Lord, new life impart,
Frefh ardours kindle in my heart;
One ray of Thy all-quickening Light
Difpels the floth and clouds of night.

Lord, left the tempter me furprife,
Watch over Thine own facrifice;
All loofe, all idle thoughts caft out,
And make my very dreams devout.

Praife God, from Whom all bleffings flow,
Praife Him, all creatures here below;
Praife Him above, ye Heavenly Hoft;
Praife Father, Son, and Holy Ghoft.

ADVENT SUNDAY.

Days Numbered.

And that, knowing the time, that now it is high time to awake out of fleep: for now is our falvation nearer than when we believed. The night is far fpent, the day is at hand; let us therefore caft off the works of darknefs, and let us put on the armour of light.—*Romans* xiii. 11, 12.

GOD a command upon me lays,
    Rightly to number all my days,
Of all paft, prefent, and to come,
    To caft the fum.

ADVENT SUNDAY.

That gracious God may be obey'd,
I call arithmetic to aid,
The sum, to which they all amount,
    I strive to count.

But soon as I begin to cast,
The number of my days now past,
All look like an evanid dream,
    All cyphers seem.

My Now when I minutely weigh,
'Tis but a moment, not a day,
My Future is to all unknown,
    But God alone.

I then arithmetic suspect,
And on the past again reflect,
To number not by days but sins,
    My soul begins.

When I thus calculate my years,
Each guilty day an age appears,
Time tedious is which we misspend
    God to offend.

My sins to such vast numbers swell,
Which no arithmetic can tell;
Their multitude, which has no bounds,
    My soul confounds.

My cyphers I to figures change,
And in a total fain would range;

But when I resurvey the score,
    I still find more.

And yet a sum much greater lies
Hid from my intellectual eyes,
Of sins forgot whose guilt remains,
    And crimson stains.

Lord, in Thy book they are enroll'd,
O might I there the sum behold,
That I the debt immense may know
    Which there I owe.

With fountains, Lord, supply my head,
A wave for every sin I'd shed,
I'd strive to pay the full in tear,
    My debt to clear.

But should the streams which from me flow,
Up to a new Atlantic grow,
'Twould not the obligations pay
    Of but one day.

The Blood of dying God alone,
Can for my vast arrears atone;
His Merits far my sins exceed:
    Them, Lord, I plead.

Accept my plea, and when that's done,
While I my future race shall run,
I'll not by sins, but duties rate,
    My future state.

I'll every morn my vows renew,
I'll God retain all day in view,
My conscience court in me shall keep,
    Before I sleep.

Conscience, you made me first awake,
Due care to keep me waking take,
Mind me of duty, steer my will,
    And guard from ill.

My past lost moments I disclaim,
My present shall at duty aim,
And all my future as they glide,
    To Heaven I'll guide.

I then no more the fool shall act,
Or friendship with the world contract,
Or squander precious time, to gain
    Eternal pain.

But duly numbering all my days,
I shall a stock of wisdom raise,
And from the hours I well employ,
    Reap endless joy.

SECOND SUNDAY IN ADVENT.

Judgment.

And then shall they see the Son of man coming in a cloud with power and great glory.—*Luke* xxi. 27.

WHEN the Arch-angel's trump shall sound,
And warn the world in stupors drown'd,
At God's Tribunal to appear,
Hell-powers the voice shall quivering hear,
The earth shall quake from pole to pole,
The orbs celestial trembling roll:

The dead shall in their graves awake,
The hearts of all the living quake,
Good Angels shall the sound revere,
And God adore with humble fear;
God-man the Judge shall ready stand,
To leave His Throne at God's Right-Hand.

Supernal Hosts who beams diffuse,
Through arched Heaven shall rendezvous;
Horses and chariots, with which God
In triumph through the waters rode,
Shall to the Heavenly Gates repair,
To wait on Jesus in the air.

The Angels at His march shall shout,
And all the way, with zeal devout,
Shall hymns to the Incarnate King
Of Mercy, and of Justice, sing;
They'll then His Throne in air erect,
That all the world He may inspect.

God-man His Angels will enjoin,
Saints' hallow'd dust to re-enshrine,
And when their souls they re-embrace,
Waft them to see His blissful Face;
The Saints they'll in their chariots drive,
'Till they at Jesus' Throne arrive.

Damn'd souls shall then too late, in vain
Bewail their sins which caused their pain,
They'll wish eternally to die,
Or buried under rocks to lie,
In vain their wishes will be made,
No guilt God's Judgment can evade.

The heavenly book shall be unclosed,
The secrets of all hearts exposed;
God and their conscience saints will clear,
They'll plead not perfect, but sincere;
To their mild Judge they'll make appeals,
Who with His Blood their pardon seals.

The guilty sinners, self-condemn'd,
Who Jesus' laws and cross contemn'd,

Defpairing to decline their fate,
With horror fhall their doom await;
No force of language can difclofe,
Saints' raptures, or curfed finners' woes.

Go, Curfed, doom'd to endlefs pain,
Come, Saints, in endlefs blifs to reign,
Good Angels thence fhall Saints attend,
With Jefus they'll to Heaven afcend;
Curfed fiends fhall drag the damn'd to hell,
In everlafting pains to yell.

All praife to God, who here below,
Prolongs my choice of blifs or woe;
My paft ill choice may I deplore,
Fear hell, but fear offending more,
Keep a tribunal in my mind,
And have by God my pardon fign'd.

THIRD SUNDAY IN ADVENT.

Refurrection.

Judge nothing before the time, until the Lord come.
1 *Cor.* iv. 5.

GREAT Day! to mortals kept unknown,
When an Archangel from the throne
Shall on his radiant wings appear,
And hovering o'er this lower fphere,

His trumpet blow, whose mighty sound
Shall undulate the globe around.

All separate souls where'er they dwell,
In the out-courts of Heaven or hell,
Soon as they hear shall summons have,
To fly to each appropriate grave,
And their corporeal bulk resume,
To wait their Everlasting Doom.

The particles of bodies dead,
Though over numerous regions spread,
By sympathetic force impress'd,
Shall haste in pristine form to rest;
While to its seat the soul reflies,
And the same man who died shall rise.

From glorious God an angel sent,
His Vial on Euphrates spent,
Should he his empty Vial fill
With Hermon dew, and thence distil,
One drop on every stream which glides,
'Till it in ocean lost abides:

Yet every drop Omniscience knows,
And where it in each billow flows,
Can every drop entirely lave
From its transfusions into wave,
Though distant as each polar shore,
Can to the Vial them restore.

THIRD SUNDAY IN ADVENT.

Should every drop in vapour rife,
Turn rain, hail, fnow, when in the fkies,
Thence falling into earth be funk,
And up by vegetables drunk,
God all their fhiftings can compute,
And into dew them re-tranfmute.

From Jefus' Body virtue came,
Which cured the blind, fick, dumb and lame;
But fince He from the grave arofe,
A nobler virtue from Him flows;
A virtue over Death to reign,
And raife all dead mankind again.

Pure fouls with rapturous joy fhall hafte,
In their loved fhells to be encafed,
While impious fouls with hideous cry,
In vain fhall loathed re-union fly.
Saints' graces them for blifs difpofe;
Guilt finners weighs to endlefs woes.

God-man be praifed, who Saints' loofe duft,
To glorious bodies will adjuft :
Tho' foul and flefh fhall parted be,
They'll meet in blefs'd Eternity.
That thought devoutly, Saints, revolve,
And live in languor to diffolve.

FOURTH SUNDAY IN ADVENT.

John answered them saying, I baptize with water: but there standeth one among you, whom ye know not. He it is who, coming after me is preferred before me.

John i. 26, 27.

AS when a visit emperors intend
    To some chief town, their harbingers they send,
To plain rough ways, to throw down every hill,
To straighten crooked roads, and valleys fill:
The Baptist for God-man thus passage made,
His work was true repentance to persuade;
To smooth rough tempers, the perverted guide,
Erect humility, and level pride.
Jerusalem, and all Judea round,
Drawn by a saint so awful, so renown'd,
Flock'd to clear Jordan's stream, their sins confess'd,
Were all with his initial washing blest;
Of their disease true penitential sense,
To a kind Saviour made them all propense:
He proselytes of all conditions gain'd,
And in his discipline for Jesus train'd.

  God to His servant this high honour gave,
Him to baptize, who the whole world should save.
The Apparition then, and Voice Divine,
Were of Messias the appointed Sign.

He, from the hour when Jesus he descried,
Exhorted all in Jesus to confide;
Commending Jesus to the world's esteem,
The Lamb of God, who should the world redeem.
With water only, I, said he, baptize,
To penitential tears excite your eyes;
But Jesus inward graces shall inspire,
Baptize you with the Holy Ghost and fire.
Blest Jesus with a fan shall purge His floor,
The wheat in His repository store;
To Saints give bliss, the bad to torment doom,
The chaff with fire unquenchable shall fume.

CHRISTMAS DAY.

CELESTIAL Harps prepare
To sound your loftiest air;
You choral Angels at the throne,
Your customary hymns postpone;
Of glorious spirits, all ye orders nine,
To sute[1] a hymn, to study chords combine.

    You all your happy days,
      Pay tributary praise,
God's mighty works you fully view,
And give your Maker praises due;

[1] *Sute*, to follow.

This day a nobler theme your powers employs,
Deserving noblest hymn, chords, love, and joys.

 This day (for you well know,
  Our time in flux below),
 You Sons of God together met,
  On a fix'd day which Godhead set;
This day God sent His Son to save mankind,
You to adore His rising, are enjoin'd.

 You first to humble swains,
  Who watch'd on Bethlehem plains,
 Glad tidings in sweet song proclaim'd,
  And them with Jesus's love inflamed;
O may my guardian, who then join'd your quire,
Me with like love in a like hymn inspire.

 You with your heavenly ray,
  Gild the expanse this day,
 You overlooking all the earth,
  To all sang God Incarnate's birth;
Fill with your splendours the expanse again,
Re-sing this day the same angelic strain.

 You all must hymn this morn,
  Not the Lamb slain, but born:
 To Bethlehem lead me now the way,
  Help me the wonders to survey,
The stable, and the manger, where God-man
His condescensions infinite began.

 My eyes the Babe may reach,
  You must His Godhead teach;

God there His Godhead deigns to hide,
　　Which he can never lay aside;
In human flesh His Majesty He shrouds,
You Godhead see, I only see His clouds.

　　I, while you God describe,
　　　Will what you sing imbibe;
　　Then stretch my powers to utmost might,
　　Till of God-man I hymns indite;
But yet I fear you all too finite are,
The Love of God Incarnate to declare.

　　I'll to my cell retire,
　　　In silence God admire,
　　Who vilest sinners to redeem,
　　Thus veil'd His Majestatic beam;
And while I in prostration speechless lie,
My love up to the Mystery shall fly.

　　Bless'd Angels, you mean time
　　　Return to bliss sublime;
　　But when at Glory you arrive,
　　The Saints in hymn with you will strive,
Their nature God assumed, not yours, and they
Will love God most, and sing the noblest lay.

　　Love on ambitious wing,
　　　Soar'd up to hear them sing;
　　And though it could not reach the height,
　　Yet when it met the Sons of Light,
It irresistibly would them intreat
The hymns of competition to repeat.

Love would ſtrict notice take
Of a Saint's heaven-ward wake,
Watch openings of the heavenly gate,
Through that to eye the bliſsful ſtate;
How God this day in brighteſt glory ſhines,
Freſh joys diffuſing o'er the heavenly lines.

God takes immenſe delight
In His own glorious ſight;
But no perfection He eſteems
So dear as His redeeming beams:
Philanthropy this day moſt bright appear'd,
And to the God of Love the day endear'd.

My love when back it came,
Brought ſupplemental flame;
Yet could not Jeſus' Love conceive,
But my deſpondence to relieve,
Since hymns all fell too low, ſaid, love would beſt
By copying Jeſus' graces be expreſt.

My love would yet incline,
Together both to join;
All praiſe to God, Who for our ſake,
Of man's frail nature would partake;
Born poor, to teach us riches to deſpiſe,
Which worldly ſouls inſenſate idolize.

God-man be ever bleſs'd,
Born naked and diſtreſs'd;
Who all terreſtrial glare declined,
And tendencies of ſenſual mind.

'Gainſt wealth, pomp, pleaſure, earthly, tranſient,
        vain,
May I a like antipathy maintain.

    Our great diſeaſe was luſt,
    Which made us Heaven diſguſt:
  God-man be praiſed, who choſe a ſtate,
  Our earthly paſſions to abate.
Inſpire me, Lord, with heavenly-minded ſenſe,
Antarctic to all foul concupiſcence.

    God-man no ſooner roſe,
    But He began His woes;
  It grieved the Babe's Omniſcient eye,
  Men's curſed rebellions to deſcry,
He knew the mighty guilt of man's offence
'Gainſt boundleſs Love, and grieved with grief
        immenſe.

    God-man I Thee adore,
    And from Thy Love implore,
  Againſt all ſin a flagrant zeal,
  Yet joys of pardon when I feel,
Sin tempts me to rejoice, which drew God down,
To raiſe vile ſinners to a heavenly crown.

    With joy I praiſes ſing,
    To our great humble King;
  Thou Heaven didſt leave for love of me,
  May I leave all for love of Thee,
With Saints above, this day I'll bear my part,
O may I Thee incarnate in my heart.

ST. STEPHEN'S DAY.

I SING, my God, the Saint this day,
Who led the suffering host the way
To rise to glory most sublime,
   The Martyr prime.

God-man debasements ne'er declined,
To shew compassions to mankind;
He servants would as masters treat,
   And wash their feet.

He joy was wont for sinners' sake,
In humble charities to take:
Bless'd Stephen kept God-man in view,
   And copy drew.

In Jesus' love the Saint up-train'd,
Would humble deacon be ordain'd,
To all men's woes to condescend,
   And poor attend.

God with the zeal benign was pleased,
Which had the Saint entirely seized,
And grace superlative design'd,
   To store his mind.

The Gracious Dove upon him came,
And kindled in him heavenly flame;

He full of faith, bless'd Jesus taught,
>   And wonders wrought.

Five Synagogues at once combined
Of various lands, to storm his mind;
He stood their fierce, confederate spite,
>   With humble might.

No wit of men, no hellish band,
His heavenly wisdom could withstand;
Their greatest sages fear'd the force
>   Of his discourse.

The Jews, who in his death conspired
False witnesses against him hired,
Who should what malice could suggest,
>   With oaths attest.

The people, elders, scribes, enraged,
To seize his person then engaged,
And to the council dragged the Saint
>   With loud complaint.

The villains falsely him accused,
That he had dangerous points infused,
Their venerable law decried,
>   And God denied.

They swore that he had spread the fame
All Salem o'er of Jesus' Name,
To darken Moses, and erase
>   Their holy place.

But God, the injured Saint to clear,
Made saintship in his looks appear;
The Council in his face saw light,
    As Angels bright.

Great Moses, when for forty days
He was ingulf'd in awful rays,
Did not with splendour more divine
    Than Stephen shine.

The High Priest then the Saint bespake,
Some answer to the Jews to make,
Who with celestial zeal began
    To preach God-man.

He taught them shadows to despise,
And on the substance fix their eyes,
Truth in those vehicles convey'd,
    Was now display'd.

He provocations high, yet true,
Laid to the unbelieving Jew,
Their harden'd heart he durst upbraid,
    Which Truth gainsaid.

He charged on them their fathers' guilt,
And blood of all the prophets spilt,
Sins cherish'd, which they should bemoan,
    Became their own.

He them reproach'd, who set at nought,
All that God-man or did or taught,

That God's bleſs'd Spirit to repel,
              They leagued with hell.

That to the croſs God-man they led,
Blaſphemed Him while His Blood they ſhed,
And whilſt He tortured hung for thoſe
              Who cauſed thoſe woes.

That they God's holy laws tranſgreſs'd,
Clear prophecies fulfill'd, ſuppreſs'd,
And ſhut their eyes againſt the light,
              In love with night.

Straight to the quick their hearts were
              gaſh'd,
Their teeth againſt the Saint they gnaſh'd,
They of their crimes reproof ſincere
              Abhorr'd to hear.

Heaven at that moment open flew,
The Saint had Heavenly Bliſs in view;
A thouſand deaths he could have died,
              When bliſs he eyed.

Angelic Hoſts together flock'd,
To Heaven's bright gates, juſt then unlock'd,
To ſee a Chriſtian Martyr's gore,
              Ne'er ſeen before.

Love ſhined ſo bright in martyr's pains,
They ready were to wiſh for veins,
That love they might with Stephen vie,
              And martyrs die.

They Jesus saw His posture quit;
He at God's Right though wont to sit,
Then stood, prepared to help with speed
   The Saint in need.

Through open Heaven the Martyrs sight
Could reach to majestatic height;
Thus rapt, he could not speech withhold,
   But vision told.

Stopping their ears, the furious crowd
Doom him to death with ravings loud;
Out of the city they him cast,
   To breathe his last.

There they the Proto-Martyr stoned,
Who them, more than himself, bemoan'd;
Midst stony showers he kneel'd and pray'd,
   Still undismay'd.

At every stone they at him threw,
Ejaculations from him flew;
"Jesus," he cried, "to Thee I cleave,
   My soul receive.

"Forgive, O Lord, my causeless foes;"
Love then put to his life the close:
He sank, and on the stony heap
   Fell fast asleep.

The Jews the murder to complete,
Their garments placed at young Saul's feet;

He to like fury then was moved,
    And crime approved.

Saints in his grave the Martyr laid,
And all due honour to him paid;
Joy'd for his blifs, for lofs they grieved
    The Church received.

God at the force of Stephen's prayer,
Decreed their loffes to repair;
To an Apoftle raifing Saul
    By heavenly call.

To Jefus praife, who midft the ftones,
Eafed all blefs'd Stephen's dying groans;
Who deign'd for martyrs' aid to ftand
    At God's Right Hand.

Heaven fent Angelic Squadrons down,
To guard the Martyr to his crown;
Saints joy'd that God had raifed his throne
    Above their own.

Rays to that crown for every ftone
Which Jews had at the Martyr thrown,
Were added to reward his woe,
    And honours fhow.

May I, my God, by faith have fight
Of Jefus ftanding at Thy Right:
And ready when this world I leave
    Me to receive.

May I, like him, the influence feel
Of faith, love, patience, courage, zeal;
Forgive my foes, for heaven prepare,
        And die in prayer.

For love of Jefus, O may I,
Like Stephen live, difpofed to die;
And gladly joys of love to reap,
        Lay flefh afleep.

ST. JOHN'S DAY.

FAITH, hope, and tear within my breaft,
   Shall, Lord, this day in filence reft,
O raife my love upon the wing,
While I the loved Difciple fing;
For Love can beft the fong indite,
Love only can of lovers write.

Blefs'd John, you young the world forfook,
Ere you too deep infection took;
The lefs fouls have of worldly taint,
The fooner they grow up to faint;
A foul towards heaven which early ftreams,
Is the offering which God moft efteems.

To God's high friendfhip, love afcends,
And dear communion ufed by friends;
Love gave you nobleft heat and light,
You feem'd below to live by fight,

You lessen'd in self humbling view
The more, the loftier heights you flew.

You when by Jesus' Love inflamed,
Were yet a son of thunder named;
O how could love soft, gentle, mild,
Be with dread thunder reconciled?
When God shines out in gracious rays,
He then aside His thunder lays.

O 'twas not thunder of the cloud,
'Twas heavenly, and benign, though loud;
Form'd to awaken, not to scare,
Such as was heard at Jesus' prayer,
When a voice sweet, yet mighty, came
From Heaven, God's glory to proclaim.

Bless'd Daniel was to rapture used,
Had evangelic truth infused,
He taught by Heaven, Messias knew
Should be cut off by impious Jew;
But he no further could aspire,
Than man of languishing desire.

Incarnate God, who bless'd your eyes,
Made you to man of love arise;
You the inflammative beheld,
Which all but Jesus' Love expell'd;
Great Moses, when God gave the law,
Sight so endearing never saw.

You had of dying Jesus view,
On His dire Cross remembering you,
His dearest Mother, deeply grieved,
He will'd by you should be relieved;
His Mother, He your Mother styled,
And in His room yourself her child.

Next to the Mother ever-bless'd,
Who gave the God of Love her breast,
(She melting, while He sweetly shined,
To co-enarmourments inclined,)
None to such height of love attain'd,
As John on top of Calvary gain'd.

All gracious wonders Jesus wrought,
All His dear loves absorb'd your thought,
You well the sinner's merit weigh'd,
With Blood of God for ransom paid,
And taught by the Eternal Dove,
Gave God the proper name of Love.

To God alone your love inclined,
The freer 'twas, the more confined;
In God vast amplitude you found,
And loveliness which had no bound;
O'er love's expanse it took its flight,
Imbibing sweetness infinite.

God-man who in pure Love decreed
For sinners on the Cross to bleed,
In you excited a fresh flame,
For all who from lapsed Adam came;

ST. JOHN'S DAY.

A love which copied Love Divine,
Of Jesus' lovers made the sign.

God Filial, ere He stoop'd to clay,
In His loved Father's Bosom lay,
And from His infinite repose,
Came truth salvific to disclose;
You most beloved, loved Jesus best,
You lean'd on loved God Filial's Breast.

What loves, what heights you there attain'd
Could ne'er be by yourself explain'd;
If envy on a Saint could seize,
All Saints would envy you that ease;
If earth with Heaven in joy can vie,
'Tis next to Jesus' heart to lie.

You with the God of Love conversed,
From Fontal Love you streams dispersed,
You saving truth o'er Jewry shed,
Glad tidings you o'er Asia spread,
Seven Mother-Churches there you steer'd,
To Jesus's love all co-endear'd.

Your love, which terrors all defied;
Was yet by martyrdom untried;
But God, who raises good from ill,
Made hell subservient to His Will,
Turn'd from its aim infernal spite,
To give your love its perfect height.

By hell the Pagans ſet on fire
Enkindled the Proconſul's ire,
He ſent you bound with guards to Rome,
To fierce Domitian for your doom;
He you into a cauldron caſt
Of boiling oil, to breathe your laſt.

But God, who furnace-fire reſtrain'd,
While Saints in flame unſinged remain'd,
The raging, fiery force o'er-ruled,
And to kind heat the liquor cool'd:
God martyr's crown for you contrived,
Though you your martyrdom ſurvived.

Your limbs decrepit, ſtiff, and cold,
Juſt crumbling towards primeval mould,
By ſuppling oil, and gentle heat,
Soon felt invigoration ſweet,
Heaven made you vital force regain,
By what hell meant ſhould be your bane.

At bliſs delay'd, you ne'er repined,
God for your love more work deſign'd;
The tyrant at your 'ſcape enraged,
In a freſh cruelty engaged,
He ſent you bound to Patmos iſle,
To a diſconſolate exile.

God ſufferings there for you ordain'd,
Which numerous ſouls to Jeſus gain'd

But when the bloody tyrant fell
To his imperial pains in hell,
Mild Nerva chosen to succeed,
You by divine direction freed.

At Ephesus abode you made,
Where neighbouring Churches you obey'd,
You with illumination stored,
When Asian guides your help implored,
The Church from heretics redeem'd,
Who raised by hell, God-man blasphemed.

In all your writings every line
Was dictated by Love Divine;
Your love the more vivacious grew,
The nearer it to glory drew;
When you a century had reach'd,
Love was the only thing you preach'd.

In vain no lover ever pray'd,
You gain'd a super-effluent aid;
And God's perfections all combined
To further what you had design'd;
The miracles which made you famed,
Your love as well as truth proclaim'd.

Your love on Heaven fix'd vigorous aim,
Though you had spent your vital flame;
Haste, O my Love, your longing heart
Cried, as it felt the welcome dart:
Love heard, and sent a seraph down
To waft you to a martyr's crown.

Praiſe, Lord, to Thee, who didſt outſtream
On John a ſweet enamouring beam,
Whoſe love diffuſing heavenly flame,
Made pagan nations love Thy Name,
O may I feel Love's gracious might,
And all I can to love excite.

THE HOLY INNOCENTS.

SOON as Great God in fleſh enſhrined,
   Began ſalvation of mankind,
     Hell utmoſt ſpite diſcloſed,
     God's boundleſs Love oppoſed;
And numerous fiends to Salem ſent,
Judaic malice to foment.

The fiends ſaw Herod deeply grieved,
That the Wiſe Men had him deceived,
     And would no tidings bring
     Of Jewry's new-born King;
And they a ſtrong detachment made,
Which ſhould the tyrant's ſoul invade.

A legion ſtraight the wretch poſſeſs'd,
Strong jealous terrors to ſuggeſt;
     Ideas dire they wrought,
     To haunt his troubled thought;

Amidst his slumbers he would start,
In dream, the babe had stabb'd his heart.

The jealous fears which tyrants seize,
Diabolize them by degrees,
    Fierce Herod swell'd to rage,
    Which nothing could assuage;
For infant blood remorseless raved,
And the arch-murderer out-braved.

But Heaven to Joseph warning gave,
The Mother and the Babe to save;
    To take to Egypt flight
    From Herod's murderous spite;
Strange land, the Babe, long dangerous way,
They urge not; but with zeal obey.

Wills which to God surrender'd are,
He makes His own peculiar care,
    His Wisdom, Goodness, Power,
    Still nigh in needful hour,
Was their support, defence, and guide,
And what they wanted, still supplied.

The tyrant troops, his rage to vent,
To murder Bethlehem infants sent;
    To kill one babe alone,
    Could not his rage atone,
A general slaughter he decreed,
In hope the Rival Babe might bleed.

The mothers' shrieks, the infants' cries,
Frighted the fiends who crowd the skies;
    And Luciferian pride
    The fact with envy eyed,
Swore since the devils learn'd to kill,
They ne'er achieved so brave an ill.

The land was deluged with a flood
Of mothers' tears, and infants' blood;
    Such a heart-bursting moan
    Was ne'er in Egypt known,
When the Destroying Angel's blade
Of the first-born massacre made.

Great God, whose Omnipresent eyes
All human actions supervise,
    Forced Herod 'gainst his will
    Heaven's purpose to fulfil;
Turn'd his efforts of hellish ire,
In his own ruin to conspire.

Just vengeance on the wretch was shewn,
By plagues and horrors on his throne;
    But reeking infant gore,
    To vengeance cried for more:
With that God damn'd him to like pains,
Which the arch-murderer sustains.

From danger when the coast was clear'd,
God back all three to Nazareth steer'd:

Praise to the Mighty Child,
   Content to be exiled,
And for our sakes in tenderest age,
In numerous hardships to engage.

There Joseph, and the Virgin blest
With her Redeemer at her breast,
   Lived in sweet, awful sense
   Of their dear Babe immense,
Both by Angelic hosts revered,
Above all Saints to God endear'd.

Both by their humble Infant taught,
No worldly joy, wealth, honour sought,
   To raptures ne'er aspired,
   Lived humble, and retired,
In love, prayer, meditation, praise,
Form'd by His imitable rays.

May I, like them, in bless'd retreat,
On Heaven employ residuous heat,
   Meek, humble, and serene,
   From wilful outrage clean,
Keep to God's Will, my own resign'd,
And fix on Jesus' Love my mind.

Bless'd Jesus, on the babes, who bled
For His sole sake, high favours shed;
   By happy deaths secure
   From ills they might endure;
Of losing Heaven from danger freed,
To heaven by making early speed.

The Guardians, children wont to aid,
In vehicles like doves array'd,
    Their innocence to paint,
    Took each his infant Saint;
'Twixt their foft wings to Heaven they fwam,
Like cygnets on a feather'd dam.

Heaven joy'd to fee the fpeechlefs flight,
All wafh'd in blood of martyr white;
    Saints and Angelic Quires
    To their refplendent lyres
The firftlings of falvation fung,
Who join'd them with their loofen'd tongue.

All praife to God, whofe gracious Might
Even fucklings can to hymn excite:
    O may I, born anew,
    Keep heaven in longing view,
From ghoftly child, blefs'd manhood gain,
Till, ripe for heaven, I heaven obtain.

FIRST SUNDAY AFTER CHRISTMAS.

God a Father.

And becaufe ye are fons, God hath fent forth the Spirit of his Son into your hearts, crying, Abba, Father.—*Galatians,* iv. 6.

'TIS, Lord, Thy Will that all mankind
　　Should love Thee with heart, foul, and
　　　　mind;
　　And of all laws fublime,
　　Love nobleft is, and prime;
But O! by whom fhall we be taught,
To love Thy Goodnefs as we ought?

Lord, 'tis Thyfelf, who haft imprefs'd,
In native light on human breaft;
　　That their Creator all
　　Mankind fhould Father call;
A Father's love all mortals know,
And the love filial which they owe.

Our Father gives us heavenly Light,
And to be happy, ghoftly fight;
　　He bleffes, guides, fuftains,
　　He eafes us in pains;
Abatements for our weaknefs makes,
And never a true child forfakes.

He waits till the hard heart relents,
Our self-damnation He laments;
    He sweetly them invites,
      To share in Heaven's delights;
His Arms He opens to receive,
All who for past transgressions grieve.

My Father! O that Name is sweet,
To sinners mourning in retreat;
    God's Heart paternal yearns,
      When He a change discerns;
He to His favour them restores,
He heals their most inveterate sores.

When pangs of the new birth they feel,
He to their pardon sets His seal;
    O Love! exceeding thought,
      Which our redemption wrought;
Which endless bliss for Saints prepares,
To reign with His own Son, co-heirs.

Religious honour, humble awe,
Obedience to our Father's law;
    A lively grateful sense,
      Of tenderness immense;
Full trust on God's paternal cares,
Submission which chastisement bears.

Grief, when His Goodness we offend,
Zeal, to His Likeness to ascend;

Will, from the world refined,
To His sole Will resign'd;
These graces in God's children shine,
Reflections of the Love Divine.

God's children love all human race,
In whom they God's dear Image trace;
More likeness they attain,
The greater love they gain;
Saints in whom God is most express'd,
Fraternal charity loves best.

God's Son co-equal taught us all,
In prayer His Father ours to call;
With confidence in need,
We to our Father speed;
Of His own Son the language dear,
Intenerates the Father's ear.

I, prodigal, to squander strive,
The portion I from God derive;
I precious time misspend,
Towards vanities propend;
On husks of worldly joys I feed,
Which nothing but frustrations breed.

Thou Father art, though to my shame,
I often forfeit that dear Name;
But since for sin I grieve,
Me Father-like receive;

O melt me into filial tears,
To pay of love my vaſt arrears.

My love, my tears can never riſe,
To a juſt filial ſacrifice;
    But Jeſus for me bled,
    Both love and tears He ſhed;
For His love, tears, O! me forgive,
That I Thy child may ever live.

O Spirit of Adoption! ſpread
Thy Wings enamouring o'er my head;
    O Filial Love immenſe!
    Raiſe me to love intenſe;
O Father! ſource of Love Divine,
My powers to love and hymn incline.

While God my Father I revere,
Nor all hell powers, nor death I fear;
    I am my Father's care,
    His ſuccours preſent are;
All comes from my loved Father's Will,
And that ſweet Name intends no ill.

God's Son, His Soul, when life He cloſed,
In His dear Father's Hands repoſed;
    I'll, when my laſt I breathe,
    My ſoul to God bequeath;
And panting for the joys on high,
Invoking Love Paternal, die.

THE CIRCUMCISION.

UPON the octave of Thy birth,
  Since Thou God-man didſt ſhine on earth,
    Thou as the blisful light
    Immaculately bright,
  Wouldſt a ſeverity endure,
Contrived to teach lapſed men they were impure.

  Thy heav'nly Father it ordain'd,
  Love to obedience Thee conſtrain'd,
    Our ſpirits to incline
    To zeal for law divine,
  From infancy Thy Father's Will,
It was Thy care devoutly to fulfil.

  Thou our affections to excite,
  Wouldſt ſtoop to an afflictive rite,
    Thou early didſt foreſhew,
    What Thou wouldſt undergo,
  Thy Croſs and agonizing pains,
Which made Thy Blood guſh out at all Thy Veins.

  But, Lord, from ſin all pain aroſe,
  Sin is the cauſe of penal woes,
    A babe Thou didſt begin
    To bear the weight of ſin,
  And by the circumciſing ſteel,
Teach that Thy Fleſh our puniſhment ſhould feel.

THE CIRCUMCISION.

All Heaven and earth which saw Thee bleed,
Saw Thee true man and Abraham's seed,
   He first received the sign
   Of covenant divine,
And 'twas by Thee from him derived,
All dead in sin, to bliss should be revived.

Thy Love, sweet Babe, with willing heart
Endured Thy Circumcision smart,
   'Twas Thy propitious aim
   To take that dearest Name
Of Jesus, at that rite imposed
Which Thy Salvation to the world disclosed.

My spirit makes its last efforts,
To think what that dear Name imports,
   One while I sin survey,
   Which Jesus takes away;
I see my Jesus bear the pains
Due to my own concupiscential stains.

My love one while suggests to thought,
The great Salvation Jesus wrought,
   And while I Jesus see
   Hang on the Cross for me,
My love trajected from my eye,
O'erflows my heart, I could for Jesus die.

Dear Jesus is a joyful Name,
And I a part in Jesus claim,

THE CIRCUMCISION.

    Sweet Jesus dries my tears,
    Sweet Jesus calms my fears,
  And I from guilt by Jesus freed,
The very Angels should in hymn exceed.

  Bless'd Angels! you my Jesus praise,
  Flesh cannot reach your heavenly lays,
    Yet since for me He deign'd,
    Not you, to be arraign'd,
  In love with you I'll strive to vie,
With all your might you love, and so will I.

  My love in this shall yours outdo,
  'Twill be the tenderer of the two,
    Into soft tears 'twill melt,
    For woes my Jesus felt;
  Our loves in different rills will stream,
Mine native, yours but foreigner will seem.

  At Jesu's Name all knees must bow,
  Their hearts for off'rings to Him vow,
    I, Jesu, would vow mine,
    But Thou must it refine,
  Till it to Thy sole Love adheres,
And at Thy Throne fit holocaust appears.

  But what have I which is my own,
  To offer, Jesu, at Thy Throne?
    The heart that I design,
    Is by dear purchase Thine,
  And I have nothing left in store,
But was Thy own, my Jesus, long before.

THE CIRCUMCISION.

O, my dear Jesus, 'twas Thy own,
I now my sacrilege bemoan,
   I stole my heart away,
   Made it to sin a prey.
Thou gavest Thyself to free the slave,
Reject me not whom Thou didst die to save.

My Jesus! O Thy Name is sweet,
To sinners mourning in retreat,
   The Name by God design'd
   To ease a troubled mind.
God Love to us had ne'er been styled,
Had He not been in Jesus reconciled.

My Jesus! while I here remain,
Affections vile, unruly, vain,
   Are ready to arise,
   My spirit to surprise;
O circumcise them from my heart,
That naught may me and my dear Jesus part.

Duration the Angelic quire
In hymning spend and never tire,
   Eternally delight
   In Beatific Sight,
When Jesus has my heart possess'd,
O I could Jesus hymn and never rest.

A thousand years is but one day,
In God's indivisible ray.

And while I Jesus sing,
   An ever-gushing spring
With thought devout supplies my zeal,
And I in singing no succession feel.

My Jesus! no seraphic flame
Has ardours fit to hymn Thy Name,
   While I to hymn incline,
   I'll love and Jesus join,
And when my hymn remits its heat,
Jesus my love a thousand times repeat.

My Jesus! I my spirit chide,
When from Thy thought it turns aside,
   O be Thou on my breast
   Still virtually impress'd,
My love will long to sing with those,
Whose hymns to Jesus never shall have close.

SECOND SUNDAY AFTER CHRISTMAS.

On the Nativity.

Luke ii. 15-21.

O GREAT God-man! my grovelling spirit raise,
To a devout sublimity of praise;
Thy beams on me Thou Fontal Wisdom dart,
Thy boundless Love incarnate in my heart,

That at full pitch of evangelic joy,
To sing Thy birth, I may my powers employ.

   The stationary priest, with lighted torch,
Had tried the Levites upper vests to scorch,
Whom at their various posts he sleeping found,
As in the Holy Place he walk'd the round,
When God Incarnate pass'd His virgin shroud,
With gentler force than rays a yielding cloud.
And lapsed man saw the first salvific gleams,
Which soon grew up to full meridian beams;
Spreading a glorious evangelic light,
And uninvadable by ghostly night;
The Virgin Mother near the manger placed,
In her soft arms the boundless Babe embraced,
As on the Ark the Shechinah reclined,
Between the cherubims' bright wings enshrined,
While all the world in sudden rapture joins,
And in high sympathetic praise combines.

   The morning stars new lofty carols sang,
And all the heavenly orbs of Jesus rang,
A cheerful splendour brighten'd all the sphere,
The air serene made clouds to disappear;
The moon wiped her disfigured spots away,
Ambitious at midnight to make midday;
The drooping flow'rs which absent sun bemoan,
Raised up their heads, grew fresh, and fully
      blown;

All strove their quintescential sweets to drain,
Perfuming earth, God-man to entertain.
Earth which with Paradise might then compare,
And felt more odorous incense in the air.
The woods, by winter of their shade bereaved,
By an extemporaneous spring were leaved;
The nightingales, just fallen asleep, awoke,
The airy quires with singing to provoke,
And thick on every tree the winged throng
Strove to out-do the nightingales in song;
The God of harmony voiced all their throats,
And sweetly harmonized their various notes,
Ominous birds, at midnight wont to roam,
Made no dire noise, but silent perch'd at home.
The fiends were all night long in Tophet chain'd,
Wondering they from their haunts should be
    restrain'd,
The ocean crystal clear lay fast asleep,
The eye might view the bottom of the deep.
Dread thunders into warblings soft were still'd,
Heaven shot kind lightnings the expanse to gild;
All the loose winds which o'er the compass flew,
In sweet, refreshing, gentle murmurs blew;
No noxious exhalations could arise,
Balsamic vapours only fill'd the skies,
And mortals drown'd in sleep alluring steams,
Of strange deliverance had transporting dreams.

    The shepherds, who near Bethlehem watch'd
        the fold,

A wondrous change could in the world behold;
There was no need to drive the wolves away,
Wolves would with fearless lambs familiar play,
When on a sudden, arched Heaven around,
Of swift angelic wings they heard the sound,
With light a thousand times beyond the sun,
All Heaven was in an instant over-run,
Bright majestatic glory fill'd the sphere,
And struck the swains with a sweet, awful fear;
Till an Archangel stay'd on wings outspread,
With heavenly mildness, thus allay'd their dread.

Fear not: Behold, good tidings I declare
Of greatest joy, in which all men shall share:
In David's city at this turn of morn,
A Saviour, Christ, the Lord, to you is born.
This sign shall Him distinguish to your eyes,
He's swathed in clouts, and in a manger lies.
Straight with the radiant herald, numerous hosts
Of glorious Angels, fill the airy coasts,
Dancing for joy o'er the expanse on wing,
In heaven-taught measures, while they loudly sing,
To God in Heaven be Glory, on earth Peace,
God-will towards men, such as shall never cease.
And while their voices in sweet chords conspire,
Each heavenly harper strikes his tuneful lyre:
Good Angels joy, when but one sinner weeps,
Heaven Jubilee for every mourner keeps.
But their ecstatic joys were unconfined,
At the Salvation of all lapsed mankind.

God, who Himself immense complacence shew'd,
With beams triunal the horizon strew'd.

   The winged host remembering God's Decree,
When Filial God they should Incarnate see,
That they should all adore Him, swiftly flew
To Bethlehem, there to pay their homage due;
But ere to make their entrance they presume,
Themselves they first proportion to the room,
They their expanded vehicles condense,
Their rays collected, shine the more intense.
Nine heavenly orders enter one by one,
The lowest shined much brighter than the sun.
Joseph and Mary's elevated sight
Remain'd undazzled at their glories bright;
Angels first, Seraphs last, their reverence made,
In proper robes resplendent all array'd.
Each order entering the bless'd humble door,
At the Babe's feet fell prostrate on the floor;
Of humble Jesus, each sang hymns sublime,
With the celestial harpers keeping time:
Soon as they had their adorations paid,
And heap'd their blessings on the heavenly Maid,
As forth they from the hallow'd stable went,
They stretch'd their radiant shapes to full extent,
And straight remounting to the realm of light,
Hymn'd God Incarnate all along their flight.

   The lowly swains, to see the wondrous Child,
Leave sheep and wolves together reconciled;

On straw they find Him in the manger laid,
Till taken up by the sweet, humble Maid;
As in her arms her dearest Babe reposed,
A wreath of heavenly glory both enclosed,
The shepherds the Immortal Child adored,
His blessings for themselves and flocks implored,
And rapt at His transporting sight, diffuse
All o'er the city the transporting news,
While David's race in David's town enroll'd,
Haste to the inn, the Infant to behold,
The faithful shepherds to the crowd declare,
The glorious vision they had seen in air,
All in amazement pleasing and devout,
Gave an exulting eucharistic shout;
Blest Mary, who in joys had greatest part,
Kept all they said deep graven on her heart;
The swains with overflowing joys repair,
Of their dear flocks to reassume the care,
And all the way returning to the field,
Praised God for all the glorious things reveal'd;
Their flocks they feeding in full safety found,
And made the plains with Jesus' praise resound.

    To guide the kings, a radiant star was sent,
Bless'd swains, celestial beams o'erspread your tent,
God Angels chose, glad news to them to bring,
They saw them dance for joy, and heard them sing,
God, who exalts the humble, honour'd you

Above all men, with God Incarnate's view.
May I, like you, life on my calling fpend,
Untainted by the world on God attend,
Devout, meek, peaceful, low in my own eye,
In God's tranfporting favour live and die.

 Jefus be praifed! Who deign'd the joyful news
By Angels into fhepherds to infufe.

 Glory to Jefus! the whole mount recites,
Who humbleft faints exalts to nobleft heights.

THE EPIPHANY.

WHEN God from Heaven came down,
 To take our flefh in Bethlehem town,
 Heaven the tranfporting news
 Declared at firft to none but Jews;
To Bethlehem fhepherds who watch'd o'er the
  fold,
A quire of Angels the glad tidings told.

  They faw God's early ray,
 And might keep feftival that day,
  From Gentiles God conceal'd,
 The faving truth to Jews reveal'd.
This day the Gentiles the glad tidings heard,
This day, by all the world to be revered.

  A ftar, new, ftrange, and bright,
 Appear'd by day as well as night,

And with its radiant beam,
Strove with the sun to be supreme,
Which Eastern Gentiles guess'd was to forerun
The wish'd-for dawn of the Eternal Sun.

By rays which from it stream'd,
One of the morning stars it seem'd,
Which from the quire detach'd,
Was to the solar sphere despatch'd,
By the peculiar pointings of its ray,
To shew the Gentiles where their Saviour lay.

Led by the wondrous star,
Three princely sages came from far,
Who made all Salem ring
Of their new-born propitious King,
And the great council Herod call'd agreed,
That for His birth-place Bethlehem was decreed.

This day the star stood still,
Its rays which brighten'd Bethlehem vill,[1]
Towards the poor stable veer'd,
Where God in swaddling-clothes appear'd:
The sages entering fell upon the floor,
The weak Almighty Infant to adore.

Next to the Infant, they
Due honour to the Mother pay,

[1] *Vill*, town.

Then cloths of state unfold,
　Which wrapt myrrh, frankincense, and gold,
Those they presented to the Infant's view,
The noblest gifts which in their countries grew.

　　　Ye eastern sages say
　When you had travell'd a long way
　　　To seek a King, and saw
　None but an humble Babe on straw,
What moved you for a King that Babe to own,
Who had a manger only for His throne?

　　　Knew you what was of old,
　By Balaam of a star foretold,
　　　Which should in Jacob rise,
　Whose beams should glad their wishing eyes?
Or had some long tradition reach'd your ear,
Of a new King to roll the Jewish sphere?

　　　O it was Light Divine,
　Which deign'd into your hearts to shine,
　　　Which ghostly clouds dispell'd,
　The star's effulgence far excell'd;
Made you the guilt of human race descry,
And long till a Redeemer bless'd your eye.

　　　You Mother saw and Child,
　She sweetly yearn'd, He brightly smiled;
　　　None of the bless'd above,
　E'er had such interchange of love.

'Twas heavenly glory which the Infant crown'd,
Dilating His pure Mother to furround.

  You faw her fweet amaze,
 How her full foul o'erflow'd with praife,
  And how her eyes fhe tried
 'Twixt Heaven and Infant to divide;
Who taught her love to Heaven the readieft way
On His reflex of Fontal Godhead's ray.

  Rapt at the Infant's fight,
 You in a dream infpired by night
  Were Salem charged to waive,
 From Herod's rage the Babe to fave,
And to your lands return'd by fecret roads,
To fcatter light o'er all your dark abodes.

  By the firft-fruits thus blefs'd,
 Of Gentiles hallow'd were the reft;
  And foon the fplendour fpread,
 Which the fweet Dove Eternal fhed;
'Twas on this happy day the Gentile world
Firft faw the banner of God's love unfurl'd.

  No penitential moan
 Should reach this day the Heavenly Throne,
  But fhould a tincture have
 Of joy, for Him who came to fave;
And His Salvation to extend to all,
Who o'er the world for mercy to Him call.

Be gracious God adored,
Who in pure pity unimplored,
  Would yet the joyful news,
O'er this my native land diffuse;
And whose Omniscience, which all persons sees,
Design'd me share in His benign decrees.

  Thou, Lord, my plague hast heal'd,
By saving-truths by Thee reveal'd;
  While I Thy pardon feel,
With a compassionating zeal,
I beg that darken'd souls Thy Light may see,
And in Thy Goodness share, which shines on me.

  For star my soul to lead,
Thy holy Word I'll daily read;
  'Twill shine all o'er my way,
And shew the right, whene'er I stray:
But when I shall approach my Heavenly King,
I votive gifts, like the wise men, should bring.

  I'll, Lord, my gold present,
On Thy poor brethren to be spent;
  Prayer shall to Thee aspire,
As frankincense fumes up by fire;
For uncorrupting myrrh, an heart sincere
I'll bring, from wilful putrefactions clear.

  Lord, on my gifts though vile,
Let Thy benignity but smile,

My love shall daily strive
  At higher offerings to arrive;
And for their daily failings to atone,
Present new hymns to Thy propitious throne.

FIRST SUNDAY AFTER EPIPHANY.

His mother kept all these sayings in her heart.
St. Luke, ii. 51.

GOD, Who is pleased bright Angels down to send,
On purpose little children to attend;
When blessed Mary first drew vital air,
Entrusted her to a bright seraph's care;
The aged Saints, who for a child had pray'd,
Sang hymns to God when joyful parents made;
Devoted God's free gift to God alone,
And more God's child esteem'd her than their own;
Her seraph kept her in his sweet embrace,
No one foul spirit durst approach the place;
The Holy Ghost His temple in her built,
Cleansed from congenial, kept from mortal guilt;
And from the moment that her blood was fired,
Into her heart Celestial Love inspired.

  The babe, when she began to speak, was taught
To consecrate to God her tongue and thought,
And, prompted by her seraph, took delight

Continual hallelujahs to recite;
Her phylacteries next she by degrees
Had learn'd, and to repeat them on her knees;
Those which the love of God sincere enjoin'd
Affected most her heaven-enkindled mind:
When she began to read God's holy book,
In which she her initiation took,
Her soul was with a heavenly manna fed,
Her spirit tasted every truth she read;
And ere she saw two weeks of years complete
She the whole psalter could by heart repeat;
From types, and what the prophesies foretold,
Which she, by Heaven enlighten'd, could unfold,
She the idea of Mesiias drew,
Pray'd for His advent, kept Him still in view;
Seven times a-day she to her closet went,
Her fervent love in fervent prayer to vent;
And her unwearied zeal was wont to pray
By warm ejaculations all the day;
She in the depth of her serene repose
At midnight to her solemn office rose:[1]
As she grew up love daily gain'd new heights,
And she from them began sublimer flights.

No Angel who e'er human likeness took
Had a more chaste, sweet, charming, heavenly look,
A look, which all at the first sight revered,
And while it struck a sacred awe endear'd;
Plain, cleanly, and becoming was her dress,
Had nothing curious, nothing of excess;

She idleness, the pest of souls to shun,
In intervals of prayer her garments spun;
Soon as herself she decently array'd,
She vestments for the poor and naked made;
Charity, next to Heaven, absorb'd her care,
The poor, in every meal she eat, had share;
Her closet-meditations, most sublime,
Where with her God alone she spent her time;
Her languors, bless'd Messias to behold,
Spring-tides of Heaven, which o'er her spirit roll'd;
Humility, which all proud thoughts suppress'd,
As if no one perfection she possess'd,
Her will transfused into the Will Divine,
Accustom'd with God's Will to co-incline;
Her sanctity to God's true Likeness grown,
Her frequent visits from the glorious throne
A silent admiration may create,
None but her guardian seraph can relate.

 To parents, next to God, she reverence paid,
They sweetly ruled, as sweetly she obey'd;
She was the subject of their prayer and praise,
Their tender nurse in their declining days;
Heaven warn'd them their dear daughter to
   commend
To reverend Joseph's care, their ancient friend,
A saint, who would her purity protect,
And treat her with angelical respect;
To her dear parents' choice she chose to yield,
And the espousals solemnly were seal'd,

AFTER EPIPHANY.

Gabriel meanwhile from bliss flew down full-speed,
To tell her as she pray'd that Heaven decreed
She the Messias in her womb should bear,
Whose sight had been the subject of her prayer;
The boundless might of Fontal Love Divine
The love co-breathed, third of the Glorious Trine,
On thee descending shall thy womb dispose
Great filial God incarnate to inclose;
She scarcely could believe her ears and eyes,
The message had such rapturous surprise,
Till Gabriel her assured it was God's Will,
Which 'twas her sole ambition to fulfil;
And as he back to Heaven his flight began
In a love-transport she conceived God-man;
While Godhead templing in her womb remain'd,
What influence from God within she gain'd,
What suavities, loves, languors, ardours, lights,
Joys, jubilations, beatific sights,
What rapts when she Magnificats composed,
Or when t' Eliza Gabriel's news disclosed,
Her spirit fill'd, no poetry can guess,
Herself could never what she felt express.
Joseph with jealous eye her change beheld,
Till a bright Angel all his doubts dispell'd;
Then both at Nazareth lived a blissful life,
Most tender husband, most submissive wife;
Their chastity was free from sensual taints,
Their mutual love pure, as in heavenly Saints;
His Angel and her Seraph could not join
In friendship more endearing, more divine.

When ſhe to Bethlehem came that happy morn,
Her virgin-eyes ſaw God Incarnate born;
How high her raptures then began to ſwell,
None but her own omniſcient Son can tell;
God-man, who deigns to temple in pure hearts,
A wondrous love to common ſaints imparts,
Gives them of heavenly love foretaſting ſight,
To comprehend its length, breadth, depth, and
    height;
Much greater love to His dear Mother ſhew'd,
Heaven in ſweet deluge on her ſpirit flow'd;
As Eve when ſhe her fontal ſin review'd,
Wept for herſelf, and all ſhe ſhould include;
Bleſs'd Mary, with man's Saviour in embrace,
Joy'd for herſelf, and for all human race;
All Saints are by her Son's dear influence
    bleſs'd,
She kept the very fountain at her breaſt;
The Son adored and nurſed by the ſweet Maid,
A thouſand-fold of Love for love repaid;
Saints, who of God have beatific view,
Such mighty joys peculiar never knew;
They to hymn God as vot'ries are employ'd,
As Mother of the God they hymn'd, ſhe joy'd.

But yet to temper rapturous exceſs,
Her joys below were mingled with diſtreſs;
When ſhe a Mother, yet a Virgin pure,
Purification legal would endure:
Simeon, who honour'd was God-man to hold,

The sword, which should the Mother pierce, foretold,
Her Son was born our griefs to undergo,
She sweetly sympathised in all His woe:
The wound which first check'd her ecstatic joy,
Was Herod's plot the Infant to destroy;
But warn'd by Heaven, to Egypt she took flight,
God cured that wound by baffling Herod's spite;
Babe, Virgin, Joseph, when the storm was o'er,
Return'd to Nazareth, where they lived before,
There humble and obscure the parents dwelt,
And of their Son, God-man, the blessings felt;
Above two lustres in sweet peace they spent,
Then with their wondrous Son to Salem went;
The Virgin there received a second wound,
Which soon was cured when the dear Child they found;
All three to pleasant Nazareth then retired,
Where Joseph in the Virgin's arms expired;
God-man Himself his absolution spake,
His spirit long'd its prison to forsake;
Son then and Mother lived exempt from noise,
Reciprocating heavenly loves and joys.

Into the world soon as bless'd Jesus came,
His mediatory-office to proclaim,
Bless'd Mary, who in her reflecting soul
Took care all Jesu's actions to enroll,
Who had of sin, and Love Divine, a sense
Next to her Son, most lively, most intense,

When she His Love, which sinful man redeem'd,
Saw daily scorn'd, insulted, and blasphemed,
The sword pierced daily through her tender heart,
And she of all His sorrows felt the smart;
But when she on the Cross beheld God-man,
Up to the hilt the dolorous weapon ran.

  Soon as He left His grave her joy revived,
She from her Son fresh springs of joy derived;
To John's dear care she by her Son consign'd,
To his sole mansion her abode confined;
The bless'd above adore their heavenly King,
Contemplate, love, converse, rejoice, and sing,
Those were her sole employments day and night,
Her conversation darted heavenly light;
To all the hours of prayer she daily came,
When any cool'd, her zeal refresh'd their flame;
She to devotion all her time applied,
She lived as if already glorified;
Her love still languish'd for the happy day,
When to the grave she should resign her clay,
Exulting when the world she was to leave,
And her divine Viaticum receive,
Fell sick, and died of an excess of love,
Hastening to her restorative above;
Heaven with transcendent joys her entrance graced,
Next to His throne her Son His Mother placed;
And here below, now she's of Heaven possess'd,
All generations are to call her bless'd.

SECOND SUNDAY AFTER EPIPHANY.

Christ-like Love.

Be kindly affectioned one to another with brotherly love, in honour preferring one another.—*Romans* xii. 10.

AS to myself, to be to others kind,
   Jesu, is by Thy Law enjoin'd,
    And how I love myself I well
    Can by my own sensation tell,
In grief, want, danger, pain, I recollect
    What love from neighbours I expect,
    By measuring myself I know
Like love sincere I to all others owe.

Thou, Jesu, in the Evangelic pact
   A love much harder dost exact,
    That all who Thy true lovers are
    Their love, shew'd with Thy own, compare,
That they should others love to like degree,
    As they themselves are loved by Thee,
    This seems of love the utmost height,
A pitch transcending far all human flight.

Thou, mighty God, out of pure boundless love
   Didst leave Thy glorious Throne above
    To sink to flesh, and to sustain
    Successive want, reproach, and pain,

And after all Thou didſt Thyſelf expoſe
    To Crucifixion for Thy foes,
    None but God-man ſuch love could ſhew,
Such undeſerved griefs could undergo.

But ſince Thou, Lord, haſt made this Love Divine
    Of cordial love to Thee the ſign,
    Since Thou haſt thus loved me, I'll ſtrive
    From Thee like paſſion to derive,
Love will think nothing grievous, nothing hard,
    While to Thy Love it has regard,
    Love of no ſufferings is afraid,
Which are with beatific Love repaid.

Lord, ſhouldſt Thou call me to the ſtake to die,
    To ſave from hell my enemy,
    O let Thy Love my ſpirit fire,
    I'll on the Croſs for love expire,
While I my ſoul for love an offering make,
    I'll love to ſuffer for Love's ſake, ⁒
    I'll joy my ſufferings are like Thine,
That I with Thee ſhall in like glory ſhine.

THIRD SUNDAY AFTER EPIPHANY.

The Saints with Jesus.

And I say unto you, That many shall come from the east and west, and shall sit down with Abraham, and Isaac, and Jacob, in the kingdom of heaven.—*Matthew* viii. 11.

SOUL, when your flesh dissolves to dust,
 To God's safe Hands yourself entrust;
Be not too curious to inquire,
    Where to aspire;

Whether to Paradise you fly,
Or in bless'd Abraham's bosom lie,
Or to that orb your flight you raise
    Where Enoch stays;

Or to the third celestial sphere,
Where wonders Paul was rapt to hear,
Or Hades bless'd where souls elect
    Full bliss expect.

Secure your Love while here below,
And dying you'll to Jesus go:
Paul long'd loved Jesus' face to view,
    For that long you.

Bleſs'd Jeſus' boundleſs bliſs Divine
In you in miniature will ſhine,
Glory for glory, beam for beam
     Will on you ſtream.

A crown, a throne at God's right Hand,
Where Saints their robes of ray expand,
Where Saints are kings, and on their ſtate
     High Angels wait.

Such bleſſings on the Saints attend,
When Jeſus-like they Heaven aſcend,
The Lamb, of joys the boundleſs ſpring,
     They'll ever ſing.

Death our fore-runner is, and guides
To Sion, where the Lamb abides,
There Saints enjoy ecſtatic reſt
     In manſions bleſt.

Death, I well know, that every day
Wiſe Providence appoints your way,
Your thirſt for blood would ſlay mankind,
     If not confined.

I long to reach the Lamb's dear ſight,
Be ſure to hit my vitals right,
Left life half left prolongs my days
     And bliſs delays.

FOURTH SUNDAY AFTER EPIPHANY.

Omnipotence.

But the men marvelled, saying, What manner of man is this, that even the winds and the sea obey him?
Matthew viii. 27.

MY God, 'tis by Thy sweet supports,
I offer Thee my last efforts;
In my declining painful years,
Thy gracious aid my spirit cheers;
Hymns on Thy Power benign I'll still compose,
From which my power to love and hymn Thee rose.

I humbly, Lord, adore Thy Might,
With Deity co-infinite;
Nothing's impossible to Thee,
Unless uncapable to be;
Which either contradiction pure implies,
Or cannot with Thy nature harmonize.

Thy Power could out of Nothing rear
Earth, ocean, the celestial sphere,
And pass the boundless gulf betwixt
Eternal Nought and Being fix'd;
Thy Power immense, which could on Nothing act,
Could, with like ease, unnumber'd worlds extract.

Thou, Lord, didst speak when Nothing heard,
And instantly a world appear'd;
To all things Thou didst space divide,
In minutes, Time began to glide;
O wondrous Power, which all things out of Nought,
By but a word, in beauteous order brought.

When all things, with coeval Light,
Were form'd by Thy Ideas bright;
All joy'd their Being to commence,
Nought could insult Omnipotence;
When Thy Almighty Word its effluence made,
Obediential chaos ne'er gainsaid.

But when Thou hadst fall'n man in view,
And Thy lapsed creature wouldst renew,
A thousand oppositions rose,
That new Creation to oppose;
Concupiscence, the World, and Hell combined,
To grieve, to outrage, Goodness unconfined.

Thy mighty Love would then redeem
The objects of Thy hate extreme,
And sent God Filial from on high,
For sinners on the Cross to die;
Thy Love was more omnipotent to save,
Than Thy creative power, which Being gave.

Since Angels, men, and all below,
To Thy sole Word existence owe;

Saints, in the moſt afflictive hour,
Recumb on Thy propitious power;
Thou, Who the world didſt by Thy Word create,
Canſt reſcue from the moſt minacious[1] fate.

All things from Thee, which Being took,
Thy Omnipreſent Eyes o'erlook;
Thy Power o'er Heaven and Earth preſides,
All things controls, ſupports and guides;
Since all events Thy Power, wiſe, gracious,
    ſteers,
Thy lovers live exempt from ſervile fears.

O happy ſouls, who in diſtreſs
Have to Omnipotence acceſs;
No Faithful ever pray in vain,
Their prayers Almighty ſuccours gain;
Omnipotence with Goodneſs ſtill is join'd,
Both to ſoft pity always are inclined.

Lord, the ſame Power which ſaints ſuſtains,
Inflicts on rebels endleſs pains;
Thy Power is by Thy Juſtice ſway'd,
And ſin is with due plagues repay'd;
O may I ne'er that awful Power diſpleaſe,
Which keeps of endleſs Life and Death the keys!

Thy friend was, Lord, to walk enjoin'd,
With Thy Omnipotence in mind,

---

[1] *Minacious*, full of terror.

  To keep, in every step he trod,
   A reverential sight of God;
May dread of the Almighty's Presence rest,
Each step I take, imprinted on my breast.

  By miracles which Jesus wrought,
  God-man His Power Almighty taught;
  Faith, to that gracious Might resign'd,
  No dolorous Martyrdom declined;
The world no blessing knows, which can in need,
Compassionate Omnipotence exceed.

  King David on Thy Power relied,
  And, single, num'rous hosts defied;
  When Death with all his terrors tries
  The Saints to frighten or surprise,
They him, disarm'd of deadly sting, outbrave,
Assured Thy Power will raise them from the grave.

  Should devils a Saint's woe conspire,
  With spite as raging as their fire;
  With them should all fierce Neroes meet,
  Inflamed with their infernal heat;
And quintessential torturing pains compound,
They might a Saint afflict, but not confound.

  Firm trust in God would him secure,
  Amidst his pains of Triumph sure;

>   His Heavenly Crown he'd keep in view,
>   His patience would their rage outdo;
> O vain efforts, the world and Tophet make,
> Souls ſhelter'd in Almighty Arms to ſhake.
>
>   To the Omnipotent, Who reigns,
>   I offer up my humble ſtrains;
>   With Saints I to the Heavenly King
>   My Hallelujahs ſtrive to ſing;
> When from frail fleſh I take ſupernal flight,
> I God ſhall hymn, at the celeſtial height.

FIFTH SUNDAY AFTER EPIPHANY.

Matthew xiii. 24-30.

> LORD, 'tis not in Thy Church alone,
>   That tares among good corn are ſown;
> Satan our hearts to diſcompoſe,
>   His tares there ſows.
>
> Soon as the amiable Dove
> Sheds in our hearts celeſtial Love;
> And our clear'd heaven-erected eyes
>   This world deſpiſe;
>
> Soon as our powers begin to feel
> The ſuavities of heavenly zeal,
> And ſtand propending to obey
>   Love's gentle ſway:

Satan his force and wiles collects,
Loose thoughts into our souls injects,
Which our imaginations lure
    To loves impure.

Thy Word, Lord, in this life declares,
That corn will mingled be with tares,
Thou separation dost delay
    Till Judgment Day.

My God, let neither tares nor weeds,
Choke in my soul Thy heavenly seeds,
Keep, Lord, what Thou Thyself dost sow,
    From the cursed foe.

From the cursed foe, for in my heart
'Tis he would fain usurp a part,
But I to Thee my heart resign,
    Keep what is Thine.

My Love shall Satan's spite oppose,
And if in me his tares he sows,
May he at Judgment bear the blame,
    I them disclaim.

Tares in the hearts of Saints remain,
Foils to the true and beauteous grain,
For love they trials are design'd
    In souls refined.

Our birth propension sensual sows
To wilful sin, which cherish'd grows;
We all our life must God invoke,
    That growth to choke.

To all the daughters of lapſed Eve,
Eve-like concupiſcences cleave,
And 'tis by power of Grace Divine,
    We them confine.

Grace, which all votaries' wants ſupplies,
Which God to no weak ſoul denies,
Strengthening the fraileſt, to repel
    The powers of hell.

Live ſatisfied to be ſincere,
Infirmities you'll ſuffer here,
None to perfection can attain,
    Till Heaven they gain.

Lord, ſow Love in our ſpirits deep,
That each a daily crop may reap,
To Thee a harveſt every day,
    Of Love to pay.

SIXTH SUNDAY AFTER EPIPHANY.
The Trumpet.

And he ſhall ſend his angels with a great ſound of a trumpet, and they ſhall gather together his elect from the four winds, from one end of heaven to the other.
                      Matthew xxiv. 31.

IN univerſal dread I waked,
    Each atom in me quaked,
Tremendous ſounds, methought, hung in my ear,
Which ſhook the circumambient ſphere,

Methought it reach'd to hell,
Where all the frighted fiends a-trembling fell.

   I starting, to my Guardian say,
     Sure 'tis the Judgment Day,
Woe, woe, is me, my soul is unprepared,
   I am unutterably scared;
     O for one minute more,
In which I may my numerous sins deplore!

   To God send penitential cries;
     My Guardian then replies,
God gives you time your wanderings to lament,
   Which should upon your knees be spent:
     What found, I then rejoin'd,
Is that, which with this horror strikes my mind?

   I saw, my Guardian said, this night
     An Angel in his flight,
One of the seven, who at God's Throne of State
   With their celestial trumpets wait,
     Him I, in darted thought,
To rest himself a while with me besought.

   He mildly yields, I him embrace,
     And as he took his place,
I saw his trumpet hang between his wings,
   As we discoursed of heavenly things,
     And his right hand contain'd
Seven thunder-bolts, for some cursed land
     ordain'd.

AFTER EPIPHANY.

Ah me! said I, how is mankind
    Turn'd deaf, dumb, stupid, blind!
To the surprise of death and endless woes,
    Each moment they themselves expose;
      This soul I tender here,
I rarely make my warnings to revere.

    I long my pupil to secure,
      And keep him Christ-like pure,
O lift your radiant trumpet to your head,
    Sound in the key which wakes the dead,
      Sound singly to his ear;
Wake all ye dead, at Judgment to appear.

    The Angel with my wish conspired,
      Sounding what I desired,
But much more dreadful, more surprising found
    Will through the hollow graves rebound,
      When the last trump begins
To summon souls to Judgment for their sins.

    I thanks to my good Angel paid,
      The warning duly weigh'd,
The sound continues lively in my mind,
    And when to ill I am inclined,
      The trumpet I recall,
To keep me watchful, and prevent my fall.

SEPTUAGESIMA SUNDAY.

Justice.

But he answered one of them, and said, Friend, I do thee no wrong: didst not thou agree with me for a penny?
Matthew xx. 13.

THY Justice, Lord, my song excites,
   Which guilty spirits frights;
As guardian it Thy Love attends,
   Thy Goodness it defends;
   Men would Thy Love despise,
Hadst Thou not awful Justice to chastise.

Ah, had we innocence retain'd,
   Love o'er our powers had reign'd;
Love which our souls to God had sway'd,
   God had with love repaid;
   Reciprocations dear,
Had made this world a beatific sphere.

O cursed sin! provoking God,
   To His avenging rod;
Which set just jealous God on flame,
   To vindicate His Name;
   Yet in God's Justice we
Benignities still tempering terror see.

Meek Moses saw with happy eye,
   Thy Goodness passing by;

SEPTUAGESIMA SUNDAY.

Thy Goodnefs, Lord, was firft proclaim'd,
   Next that Thy Juftice named;
  Both amicably join'd,
But the firft place to Goodnefs was affign'd.

Thy Wifdom with Thy Juftice fides,
   And Thy vaft empire guides;
Nothing unworthy thence can flow,
   On finners here below;
  Thou never couldft create,
A creature purpofely to damn and hate.

Our being from Thy Goodnefs ftreams,
   Suftain'd by gracious beams;
And 'tis Thy Will we fhould love Thee,
   With love entire and free;
  But we, propenfe to ill,
Crofs the juft native purpofe of Thy Will.

Thou, Lord, rebellious man to fave,
   Wouldft Thy dominion waive;
A covenant Thou didft begin,
   To refcue him from fin;
  By powerful hope, and fear,
Hell to embitter, glory to endear.

Thy Juftice which conftrains Thy Will,
   Thy Promife to fulfil;
Creates condecencies as ftrict,
   Woes threaten'd to inflict;
  Thou, Lord, in both are true,
The faint and finner both fhall have their due.

When sinners boundless Love repel,
    'Gainst gracious God rebel;
For things vain, hurtful, transient, ill,
    Which in fruition kill;
    When they make God so cheap,
'Tis just they of their crimes the fruits should reap.

Though, Lord, Thy distributions here,
    Oft clouded may appear;
And we into Thy conduct strive,
    In vain, by guess, to dive;
    At the all-clearing Day,
Thy Justice will emit unblemish'd ray.

No damned wretch shall then complain
    Of undeserved pain;
Thy Justice will abatements make,
    For frailty and mistake;
    Thy ears will open be,
To hear the least commiserable plea.

Each guilty and upbraiding breast
    Shall their just doom attest;
And as they into hell are thrown,
    Their cursed option own;
    'Twill be their torturing woe,
That to themselves they their damnation owe.

Thy punishment shall sinners grieve,
    While chastening Saints receive;

That, from effential juftice flows,
    This, love paternal fhows;
    For poifon that's defign'd,
For medicine this, to cure a fickly mind.

To none, juft God, Thou partial art,
    Thy favourite is the heart;
All who to Thee whole hearts direct,
    Thou wilt pronounce elect;
    They'll urge no dark decree,
But plead prayers, tears, and Jefus on the Tree.

Saints at the Day which finners dread
    With joy fhall raife their head;
They'll Jefus fee enthroned on high,
    Who would to fave them die;
    He, Who their nature bore,
Will mildly judge the failings they deplore.

We, Lord, Thy juftice plainly read,
    When common death we heed;
It is of fin the wages due,
    Drawn from the fontal two;
    Though death I muft endure,
From fin, which gives its fting, my foul fecure.

May I in view of the great Day,
    My fins diftinctly weigh;
On all efforts of worldly luft,

Pafs condemnation juft ;
Before the Judge enthroned,
Plead my guilt, felf-condemn'd and ftain-bemoan'd.

All praife to God Who joys and woes
 Will in juft lots difpofe ;
Whofe juftice, fhining in true light,
 Will faints to hymn excite ;
 O then, with confcience clear,
May I my joyful Abfolution hear !

SEXAGESIMA SUNDAY.

If I muft needs glory, I will glory of the things which concern mine infirmities.—2 *Cor.* xi. 30.

FRIEND, for my pain your moan forbear,
 It comes from God's paternal care ;
From pain I ghoftly health derive,
It is my foul's reftorative.

When you obferve a father mild
Correct his dear beloved child,
You fee the yearnings he betrays,
At each foft ftripe he on him lays.

If fathers here, who fons chaftife,
Thus with their children fympathife

Thence eſtimate the boundleſs Love
In our bleſs'd Father, God above.

All loves paternal here below,
From Fontal Love Paternal flow;
If finite nature is thus kind,
What is the Love that's unconfined?

You by the rills the ſource may gueſs,
You'll then leſs pity my diſtreſs;
Love Infinite my medicine ſends,
And nothing but pure love intends.

Let Love immenſe His work fulfil,
My pains inſtructive cure my will;
Love ſaw me cool, I by His rod
Shall re-enamour'd be of God.

QUINQUAGESIMA SUNDAY.

Though I ſpeak with the tongues of men and of angels, and have not charity, I am become as ſounding braſs, or a tinkling cymbal.—1 *Cor.* xiii. 1.

ALL praiſe to Thee, great God, we owe,
To Thee, from Whoſe inſpirings flow
Our ſouls immortal, unconfined,
    For Heaven deſign'd.

In vain, though like the seraphs bright,
Should be our intellectual light,
Shouldst not Thou with that light instil
      Unbounded will.

Will, which all other powers transcends,
By native weight to Thee propends;
And when propension is entire,
      'Tis love on fire.

Love, O my God, my soul esteems
The dearest of Thy gracious beams,
Saints no delight in life would take
      But for Love's sake.

Thou boundlessly enamouring sense
Hast of Thy Loveliness immense;
And souls who at Love boundless aim
      Have God-like flame.

Thy Beauties seen obscurely here,
Our souls transportingly endear:
In the attractives all combine
      Of Love Divine.

Soft yearnings of a Father mild,
On His lost miserable child.
God-man Who suffer'd pangs extreme,
      Foes to redeem.

The hoverings of the gracious Dove,
To fire, and fuel Heavenly Love,

Rewards, which utmost thought exceed,
  For love decreed.

Love was God's native, prime design,
In mutual love with souls to join:
But God and souls sin disunites,
  And hate excites.

O helpless! O tremendous state
Of souls, who God all lovely hate;
By like aversion angels fell,
  To people hell.

To love Thee, Lord, sure human-kind
Need not by Thee to be enjoin'd:
All who Thy Love but dimly know
  Must lovers grow.

Rewards, attractives, object, aid,
Love irresistibly persuade;
Yet Love to raise a gentle awe
  Became a law.

Of laws, the dearest and the best,
The happiness of spirits bless'd:
Saints here those hours they spend in love
  Taste joys above.

That I should love Thee is Thy Will,
Which I live longing to fulfil;
Since, Lord, in love we both conspire,
  Keep bright the fire.

Fire, which with such sweet force may burn,
That even my ashes in my urn
Towards Thee, may till the day of doom,
  Like incense fume.

ASH WEDNESDAY.

HARK, O my soul, the trumpet blows,
 The sound each mind considerate knows;
It is a grave and solemn note,
Fit serious passion to promote;
It warns the faithful to repair
Devoutly to the house of prayer.

The sound, methinks, comes from on high,
My soul, toward Heaven erect your eye;
Soon as my eye towards Heaven I rear'd,
A Woman in the air appear'd,
A comelier face I never saw,
She struck sweet reverential awe.

She came through the ethereal globe,
Array'd in a long, mourning robe,
On a thick cloud her stand she took,
And all the world could overlook,
Down her Archangel with her flew,
And it was he the trumpet blew.

Up then I saw the Angel take
His speaking-trump, dull souls to wake,

Then sounded, To the Church give ear,
Whom God commands all souls to hear.
When Holy Church I knew, I guess'd
What made her change that day her vest.

Her mantle was the sun till now,
A crown of stars adorn'd her brow;
But off her glories all were thrown,
When she was clothed for sacred moan,
The darkest solar spot she chose,
Which should her goodly form enclose.

The saints their Mother all revered,
The Angel straight the medium clear'd,
His wings away the vapours swept,
Left they her voice should intercept,
To souls below she thus address'd,
While tears ran down her mourning vest.

Dear children, whom with pain I bore
To people Heaven, and God adore,
I grieve to see the ghostly foes
Who your eternal bliss oppose,
How you to damn yourselves combine,
And hourly dare the wrath Divine.

My tender bowels towards you yearn,
While your sad dangers I discern;
I oft, your ruin to prevent,
Gave you loud warnings to repent;
But you at nought my warnings set,
Or heed them not, or soon forget.

To make you heed, and to retain
Repentance, which prevents your bane,
I solemn, annual fasts enjoin'd,
For you restoratives design'd;
But my injunctions you reject,
And sick of guilt, your cure neglect.

How have hell-powers their empire spread!
How are my children captive led!
Ah me! their arms they throw away!
Did they devoutly fast and pray,
Should all apostate ghosts unite,
One saint would all to Tophet fright.

Jews kept of fasts a yearly round,
Though by no heavenly precept bound;
God no command for fasts would lay
But on their Expiation-day;
In sin you daily persevere,
Which you should expiate all the year.

Your nature, when you suffer woes,
Of course your usual meals foregoes;
Did you for sin but truly grieve,
Though you should no command receive,
You fasting would esteem a rite
Con-natural to hearts contrite.

Your Kalendars for fasts present
Rogation, Vigil, Ember, Lent,

While you to keep thofe names contend,
Licentious guides loofe volumes vend,
Their real fubftance to evade,
And have their force fruftaneous made.

Ah! had you them devoutly kept,
For your own provocations wept,
And public guilt on them bemoan'd,
You then God's anger had atoned,
You had the growth of fin reftrain'd,
And penitential zeal maintain'd.

All my firft-born, with facred heat,
Their ftations weekly would repeat,
The more they curfed fin bewail'd,
The more celeftial truth prevail'd.
But now, alas! throughout the year
I few can find who fhed a tear.

On public fafts faints heretofore
Were wont tranfgreffions to deplore,
Thofe facred days they ne'er ordain'd,
But fignal benedictions gain'd;
Read the memoirs of ages paft,
They conquer'd by their prayer and faft.

O'er Benjamites, Faft got the day,
O'er Philiftines and hofts of Ai,
Made Moab and proud Ammon bleed,
All Ifrael from maffacre freed,
And to repent great God inclined
Of plagues for Nineveh defign'd.

When they the public guilt confess'd,
Sackcloth with ashes was their vest;
They sadly mourn'd, their garments tore,
Fell prostrate, mercy to implore,
Earth was the covering of their head,
As if unworthy earth to tread.

Their souls they with afflicting pain'd,
E'en from fair water they abstain'd;
The breasts to infants were denied,
The beasts were up from pasture tied,
Whole nights and days their hearts they rent,
In penitential rigour spent.

If Jews 'gainst sin such zeal express'd,
Much more should Christians it detest,
Like motives in you both conspire,
Like sins, and like impending ire,
Like ghostly, and like temporal ills,
Like worldly minds, and sensual wills.

In public guilt you both partake,
Both God, the Source of Good, forsake;
Yet on both states while I reflect,
In you I greater guilt detect;
You 'gainst the greater light rebel,
Your grief should Jewish far excel.

Your sins contribute to fill up
Of God's dire wrath the bitter cup,
And to the part of guilt you bear,
Proportion'd draughts will be your share;

But mourners by God's Angel sign'd,
Midst thunder-bolts shall safety find.

My watchmen all my lines around,
Should on this day their trumpets sound,
If to sit silent they presumed,
They'll for your blood to flames be doom'd;
If you neglect them when they blow,
On your own heads will fall the woe.

You, dearest saints, who sympathise
With all the tears which waste mine eyes,
Assist my grief while I bemoan
All outrage 'gainst Jehovah's Throne,
And o'er your land with sorrow deep,
Like Jesus o'er the city, weep.

Of sin you'll have the livelier sense,
If fasts in secret you commence.
Bless'd Jesus, in devout retreat,
Full forty days abstain'd from meat;
There He devout, ideal Lent,
In prayer and contemplation spent.

Should you from Jesus kindle flame,
And now at like retirement aim,
With humble fasts, prayer, alms and tear,
Though mix'd with frailties, yet sincere,
A penitential Sabbath keep,
Heaven on your heads would blessings heap.

Your fouls from drofs you would refine,
To copy purity Divine,
When the laft trump fhall wake the dead,
You'll then exulting raife your head;
And when at Judgment you appear,
Joy you obey'd the trumpet here.

This faid, the Church to Heaven reflew,
I keep her ftill in ghoftly view.
All praife to God, whofe trumpets found
To waken fouls from fleep profound;
O, may I all God's warnings take,
And, raifed from fin, die broad awake!

FIRST SUNDAY IN LENT.

The Temptation.

Then was Jefus led up of the fpirit into the wildernefs to be tempted of the devil.—Matthew iv. 1.

BLEST Spirit, who the woman's Offspring led
    Into the wild, to bruife the ferpent's head,
Help me in facred numbers to recite
His glorious conqueft, and the tempter's flight.

Soon as great God amidft clear Jordan's wave,
To His loved Son His atteftation gave,
The Holy Spirit His retreat infpired,
And Jefus to the wildernefs retired,

There to encounter the full power of hell,
And teach mankind temptations to repel;
Curfed Satan then, alarm'd with fpiteful fear,
Flew fwiftly to the Luciferian fphere,
With the arch-rebel mifchief to invent,
Who inftantly applauded his intent;
And Lucifer, at Satan's dire requeft,
The fall'n archangels, who whole realms infeft,
Call'd from their feveral ftations to his aid,
And three mock-thunders were the fignal made.
In a fhort time when the abaddons came,
Satan thus ftrove their fury to inflame.

Great Lucifer, and brave abaddons all,
Advanced to govern kingdoms fince our fall;
You the man Jefus know, that hateful Name,
Who dares a war againft hell's powers proclaim:
Man I muft ftyle Him, for He feems no more,
Both He and Adam feem of equal ore;
If man, He to temptation open lies,
I Him, as well as Adam, may furprife;
Yet fomething more than Adam, I fufpect,
When on fome ill abodings I reflect;
Dark prophecies predict our falling ftate,
The wonders at His birth fome dread create,
His Baptifm, and the bright appearance there,
Affright our realm with a tremendous glare.
Yet to fit ftill would be eternal fhame,
And we too late our cowardice may blame;
Lend me your help, I'll to confound Him try,

I'll with this Son of God for conquest vie:
You must in the encounter me attend,
Though I shall more on wile than force depend.
I saw Him in the waste alone abide;
And we can muster thousands on our side.
Come all well arm'd, and keep me in your eye;
In ambuscado, till I call you, lie.
There is a mount, which you remember well,
Which none of Jury's hills in height excel,
If by smooth guile the wretch I cannot court,
This Son of God I thither will transport;
You must all subterraneous fires foment,
Of all effluviums quicken the ascent;
The exhalations which earth's moisture drain,
All vapours streaming from the spacious main,
And spirits which from subtiler bodies rise
In that horizon artfully comprise;
From various tinctures various colours mix,
Such as may in the cloud surrounding fix;
Each, dipping in the paint his taper'd spear,
Must draw his proper kingdom on the sphere,
And all its glories to the life describe,
That at one view the eye may all imbibe,
Thrones, sceptres, crowns, gems, robes, wealth,
    power immense,
Lascivious beauties, all that charms the sense;
I'll offer all, His constancy to shake,
If He's a mortal man, the bait will take;
If take, we shall on God revenge our doom,
And boldly may on nobler aims presume.

I'll watch the lucky moment for assault,
This Son of God to Satan shall revolt.
With that each flew to his appointed post,
While he patroll'd along the sandy coast.

While God Incarnate in the desert stay'd,
The fiercest beasts their homage to Him paid;
Beasts more humane than the obdurate Jew,
They with less savage fury men pursue;
There He His hours in contemplation spent,
Gave His unbounded Spirit boundless vent.
The fiend, whose malice could endure no rest,
Strives thoughts impatient, impious to suggest;
Putting his hellish malice on the rack,
Twice twenty days he plied the fierce attack,
That he at last might overwhelm His strength,
By number, importunity, and length;
But Jesus fix'd on Heaven His steady mind,
And no suggestion there could entrance find;
The Father with pleased eyes His Son beheld,
Saw Satan by the woman's Seed repell'd;
Till, after forty days' continued fast,
He to keen hunger condescends at last.

The watchful tempter soon the hunger knew,
And up to air in twice three minutes flew,
Where he of brightest lightning wove a vest,
And his foul spirit in feign'd glory drest;
Mock-thunderbolt in his right hand he grasp'd,
His left, a flaming, dazzling sceptre clasp'd;

A crown of meteor-stars adorn'd his head,
All calculated for exciting dread;
Then on the stream of a tempestuous wind,
He flew to act the malice he design'd;
His voyage at the locust-tree he closed,
Where Jesus in the barren wild reposed;
Son of that God, said he, above enthroned,
While I sole god am of this region own'd,
Upon the mountain I to Moses spoke,
The sphere was then fill'd all with fire and smoke;
But I to you descend in kindly flame,
Your welcome to my empire to proclaim;
Your hunger some mortality betrays,
Which yet your power can ease unnumber'd ways;
Command these stones to turn to bread; that sign
Will witness your original Divine.
Man best, said Jesus, by God's Word is fed,
And lives not merely by his daily bread.

Then to the Temple battlement, through air,
The fiend wafts Jesus, Jesus to ensnare;
God, said he, charge upon His angels lays
To keep your feet unhurt in stony ways,
Cast yourself down, the angels in their arms
Will catch you falling, and secure from harms.
The sacred writings, Jesus said, declare,
To tempt the Lord thy God, thou shalt not dare.

Thence Jesus to the mountain he conveys,
And all his confluence of charms displays;

All that could ravish, tempt, delight mankind,
Was there in lively images combined.
You, said the fiend, the Lord of all shall be,
If you but prostrate fall and worship me;
For all this lower universe is mine,
I to bestow it have the right divine.
Let me cease to be god, if I delay
To give you over all despotic sway.
Get thee behind Me, Satan, Christ replied,
Thou by God's Word art as His creature tied;
The Lord thy God to worship, Him to own,
And pay obeisance to His sovereign throne.
The fiend, who heard himself by Jesus named,
Confounded was, but could not be ashamed;
And raving at discovery of his cheats,
As towards his ambuscado he retreats,
He Michael met, with the angelic bands,
Who lay encamp'd upon the desert sands,
All arm'd, at call their Lord to have relieved,
Had they not His victorious might perceived.
Bright Michael, left proud Satan should escape,
Seized the fiend flying, tore his glittering shape;
Satan assumed his horrid form again,
And Michael bound him with a double chain,
Sent him to the abaddons' ambuscade,
His feeble spite to punish and upbraid.
The radiant host put them in dreadful fright,
They felt their strength in the angelic fight;
All were just taking wing, when Satan came
In chains, and stripp'd of his prestigious flame;

All vow'd of pains he should have Tophet's store,
And, what would grieve him most, should tempt
    no more.

Brave Michael and his host to Jesus haste,
And brighten'd with their wings the dismal waste.
Soon as they Jesus saw, they Him surround,
And fell in low prostrations on the ground;
The seraphs sang a new triumphant song,
And to their harps sang all the radiant throng,
With loud Hosannahs they each stanza closed,
And to obey His orders stood disposed;
Our Lord their zeal approved with gracious eye,
And sent them to resume their bliss on high.

Though Jesus in the wild had nought to eat,
To do His Father's pleasure was His meat,
And a return He to the world design'd,
To perfect the Redemption of mankind;
There He vouchsafed His mortal food to take,
And suffer human frailty for man's sake.
Bless'd Jesus, to the lonely waste retired,
Ere to His charge prophetic He aspired;
And saints, ere they on public posts attend,
Choice hours in prayer, retreat, and fasting spend.
Writ Sacred for His magazine He chose,
Hell better to unmask and to oppose;
He of God's Presence taught a constant awe,
From Satan with abhorrence to withdraw,
That he with zeal resisted, always flies,
Can conquer none, who this vain world despise;

That all in aid Divine fhould acquiefce,
Diftrufting neither fuccour nor fuccefs:
For daily food take no unlicenfed way,
Beft feafted, when they beft God's Will obey:
By no rafh acts God's promife to abufe,
And by prefumptuous pride the bleffing lofe:
That ficrceft fights fhew virtues moft fublime,
Like Jefus to be tempted is no crime;
That when curfed Satan feems to be fubdued,
Souls his return by watching muft preclude;
That angels ever take a lover's part,
And help him to repel each fiery dart;
That Jefus, Satan of his force bereft,
And conqueft eafy to His votaries left.

All glory to God's Son, whofe humble might
Taught feeble man victorioufly to fight.
Glory to Jefus all the quire repeats,
Who the full force and fraud of hell defeats.

SECOND SUNDAY IN LENT.

We befeech you, brethren, and exhort you by the Lord Jefus, that as ye have received of us how you ought to walk, and to pleafe God, fo ye would abound more and more.—1 *Thefs.* iv. 1.

WE, like the fly, muft from the world retreat,
And wifely manage our fhort vital heat;
What is our life but a repeated day?

We quickly paſs our noon, and waſte away;
We daily the like ghoſtly dangers meet,
We the ſame duties every day repeat:
Strive that this day may yeſterday out-do,
Of virtue nobler heights each day purſue;
God to the preſent day our view confined,
Would have us for the future live reſign'd;
Taught us to pray for only daily bread,
And truſt on Him to be to-morrow fed;
Lord, daily bread, but love perpetual give,
Without Thy love we can no minute live;
We'll to the preſent day our cares conſign
And live in reverence of the Eye Divine:
We may our flocks aſſiduouſly inſpect,
With minds to Heaven habitually erect;
Each day we from the world as looſe ſhould ſit,
As if aſſured the world at night to quit:
Accounts with Heaven we'll daily even keep,
Should the laſt trump ſurpriſe us in our ſleep;
But death can truly ſudden be to none,
Who by repentance daily God atone.
We'll live God's children, and, to God reſign'd,
A brother and a ſiſter to mankind.
We'll to our fly give freedom, that he may
Live his age o'er with happineſs to-day;
He with his lot was in the garden pleaſed,
Till you the well-contented creature ſeized;
From him each day we'll learn to live content
Upon the daily manna God has ſent;
With thanks to God we'll now our meal begin,

Sweet is the meal which is not foured by fin;
Sweet is the meal which wafted ftrength recruits,
That God may of our vigour have the fruits;
Sweet is the meal, when as our body's fed,
Our fpirit hungers for fupernal bread;
This day to future days fhall be the plan,
We'll every day do all the good we can:
By God's fweet aid no minutes we'll mifpend,
On thefe time-drops eternal joys depend.
A thoufand years to God is but a day,
Eternity of Love feels no decay.
We'll ftrive to imitate our God above,
And live each day a thoufand years of love.

THIRD SUNDAY IN LENT.

And it came to pafs as He fpake thefe things, a certain woman of the company lift up her voice, and faid unto Him, Bleffed is the womb that bare thee, and the paps which thou haft fucked.—*Luke* xi. 27.

OF all who e'er, with heart unfeign'd,
 Kept virgin-love for God unftain'd,
  Propending to no ill,
  With full confent of will,
  Blefs'd Mary far excell'd,
Who all rebellious paffions quell'd.

She Jefus in her womb inclofed,
 There thrice three months the Babe repofed,

Then, from His prison loosed,
His morning beams diffused;
But in her heavenly mind
God-man for ever was enshrined.

God-man His Mother pure revered,
And with a thousand loves endear'd;
She form'd Him in her breast,
By that more nobly blest,
Than while her womb Him bore,
As Saint than Mother honour'd more.

She, super-effluently graced,
Away the powers infernal chased,
Her heart with God was fill'd,
No thought could be instill'd,
Her innocence to foil,
But her chaste spirit would recoil.

In reading, meditation, praise,
Prayer, charity, she spent her days;
Ne'er in the world immersed,
With her dear Son conversed,
His beams to recollect,
And in love-languors to reflect.

Her heart bless'd Jesus' ark she made,
Where He His loveliness display'd,
Where love and hymn should wait
On majestatic state,—

> They, like the cherubs placed,
> The gracious Shechinah embraced.

> Her ardent love her hymn fupplied,
> Hymn fuel would for love provide,
>   Alternately both fired,
>   Alternately infpired,
>   Alternately increafed,
> Their alternations never ceafed.

> All faints, like Mary, are enjoin'd
> To form God-man in hearts refined,
>   Each imitable grace
>   Muft there poffefs its place;
>   May I to Jefus cleave,
> And Jefus in my heart conceive.

> When Jefus in my heart is form'd,
> I fhall no more by hell be ftorm'd,
>   His graces He'll infufe;
>   I ne'er fhall Jefus lofe;
>   My love can ne'er grow cold,
> While the inflammative I hold.

FOURTH SUNDAY IN LENT.

The Life of Jesus.

And a great multitude followed Him, becaufe they faw His miracles which He did on them that were difeafed.
John vi. 2.

BLEST Spirit, who on Jefus' facred Head
Didft boundlefs grace like precious ointment fhed,
One drop vouchfafe me of that holy oil,
To fing my Lord's falvific care and toil,
Whofe love immenfe unwearied day and night,
O'er the dark world diffufed celeftial light.

Chaotic mafs in darknefs buried lay,
Till God commanded antefolar day,
In intellectual chaos thus mankind
Lay ignorant, confufed, erroneous, blind,
Till the bright Sun of Righteoufnefs arofe,
Propitious beams and influence to difclofe,
Infernal mifts the univerfe o'erfpread,
And lying fpirits human minds mifled;
The world was with unhallow'd temples ftored,
Foul devils for Jehovah were adored;
Religion fank to diabolic rites,
Apoftacy extinguifh'd native lights.
God's own peculiar care, the chofen Jew,

Who God by wondrous revelation knew,
With numerous sects, and with traditions vain,
Strove truths reveal'd to blend, pervert and stain;
Above God's law exalted their own dreams,
Damp'd of Messiah all prophetic gleams,
Zealous their superstitions to obtrude,
Zealous their own salvation to elude,
When the great Prophet, long ago foretold,
Was sent from God, God's pleasure to unfold.

Forth from the bosom of the fontal fire,
Where Son and Father the blest Dove co-spire,
Came the Eternal Word to wear our clay,
And Godhead unafflictingly display.
Truths, which the prophets partially discern'd,
By vision, dream, voice, inspiration learn'd,
He not from faith, but beatific sight
Presented in their full enamouring light;
God-man exposed Himself to mortal eyes,
His laws to sweeten and familiarise,
Paternal God with filial always join'd,
And God co-effluent fill'd His human mind.

When Jesus in the wild the conquest won,
Then His prophetic office was begun,
He faithful, no one saving truth conceal'd,
He gracious, the right way to Heaven reveal'd,
Some He exhorted, others He reproved,
Our fears and hopes by threats and blessings moved,
Condemn'd the errors which in public reign'd,

Mysterious types and prophecies explain'd,
Spake things celestial with celestial grace,
All prejudice inveterate to erase;
In obvious parables taught truth sublime,
Spent in illuminating souls His time.
Disseminated light where'er He came,
Breathed heavenly love the frozen to enflame,
Confirm'd by Sacred Writ whate'er He taught,
Down to our weakness all His precepts brought,
Preach'd truths divine, few, necessary, clear,
Which might to Heaven a simple votary steer;
The worst of men He mildly would instruct,
Glad when to Bliss He sinners could conduct;
No raptures, no austerities enjoin'd,
Nothing too high, too grievous for mankind;
No whips, no hair-cloth, His mild yoke imposed,
No souls in constant solitudes enclosed;
Pagans in these of saints might have the start,
They wound the flesh, but cannot break the heart.
Saints Heaven by prayer, alms, gentle fasting,
  scale,
The prophet could by single prayer prevail,
While Baal's priests endured unpitied pain,
Gashing their bodies all day long in vain.

 His life the comment was on what He taught,
That lovely Image ravishes my thought;
None could that life considerately know,
But he of Jesus must enamour'd grow;
In Him ideal graces all combined,

Friend, Benefactor, Saviour to mankind,
Love incommunicable, filial fear,
A conscience un-upbraidingly sincere;
Obedience perfect, free from venial ill,
Full resignation to His Father's Will;
Propensions centrally to God inclined,
Unshaken trust, a heaven-conversing mind;
Intentions which at God's sole glory aim'd,
Zeal which for God's word, house and worship
    flamed;
A temperance, which all excesses curb'd,
Contentedness, by troubles undisturb'd;
Each sense subdued, affections all confined
The dove and serpent amicably join'd;
Virginity, with filthy thought unstain'd,
Which in perpetual holocaust remain'd;
A meekness which no malice could provoke;
A patience to endure a tyrant's stroke;
A courage to encounter all things dire;
A perseverance which could never tire;
A purity which nothing could defile;
A wisdom which hell powers could not beguile;
Humility, which all debasements prized,
Exulting for God's sake to be despised,
Which human confidence would ever waive,
And of all good, to God the glory gave;
Which made disciples, not deep-learn'd, but good,
Who wise for Heaven, Heaven only understood,
Whose warm devotion kept its heaven-born heat,
Oft would to sacred solitudes retreat,

In fasting, meditation, prayer, and praise,
And ghostly watching, spend whole nights and
    days;
No wanderings, damps, or chills, His soul annoy'd,
He no one minute ever misemploy'd;
He troubled minds with consolations cheer'd,
His sweet reproofs the guilty soul endear'd.
To all in need He pity shew'd Divine,
Which unregarded would no cry decline;
His charity all malice could transcend,
To lowest offices inured to bend;
In good return'd all evils to exceed,
To save His foes, content Himself to bleed.
He, to gain souls, wept, travell'd, labour'd, pray'd,
Their bliss eternal His sole business made;
Discourse salvific He at meals instill'd,
And souls with food super-celestial fill'd;
As they could bear, He dropp'd it by degrees,
At once He sweetly could instruct and please.
His justice render'd to all men their due,
Would righteous ends by righteous means
    pursue;
To all estates He proper honours paid,
Revered the priesthood, sovereign power obey'd.
His mind, His own inferior will denied,
The transient world opposed, contemn'd, defied;
Its maxims, customs, companies, designs,
All joys, to which concupiscence inclines;
He Source and Lord of all, knew all things best,
And gave the world no harbour in His Breast;

He here below nor fought, nor felt repofe,
Continued Crofs, He for His portion chofe;
Gave higheſt proof of all that He reveal'd,
When His own Blood its confirmation feal'd.
Angels their graces by His grace refined;
He's the averfion of the worldly mind,
His felf-denials fenfual men difguſt,
Vex'd, that He no indulgence gave to luſt;
Luſt, which impoſtors patronife, and gain
Of loofe difciples an unnumber'd train;
All Jefus' graces had a God-like mien,
By them His heavenly miffion might be feen;
That perfect goodnefs could no man deceive,
That perfect goodnefs none could difbelieve.

When to His doctrine and His life Divine
His fuper-human miracles we join,
They love and admiration both excite,
Conviction will attain its utmoſt height.
He made all creatures ferve His blefs'd defign,
He water tranfubſtantiated to wine;
He trod the wave, and bid the winds be ſtill;
He made rude ſtorms fubmiffive to His will;
A fiſh to Him His tribute-money brought,
Shoals, at His call, came crowding to be caught.
Curfed by His Lips, the fig-tree ſtraight decay'd;
Invifible, He dangers could evade.
He feaſted thoufands with feven loaves of bread;
Two fiſhes and five loaves five thoufand fed;
And of the food thus multiplied remain'd

Twelve baskets, which fresh followers sustain'd;
He made the lame walk, dumb speak, deaf to hear,
And men born blind to see all objects clear;
He dropsies drain'd, and trembling palsies still'd,
The blood inflamed by fevers, gently chill'd;
He lepers cleansed, restored the wither'd hand;—
No ailment could His healing might withstand;—
The bloody-flux, which twelve long years had reign'd,
The poor bow'd woman twice six winters pain'd;
The wretch, who thirty-eight his grief deplored,
And multitudes to soundness He restored.
Even at a distance, by His word alone,
He made His power irrefragably known;
He devils at His pleasure dispossess'd,
Constrain'd by Him, His Godhead they confess'd,
Seven out of tortured Magdalen He drave,
Chased in foul swine a legion to the wave;
Jairus' young daughter, by her friends bemoan'd,
The son for whom his widow-mother groan'd,
And Lazarus, who four days had been entomb'd,
All at His word their vital heat resumed;
Saints at His rising, though long dead, revived,
And risen, at Jerusalem arrived.
From profanations He the Temple clear'd,
Profaners, His majestic voice revered,
Their treasures He o'erthrew, and at His look
The avaricious their dear wealth forsook;
The worldly, at His heart-enamouring call,
Became His votaries, and renounced their all.

He, God Incarnate, could the mind infpect,
And with fweet force the heart to God inflect.
His life, from His conception to His grave,
Strong demonftrations of Meffiah gave;
Divinity fhined bright in all He taught,
God-like benignity in all He wrought;
His miracles He gracioufly defign'd,
To cure, convince, convert, endear mankind.

Eternal Word, who, clothed in human duft,
Didft teach lapfed man the wifdom of the juft;
Illuftrate by example Thy difcourfe,
Confirm it by a wonder-working force;
Open my ears, my eyes, my tongue unloofe,
Into my heart Thy heavenly truth infufe;
That I Thy praife inceffantly may fing,
That love may give my heart a heavenward fpring!
That I may never more towards earth propend,
In vigorous, fweet efforts to Thee afcend;
Thy bright idea in my heart enchafe,
To copy out each imitable grace.

All praife to our great Prophet, by whofe light
The world, born blind, receives its ghoftly fight;
Glory to Jefus, o'er the mount was heard,
For doctrine, life, and miracles, revered.

FIFTH SUNDAY IN LENT.

God's Attributes.

Jefus faid unto them, Verily, verily I fay unto you, Before Abraham was, I am.—*S. John* viii. 58.

ERE the intelligence, from nothing rear'd,
To fpin fucceffion on the fphere appear'd,
To give duration drop by drop, to move
Frail man each fleeting minute to improve;
Thou felf-originated Deity,
In indivifible eternity;
Thou, felf-fufficient, by Thyfelf didft reign,
And with Thyfelf, Thyfelf didft entertain;
No rival infinite could fhare Thy throne,
There no more infinites can be but one;
For were there more, each would each other bound,
All join'd, an infinite could ne'er compound;
All parts are bounds, the thing compounded piece,
And bounds to boundlefs never can increafe.

Bleft Spirit, void of mixture, fhape, or part,
Beft known by not conceiving what Thou art;
Thy Majefty ten thoufand funs outvies,
A fight too radiant for the feraphs' eyes;
Their dazzled view they with their feathers cafe,
Unable to behold Thy glorious Face;

'Tis hard for our arithmetic to count
How much th' Atlantic may one drop surmount;
More difficult the difference to adjust
'Twixt the terraqueous globe and single dust;
But 'tis impossible for man to guess
'Twixt infinite and finite the excess;
If, Lord, with Thee we heaven and earth compare,
They not proportion of one atom bear;
When Moses humbly ask'd Thy glorious Name,
That he might tell the tribes from whom he came,
Jehovah, and I Am, Thou then didst own,
The awful names by which Thou wouldst be
    known;
Thou only canst be truly said to be,
All creatures nothings are, compared to Thee;
Thou art the boundless, everlasting Source
Of all existence, of all vital force.

  Thou Rock of Ages dost the same abide,
While our durations by short minutes glide;
We live in flux, and by degrees, but Thou
Art all at once, in an eternal now;
What's infinite no dissipation knows,
Self-stagnating, it neither ebbs nor flows;
Itself collected with itself consists,
It uniform, immutable exists;
Above all change unchangeable abides,
And as it pleases casual changes guides;
Thy Deity, uncircumscribed by place,
Fills heaven and earth, and extramundane space.

Thou prefent art in the infernal fhade,
The damn'd are of Thy vengeance there afraid;
Thy boundlefs glories in eternal light
Angelic hierarchies to hymn excite;
Thou prefent art in this terreftrial fphere,
Where'er we fly, or hide, Thou ftill art near;
Thou prefent art, when finners dare Thy ftroke,
Thou prefent art, when faints Thy aid invoke;
Thou, in all fin's receffes, doft furvey
Pollution with an unpolluted ray;
Thou prefent art all creatures to fuftain,
And influence Thy univerfal reign;
Thou in the temple of the world doft dwell,
All bleffings to confer, all ills expel;
Benign, or dreadful, Thou ftill prefent art,
In every faint, in every finner's heart;
Thy faints there for Thy Godhead temples build,
Which with Thy gracious Shechinah are fill'd;
And from Thy prefence finners feel within
Anticipations of wrath due to fin.

Thy fuper-immenfe Godhead, Lord, to none
But Thy unmeafurable Self is known;
And in Thy own felf-comprehending Thought
The clear ideas of all things are wrought;
What future fhall, what poffible may be,
Thou in Thyfelf eternally didft fee;
The prefent, paft, and future, all unite
In Thy eternal unfucceffive Sight;
Thou doft the fecrets of all hearts infpect,

And to Thy glory sinful acts inflect;
To all ideas in Thy mind immense,
Thy power an actual being can dispense;
Millions of multifarious worlds, and more,
Thou canst produce out of Thy boundless store;
Thou who didst other possibles refuse,
This series for futurity didst choose;
Thy wondrous works Thy mighty power declare,
Which yet faint sketches of Thy glory are,
By them Thy might we cannot fully rate,
Thou nobler canst to eternity create;
And shouldst Thou endless new creations tend,
Thou yet Thy force couldst not fatigue nor spend.

Holiest of holies, Thou art God alone,
On Thy all-glorious, everlasting Throne;
Thy Nature is immaculately pure,
Cannot the least approach of ill endure;
To Thee all excellencies we ascribe,
Which from Thy fontal fullness we imbibe;
We thoughts distinct of Thy perfections frame,
In Thee all undistinguish'd and the same.

Great God, I Thy infinity adore,
Admire devoutly what I can't explore;
Congratulating, with a joyful heart,
All that Thou dost possess, all that Thou art;
Thou art immutable, I change like wind,
Fix my backsliding and instable mind;
O let Thy Presence o'er all nature spread,

Strike me with constant reverential dread;
I cannot sin but in Thy awful view,
Sin nowhere can escape Thy vengeance due;
O ravish with Thy endless bliss my eyes,
That I may sublunary joys despise;
Thou Searcher of my heart, my heart possess,
Thy own idea deeply there impress;
May I in dangers on Thy power rely,
Safe shelter find, whene'er to Thee I fly;
O purify me, Lord, as Thou art pure,
From the polluting world my soul secure;
Thy image re-engrave; to copy Thee
Is my chief prayer, shall my ambition be.
Though no one mortal e'er Thy face survey'd,
Yet we can love Thy goodness when display'd;
Within the rocky cleft O may I stand,
Supported by Thy own propitious hand;
That as Thy awful glory passes by,
I may like Moses Thy back parts descry.

 Lord, when Thy mighty notion fills my mind,
No words to vent that boundless thought I find;
Thou all perfection, Thou all lovely art,
And shouldst Thou not Thyself to us impart;
Shouldst Thou bare being give, and heaven detain,
Thou yet all intellectual love wouldst gain;
Thy Loveliness no mind could ever know,
But must enamour'd of Thy Godhead grow;
In Thee all that is amiable or sweet,
All irresistible attractives meet;

Nothing or charms or beauty can poſſeſs,
But what it borrows of Thy Lovelineſs;
Incomprehenſible Thou art, above
My utmoſt thought, but not beyond my love;
High as Thou art, Thou canſt not love tranſcend,
I love Thee more, the leſs I comprehend;
The more Thou art above expreſſion raiſed,
Thou art the nobler Subject to be praiſed;
But ſhould I love in moſt intenſe degree,
How incommenſurate is all to Thee!
Lord, I now love by faith, a loftier flight
My love will take, when I ſhall love by ſight.

SUNDAY NEXT BEFORE EASTER.

Name of Jeſus.

Wherefore God alſo hath highly exalted Him, and given Him a Name, which is above every name: that at the Name of Jeſus every knee ſhould bow, of things in heaven, and things in earth, and things under the earth.—*Phil.* ii. 9, 10.

MY God, Thy wiſe, propitious Will
   Raiſed greateſt good from greateſt ill,
  What Adam did amiſs,
    Turn'd to our endleſs bliſs;
O happy ſin, which to atone,
Drew Filial God to leave His Throne!

Should all the race of Adam meet
In a convention as complete
    As that at the Last Day,
    When they resume their clay,
To ask of Heaven what all desire,
They all in Jesus would conspire.

Not all the music of the spheres
Sounds half so sweet in angels' ears,
    As when to hearts contrite
    We Jesus' Name recite,
That Name with sweetness overflows,
Creates full joys, and damps our woes.

The angels never sang an air,
Which could in melody compare
    With that at Jesus' birth,
    When sent to tell the earth
That the co-gracious Three design'd
Great Filial God to save mankind.

When Gabriel first spake Jesus' Name,
The heavenly orbs, the earthly frame,
    Which direful shocks sustain'd
    E'er since the deluge reign'd,
Felt instantly disorders cease,
The universe was bless'd with peace.

When Jesus human air first drew,
Sun, moon, and stars, to gain His view,

Painted their beams to meet,
To kifs His facred Feet,
And fent an envoy ftar, whofe ray
Should fhew the world where Jefus lay.

In Heaven angelic Orders nine,
From fingle to thrice treble fhine,
Of Jefus ever fing,
Adore their humble King,
Each in man's purchafed blifs delights,
And Jefus them to hymn excites.

On earth, fince God the promifed feed
In pure philanthropy decreed,
The Faithful, glory gain'd
By Jefus, unexplain'd,
Clouded in prophecies and type,
'Till men were for the fubftance ripe.

The ghofts apoftate doom'd to dwell,
Since banifh'd Heaven in loweft hell,
Lapfed man with envy eye
On Jefus who rely;
And when of Jefus faints difcourfe,
Tremble at His falvific force.

My Jefus, at Thy Name I bow,
Myfelf Thy holocauft I vow,
Of Jefus all day long
Shall be my grateful fong,
I'll ftrive each fong which I commence
To fing with love ftill more intenfe.

MONDAY BEFORE EASTER.

On the Agony.

BLESS'D Jesus, who didst wondrous grief sustain,
Eternal joy for wretched man to gain,
Fill me with an intenerating sense
Of all the dolours of Thy love immense,
That I, in melting verse, with gushing eyes
May with Thy Agony co-agonize.

Upon a mount near Salem, whose fat soil
Cheers Judah's face with soft distilling oil,
Which shrouds its head in olive-groves from heat,
And in cool Kedron bathes its parched feet,
There is a garden in whose solemn bowers
Our Lord oft spent His consecrated hours;
He thither, with His faithful train, repairs,
And from the Altar leads them to their prayers,
James, John, and Peter thither with Him go,
While the rest waited His return below:
You three, said Jesus, shall My stay attend,
In prayer and watching those choice minutes spend,
Then, heavy and afflicted, He complain'd,
As if already He death's pangs sustain'd;
Grief infinite, and dire internal pain,
Forced His warm Blood to gush from every Vein.

Curſed Invida her ſummons ſtraight diffuſed,
And all the fiends at Salem rendezvouſed;
The leading devils waited by her ſide,
Whoſe malice had in miſchief long been tried;
In arts of tempting moſt minutely verſed,
The reſt ſhe o'er Jeruſalem diſperſed;
As a tired traveller, who ſlumbering lies
Near Zembra's lake, ſtarts up in dire ſurpriſe,
When unicorns, who tread the neighbouring
    ground,
With taper'd horns his moſſy ſhade ſurround;
Inſultingly the wretch they toſs and gore,
He wounded is, and bruiſed, and bleeds all o'er;
Hell powers and furious Jews were thus intent
In fleſh, in ſpirit, Jeſus to torment;
For every paſſion they their batteries built
To raiſe by force, or by vexation, guilt.
His Father's anger, ſin, the bitter cup,
Whoſe dregs He was devoted to drink up,
His ſpirit gored, Hell the advantage weigh'd,
And general aſſaults upon Him made;
Horror, His dangers and His pangs ſuggeſts,
Impatience, with repinings Him infeſts;
Jealouſy, oft His Father's Love would blame,
Diſdain, urged of the Croſs the ſmart and ſhame;
Hate, moved Him to deteſt outrageous Jews,
Revenge, retaliations would infuſe,
Fear, tempted Him approaching pains to fly,
Deſpair, His cruel Father to deny,
Inceſſantly they toſs'd Him, gave no reſt,

Yet no ill thought upon His soul imprest;
Amidst the horns of unicorns he pray'd,
And God dispatch'd a seraph to His aid.
Swift flew the glorious envoy from the Throne,
Saw Jesus sad, and made for Jesus moan;
The blissful spirit, who ne'er grieved before,
Into compassion melted was all o'er,
His vehicle into bright tears condensed,
While thus his heavenly message he com-
  menced.

 God Filial, second of the glorious Trine,
To Whom we adoration pay Divine,
For you, though thus debased, my God I style,
Your heavenly joys suspended seem awhile,
God ne'er abandons His Beloved Son,
God and You co-eternally are One,
'Tis Your good Father's Will, and 'tis Your
  own,
That You for human guilt should thus atone.
Since cursèd sin the righteous God disclaims,
And daringly at God's destruction aims;
For every harden'd sinner has the will
To murder God, could he his wish fulfil.
You the suspense of Deity must bear,
For nothing less the outrage can repair;
You still to God immutably are dear,
God is not to His Son, but sin severe,
Man's guilt, and God's fierce wrath, to sinners
  due,

By God's decree tranflated are on You:
The greater load is on your Spirit laid,
God will be more commenfurately paid;
All the vicarious vengeance you fuftain,
And all your unimaginable pain,
Will God's effential attributes adjuft,
Purchafe immortal Life for mortal duft;
Make finners in Your Name for pardon plead,
Infernal powers fubdue and captive lead,
Make faithful fouls You their Redeemer own,
Exalt Your human nature to God's Throne,
At God's right Hand eternally to reign,
All Heaven in hymns will worfhip the Lamb flain.

Thus fpake the feraph, and to blifs reflew,
He fcarce reach'd Heaven but Jefus grieved anew;
Sin and God's anger were a mighty weight,
Which no feraphic comfort could abate.
Thus grieved, from His three votaries he withdrew,
His awful Face on earth He humbly threw;
Addrefs moft ardent to His Father made,
And with unutterable paffion pray'd.
If, Father, it confifts with Thy decree,
Set Me from this outrageous anguifh free;
Yet, Father, not My will be done, but Thine,
My will, I wholly to Thy Will refign.
With that, bleft Jefus rifing from the ground,
Chid His three votaries, whom He fleeping found;
Could you not for one hour forbear your fleep,

And with devotion this short vigil keep?
O watch and pray, lest Satan you assail,
The spirit willing is, the flesh is frail.
From them the second time He then retreats,
With double fervour the same prayer repeats;
Then, coming back, their eyelids fast were closed,
Strong grief to stupor had their souls disposed;
Again with trebled ardour He retires,
Reiterating still the same desires.
The three He then revisits, and was grieved
That sleep again of sense had them bereaved.
Ah! can you sleep, says He, when trouble's near?
The traitor soon will raise a wakeful fear;
Arise, I'll the approaching danger meet,
Saints, when God wills the sufferings, ne'er retreat.

 Foul Invida, who took no rest at all,
But lived self-tortured ever since her fall,
Her black design to full perfection brought,
And Jews to her own height of malice wrought:
Even elders and high priests ambitious were
In all the envious cruelties to share;
All arm'd with swords and instruments of rage,
And envy, which no yielding could assuage.
The moon in clouds had veil'd her orb of light,
The stars withdrew from the detested sight;
And to supply their room, the savage bands
With lanthorns came, and torches in their hands.
And Judas, lest the soldiers should mistake,
His kiss, the sign, would to direct them, make.

Meeting our Lord, Hail, Master, Hail! he cried,
Then kiss'd Him, and the band the foe descried.
Friend, said meek Jesus, why such force as this?
Canst thou betray thy Master with a kiss?
Whom seek ye? said our Lord, His heavenly Breath
Straight thunder-struck the band, as pale as death;
They, trembling, backward fell upon the ground,
His heavenly rays the armed force confound.
Meek Jesus suffering them to rise again,
Demands, Whom seek ye, with this armed train?
Jesus, they cry; if Me ye seek, said He,
Let these My faithful votaries then go free,
Fulfilling what He spake, that the Elect,
Whom God had given, He would from force protect.

Peter, his Master's champion to appear,
Drew out his sword and cut off Malchus' ear.
Our Lord rebuked his rash, revengeful zeal,
And by His touch vouchsafed the wound to heal.
Shall I, said He, from that dire potion shrink,
Which 'tis My Father's pleasure I should drink?
Twelve arm'd angelic legions ready stand,
Would I use force, to come at My command.
Why as a thief, said Jesus to the crew,
Do you thus arm'd My innocence pursue?
I daily in the Temple taught, and there
None to commit this violence would dare;
But I must suffer, 'tis My Father's Will,
And by My sufferings Holy Writ fulfil:

For Jew and Hell, 'tis the infulting hour,
You to afflict Me, have permitted power.
With that the armed rabble Him furround,
While with rude cords His facred Hands they
    bound;
Accurfed Invida in every breaft
Her fury fo indelibly impreft,
That nor His God-like Look, His heavenly
    Tongue,
(Which to the earth the trembling warriors flung)
Nor the kind miracle on Malchus wrought,
Could raife fo much as one relenting thought;
So wholly unreclaimable are they
Who Love immenfe with outrages repay.

    Like Thy bleft Self, Lord, teach me to fubmit
To all my Heavenly Father fhall think fit;
To yield the full fubjection of a fon,
Pray, Father, not my will, but Thine be done.
He ever lives unviolenced by ill,
Who to His God devoted, has no will;
Since Thou my Father art, O God, I right
Claim in Thy boundlefs Goodnefs, Wifdom,
    Might:
Thy Wifdom will my foul in doubts direct,
Thy Might will in calamities protect,
Thy Goodnefs ne'er will caufelefsly afflict,
With all the three I'll keep a union ftrict;
They'll me proportion what for me is beft,
In their difpofals I entirely reft;

I into Thee refund my borrow'd mind,
To centre in Thee by a will refign'd.

All praife to Jefus! Who our griefs to cure,
Would agonies unfpeakable endure.
Glory to Jefus! ran the mountain o'er,
Whofe limbs were bathed in His own Tears and Gore.

TUESDAY BEFORE EASTER.

The Arraignment of Jefus.

JESU, Who, man in blifs to reinftate,
 Wouldft be the object of Judaic hate,
Help me to fing of the unbounded woes
Which in Thy Soul at Thy arraignment rofe.
 Curfed Invida now thought her plot fecure,
Yet that fhe Jefus' death might more infure,
She orders gave to all the fiends that night
Anew to irritate the Jewifh fpite.
The guard, our Lord now bound, to Annas led,
His envy with that wifh'd-for fight was fed,
And having took his diabolic fill,
Sent Him to Caiaphas to complete the ill.

Soon as they at the palace gate arrive,
The council meet, His ruin to contrive.

Some perjured wretches studiously they sought,
Whose testimonies might with bribes be bought.
O'er all Jerusalem they search'd in vain,
His very foes durst not His virtue stain;
Till Invida with Avarice combined,
And two base villains to the fact inclined,
Who swore that Jesus offer'd in three days
The Jewish Temple to destroy and raise,
But yet in circumstantiating the deed,
They in their depositions disagreed.
Caiaphas strove the crime to aggrandize,
Which yet to capital could never rise:
Then asks His answer. Jesus the mistake
Well knew, disdaining a return to make.
Next he abjures Him in God's Name to shew,
Whether He were the Christ, God's Son, or no?
You, Jesus said, the Son of Man shall eye,
Enthroned one day at God's right Hand on high,
And in a cloud of glory thence descend,
To judge those judges who His death intend.
That answer sacerdotal rage foments,
His sacred vesture he in madness rents;
What need, he foam'd, of witness? ye all hear
The blasphemy which defecrates our ear.
Worthy of death all Jesus then conclude,
And treat Him with insults profane and rude,
They buffet, scoff, spit in His sacred Face,
All ways they strive to grieve Him, or disgrace;
They smite Him blindfold, and then urge to know,
By His prophetic skill, who gave the blow;

A thousand more bold blasphemies they spoke,
Yet not the least impatience could provoke.

But our dear Lord was more by Peter grieved,
Than by the wrongs He from His foes received.
Getting admittance at the High-Priest's gate,
He curious was to learn his Master's fate;
While with the rabble at the fire he stay'd,
And every passage punctually weigh'd,
Apistos urged him Jesus to abjure,
Who nor Himself, nor votaries could secure.
Fear next strove frightful fancies to inject,
That Jesus' votaries must His fate expect:
Apistos could not unbelief persuade,
But Fear prevail'd confession to evade.
Thou wast with Jesus, then a damsel cried;
The Man you name, I know not, he replied:
And for a while into the porch withdrew,
While his first crow the cock at midnight crew;
A second damsel the same charge repeats,
And with like obstinate denial meets.
Some boldly him a Galilean named,
And that his dialect his birth proclaim'd:
One vow'd, that man he with the prisoner saw
Against state officers his sabre draw;
And he by terror the third time attack'd,
With oaths and curses his denial back'd:
As from his lips his third denial came,
The cock began the morning to proclaim:
Our Lord, whose Heart, by that denial gored,

Lapsed Peter, next to His own pains, deplored,
Cast on His guilty lover standing by,
Such a soft, chiding, sweet, endearing eye,
Which penetrated with a force so kind,
Each power of his love-violating mind,
That hastening out, a lonely place he spies,
And there unsluiced the cataracts of his eyes.

While Jesus, worried by the Pagan crew,
Storm'd by hell powers, and the co-hellish Jew,
In piercing cold, void of friend, comfort, rest,
With grief incomprehensible oppress'd;
With patient meekness His tormentors tired;
Cursed Invida afresh their malice fired;
Early the Council met, the second time
Consult how they may charge Him with a crime,
But could no credible invention frame,
And the High-priest was forced to ask the same,
Art Thou the Christ, the Son of God, or no?
Yourselves, said Jesus, often style Me so.
Hear the tremendous blasphemy, they cry,
And the Blasphemer by our law must die.

Satan, who in false Judas kept abode,
And in his heart fix'd his malicious goad,
Since he had now play'd all the traitor's parts,
A fierce despair into his conscience darts;
With horror tortured, and confounding shame,
Too great to lay to any pardon claim,
He to the Council hastes, confession made,

That he had spotless Innocence betray'd,
His bribe he would refund, which they reject,
Treating him with contemptuous neglect.
Swell'd up with rage he to the Temple goes,
And on the floor the thirty pieces throws,
'Twas the vile price of a despised slave,
Which vilest Jews for God Incarnate gave,
All there conclude the price of blood, not fit
Into the hallow'd treasure to admit,
And bought with that cursed sum the potter's field,
Which should a burying-place to strangers yield,
Now styled the field of blood, that all might own,
'Twas the event by prophecy foreshewn.

Judas, of mercy having lost the hope,
Resolved his life to shorten by a rope;
A sliding cord he threw his neck around,
One end upon a lofty bough was bound,
Then headlong falling, that he soon might choke,
His heavy carcass the strong halter broke,
And falling on a stake, the wretch accursed,
In horrid manner straight asunder burst,
And while his limbs in blood and bowels roll,
He devils importunes to snatch his soul.
O unrepealable, and dreadful doom
Of those, who to betray their Lord presume.

The Jews to Pilate's palace Jesus lead,
Resolving there the prisoner to implead,
Yet enter'd not, left by impure contact

Of Gentiles, they uncleanness should contract,
That they might eat the Passover unstain'd,
And Jesus was within the hall arraign'd.
The chief-priests, scribes, and elders, in the name
Of the whole land, against our Lord declaim,
Cry Him a malefactor, and demand
His speedy doom, from his impartial hand.
But Pilate, who their furious ravings saw,
Remits Him to be judged by Jewish law.
We have no power, they said, of life and death,
That, now depends upon the Roman breath.
Thus Jesus' word minutely was fulfill'd,
Into His votaries often pre-instill'd,
That by a Roman crucifixion He,
Not by a Jewish death, should martyr'd be.

   We to your bar, they said, this wretch have brought,
Who impious doctrines o'er the land has taught;
Of Cæsar's due the payment He dissuades,
Styles Himself King, and Cæsar's throne invades.
The name of king made jealous Pilate start,
Withdrawing, he examined Him apart;
Art Thou a Jewish king, as people rave?
But no reply determinate He gave.
You hear, said Pilate, what momentous things
The awful Sanhedrim against you brings:
But Jesus silent, all defence declined,
To meet that fate Paternal God design'd.
Pilate, who by His silent meekness guess'd

His innocence, Him innocent profefs'd.
With envious rage His perfecutors fume,
And Pilate urge the hearing to refume.
Art Thou a king? faid Pilate.   Jefus fpake,
Afk you this for your own, or Judah's fake?
I am no Jew, faid Pilate, nor am fkill'd
In prophecies they dream fhall be fulfill'd;
The Council and all Ifrael hither run,
To charge you: fay, what evil have you done?
My realm, fays Jefus, waives all worldly might,
My fubjects elfe would for my refcue fight.
Did ever crown, faid Pilate, you adorn?
I am a King, faid Jefus, and was born,
That I on earth a ghoftly realm might fway,
And make My fubjects heavenly truths obey.
Then Pilate publicly declared his mind,
I in this Man no fault at all can find.
The Jews with a frefh fury clamour loud,
That He had fown rebellion through the crowd,
From Galilee to Salem men amufed,
With peftilential maxims He infufed.
Pilate, when Galilee was named, would know
Whether He Galilean was or no;
Inform'd he was, he Him to Herod fends,
While Pafchal Rites at Salem he attends.

 That tyrant had his life in inceft led,
At his command our Lord's forerunner bled,
O'er Galilee he cruel tetrarch reign'd,
And in the Jewifh law had long been train'd;

Oft he had heard of Jesus' mighty fame,
And joy'd when Jesus to his palace came,
With expectation that from Jesus he
Should mysteries hear, or miracles should see
Our Lord, Who well their hearts obdurate knew,
No answer gave to Herod, or to Jew:
They strong convictions had contemn'd before,
And God thus outraged would vouchsafe no more.
The king who saw Him resolutely mute,
Concludes Him idiot, and of no repute;
He and his furious guards our Lord deride.
The Animal with fierce insultings plied,
In a white robe, they the mock King array'd,
And to their fill their cruel pastimes play'd;
Herod, who thought his majesty debased
His indignation on a Sot to waste,
To Pilate sends Him to receive His due,
Where His malicious foes their rage renew.

Rome's Justice, Pilate said, this man acquits,
And Him even Herod uncondemn'd transmits;
No crime in Him, or he or I can see,
He shall chastisement suffer, and go free.
'Tis customary at this solemn feast
One prisoner for your sake should be released;
And this shall be the Man: for well he knew
Their envy, not His guilt, the odium drew.
At freeing Jesus, they with fury rave,
We not this Man, but we Barabbas crave;
Whose horrid crimes to all the Jews were known,

They chose the villain, and the Saint disown.
What shall I do with Jesus, he rejoin'd,
Whom, oft examined, I still guiltless find?
Then with a rage unanimous they cried,
Let Jesus be condemn'd, and crucified.
To satisfy, said he, the nation's cries,
I will the guiltless, the oppress'd chastise.
No sober counsel could allay their heat,
Crucify, crucify! they all repeat.

    While Pilate thus the rapid torrent stemm'd,
He striving to acquit, Whom they condemn'd;
His wife entreaties sent, he should take care
In murdering that Just Man to have no share;
By a tremendous dream she well foreknew,
That God the fact with vengeance would pursue.
Pilate then, Jesus' spotless life to save,
Command to soldiers, for His scourging gave;
Within the common-hall the armed bands
Strip Him, and to a pillar tie His Hands;
With knotted cords His tender Flesh they lash'd,
Long gaping furrows in His Muscles gash'd;
His Blood which gushing ran from every pore,
Bathed Him a second time in His own Gore;
His Head they with a wreath of thorns surround,
And every thorn gave a peculiar wound;
His Blood afresh in showers came trickling down,
From the sharp, numerous gorings of His crown;
Mock-purple robes He on His Shoulders wore,
For sceptre, in His Hand a reed He bore;

With bended knee His patience they abuse,
Spit in His Face, and cry, Hail, King of Jews!
Then smite Him with His own mock-sceptre reed,
Even Jews could scarce their outrages exceed.

 Thus robed, crown'd, sceptred, bleeding, full
  of woes,
Pilate, to move some pity, Jesus shows;
Behold the Man! Whose innocence I urged,
Yet for your sakes have thus severely scourged;
It were a shame I should afflict Him more;
Crucify, crucify! they foaming roar,
We have a law, with clamour they reply,
And by our law blasphemers ought to die.
This proud, ambitious Wretch, meek as He
  seems,
Styles Himself God's own Son, and God blas-
  phemes.
That Name struck Pilate with an awe profound,
And he withdrew, this question to propound;
Whence art Thou? Jesus silent stood, then he,
Have I not power to crucify or free?
And art Thou silent? Jesus made reply,
The power you have is given you from on high,
If you that power abuse, you God offend,
Jews, who know more, your guilt the more tran-
  scend.

 Still Pilate strove their malice to assuage,
Urged His release, which raised impetuous rage;

All loudly bellow, he himſelf would ſhow
Not Cæſar's friend, ſhould he let Jeſus go,
Who courts by magic popular renown,
Styles himſelf King, and aims at Cæſar's crown.
Pilate then Jeſus, in His royal weed,
Crown'd with ſharp thorns, and ſceptred with a reed,
In the Prætorium placed in all their views,
Behold your King, ſaid he, the King of Jews.
We no king, they return, but Cæſar own,
And you with watchful care ſhould guard his throne.
Away with Him, away with Him! they cry,
And let the Wretch by crucifixion die!

When Pilate ſaw their malice higher ſwell,
He thought it vain their fury to repel:
But waſh'd his hands; I guiltleſs am, he ſaid,
From this Juſt Perſon's Blood you thirſt to ſhed.
In horrid curſe their anſwer they expreſt,
His Blood on us, and on our children reſt.
Pilate, Tiberius to incenſe afraid,
And by the clamours of the Jews diſmay'd,
Deſpairing ſafely to prevent the ill,
Delivers Jeſus to their envious will;
Commands the guards Barabbas to unbind,
And Jeſus to the dolorous Croſs conſign'd.
May I devoutly, Lord, Thy patience weigh,
Oh, let no ills me rancour or diſmay!

On Thy support may I in troubles lean,
And keep in worldly storms a soul serene.

All praise to Jesus! Who with sin unstain'd
Was for our guilt content to be arraign'd.
Glory to Jesus! o'er the mountain goes,
Who for lapsed man endured such bitter woes.

WEDNESDAY BEFORE EASTER.

The Passion.

MELT me all o'er, eternal, gracious Dove,
Into the utmost tenderness of love:
That while I suffering Jesus have in sight,
Condoling love may a soft song indite.
Oh! tune my heart to that sweet, tender strain,
In which the virgins worship the Lamb slain;
While on their sympathetic harps they play
To the new song, which none can learn but they.

When timorous Pilate Jesus' death decreed,
And that He should by crucifixion bleed,
The Jews, by Invida possess'd, to please,
The rude, remorseless soldiers on Him seize.
Then His mock-purple robe away they tear,
That He might only His own garments wear;
His ponderous Cross they on His Shoulders lay,

With spears they goad Him through the dolorous
    way.
But Jesus, spent with loss of blood and pain,
Unable was the burden to sustain.
They saw Him sink, yet would no pity show,
But to reserve Him for His dying woe;
Good Simon, whom they for his friend suspect,
To bear His Cross they from the crowd select.
O happy saint! in Jesus' griefs to share,
To ease blest Jesus, Jesus' Cross to bear!
Two thieves they with Him couple, to imply,
He for like crimes with them alike must die.
The evangelic prophet this foretold,
That He should with transgressors be enroll'd.

  His faithful votaries follow'd the sad train,
And sympathised with Him in every vein.
The tender sex His view afflicting kept,
Their hearts bled faster than their eyelids wept.
With re-condoling Love and melting eyes,
Jesus to their afflicted love replies:
Drain not your tears, My anguish to deplore,
Weep for yourselves and for your children more:
I by My sufferings shall to glory rise,
But dreadful vengeance shall this land surprise.
Ah! Salem's daughters, near is the sad day
When in extremity of grief you'll say,
Thrice happy are the wombs once barren styled,
Thrice happy paps which never suckled child.
Then to the hills and mountains men shall call,

To shelter us from wrath, upon us fall!
Nor hills, nor mountains will regard their woes,
Obdurate and relentless as their foes.
Like a green tree with a well-water'd root,
I yielded for your food, life-giving fruit;
The faithless, like trees with no moisture fed,
Cumbering the ground, unfruitful are and dead;
God, who permits the green shall trampled lie,
Justly decrees the felling of the dry.
If such afflictions Innocence attend,
Think what dire judgments over guilt impend!

 Soon as they at Mount Calvary arrived,
Where malefactors were of life deprived;
For anodyne, to criminals then used,
Of wine, with frankincense and myrrh infused,
The envious Jews, His angours to augment,
A cup of gall and vinegar present:
He thirsty, of the odious potion sips,
And from it straight withdrew His injured Lips.
Naked they stript Him, to increase disgrace,
Then on the Cross His Frame supine they place;
His tender Hands and Feet with cords they retch,
And when extended to their utmost stretch,
With nails, to fix Him to the Tree, they gore,
Of a large size, to make the wider bore:
Jesus thus nail'd, the Cross on high they heaved,
And that He might be with fresh torments grieved,
Each, the same moment, letting go his hand,
Into the hole in which it was to stand,

With such a mighty torturing jerk it fell,
The malice could not be outdone by Hell.
His Body, which His Wounds alone support,
Feels now of torment the extreme effort,
It racks His Joints, unsockets all His Bones,
Each Muscle in Him agonizing groans,
Each Artery, Nerve, Tendon, Fibre, Vein,
Each atom felt strong confluential pain.
But midst His dire convulsions, pangs and throes,
No wrongs His charity could discompose;
He pardon begs for Pagan and for Jew,
Father, forgive, they know not what they do.

   The crime for which the malefactor bled,
Was by old custom labell'd o'er his head;
This sole inscription Pilate chose to use,
Jesus of Nazareth, the King of Jews.
As He in torment hung, contemn'd and scorn'd,
God with this public witness Him adorn'd.
Of sacred Truth, though Pilate nothing knew,
He gave the title to Messias due.

   The thieves on either hand on crosses hung,
And one reviled Him with a hell-fired tongue;
If Thou art Christ, Thyself and us now free,
And save us from this painful, murdering tree.
The other made a pious, grave reply,
How darest thou with words reproachful die?
We of our crimes the just chastisement bear;
Pilate was forced Him guiltless to declare;
Of God's tremendous bar hast thou no fear,

At which we in few minutes muſt appear?
With that, he deeply ſighing for ſins paſt,
Soft, penitential eyes on Jeſus caſt,
Ah Lord, remember me, he humbly cried,
When Thou art in Thy kingdom glorified!
At the firſt triumph which His Croſs had made,
Jeſus, amidſt His pains, was pleaſed, and ſaid,
Die with this conſolation, thou ſhalt be
This very day in Paradiſe with Me.
One act intenſe may in God's mild repute
For a whole age of penances commute.

   High Heaven, which could not the ſad ſight endure,
To ſee the Source of Light Divine, obſcure,
Its cheerful glories on a ſudden ſhrouds,
In thick, black, mournful, confluential clouds;
The ſun, who of its light then wholly fail'd,
The full-cheek'd moon which hinder'd it, bewail'd;
The ſpheres, which moved in harmony before,
Began in groans their Maker to deplore;
Sun, moon, and ſtars, withdrew their conſcious light,
Egypt ne'er felt ſuch horrid, diſmal night;
From the ſixth hour until the ninth, the realm
Of darkneſs ſeem'd the land to overwhelm;
The ſoldiers in four parts His veſture tear,
Each ſcoffing claims a remnant for his ſhare;
But for His ſeamleſs coat, they lots would throw,
Fulfilling what the prophecies foreſhew.

As on the Cross afflicted Jesus hangs,
Oppress'd with strong, innumerable pangs,
To heighten inward dolours, all the pains
He for His persecutors there sustains,
He's contemn'd, scorn'd, mock'd, and pastime made,
By those for whom He so dear ransom paid.
Nothing can more heart-breaking grief excite
Than utmost love, repaid with utmost spite.
The Jews, by torch-light, as His pangs they eye,
Wagging their heads, in loud derision cry,
Thou, Who didst boast the Temple to destroy,
And in three days rebuild, Thy power employ
To save Thyself; now from the Cross come down,
And take possession of the Jewish crown;
The scribes, chief-priests, and rulers, scoffing rave,
Let the world's Saviour try Himself to save.
If Thou art Christ, God's Son, and Israel's King,
Come from the Cross, and we'll Thy triumph sing;
In God He trusted, Who no saint forsakes,
God Him abandons, and no pity takes.
The cruel soldiers at His groans exult,
And with rude mockery o'er Him insult.
Cursed leading ghosts, and all their hellish train,
Feasted their malice with His boundless pain;
Even Envy, never sated since the fall,
Stood nonpluss'd, boasting she had done her all;
And the damn'd ghosts from Tophet with her flown,
All envied her the envy she had shown.

But the moſt tender Wound our Lord received,
Was to behold His deareſt Mother grieved;
The Virgin, John, and Saints of either kind,
Who thither came, themſelves to grief reſign'd:
He in the weeping crowd, His Mother ſpies,
Bemoaning Him, with ſoft, heart-draining eyes;
Maternal pity pierced her through and through,
Up to the hilt her ſword-like ſorrow flew,
At the wide-gaping wound her ſoul took vent,
And in outflowing yearnings was nigh ſpent;
When His ſoft, melting Eyes towards John He
    roll'd,
Bleſs'd Woman, there thy Son, ſaid He, behold,
Then John's regard He towards His Mother drew,
Loved John, He adds, thy future Mother view.
Thence John his houſe the Virgin's manſion
    made,
And always filial duty to her paid.

    Our Lord, with anguiſh infinite o'erpreſs'd,
Was, with man's guilt and wrath it drew, diſ-
    treſs'd.
While Godhead, from humanity withdrawn,
Gave Him no one conſolatory dawn;
No tongue His unimaginable woes,
During that ſhort ſuſpenſion, can diſcloſe.
What is the loſs of Godhead? Who can think,
To finite, from infinity to ſink?
A loſs like this, our ſuffering Jeſus grieved,
Of influential Deity bereaved;

While in a dying paroxyfm He fpake,
My God, my God, why doft Thou Me forfake?
Strong dolours, not diftruft, made this complaint,
My God, implies affurance of a faint.
Then, all His death-predictions to conclude,
He cried, I thirft! and a tormentor rude
A hyffop-reed, which with a fponge was tipp'd,
In vinegar and gall by malice dipp'd,
Prefented, to embitter His laft breath,
And irritate the agonies of death.
Our Lord received the loathfome drops, and cried,
The prophecies are now all verified;
O Father, I Thy Prieft, to Thy mild eyes
Prefent Myfelf for men a Sacrifice;
Their fhame, guilt, woes, concentre on My Head,
For them I now My Blood vicarious fhed;
If this Thy wrath, O Father, not atones,
O ftill prolong and multiply My groans!
In pity to loft man I'll fuffer more,
That to Thy favour I may him reftore;
That I may fave him from eternal pain,
Though love for Love he pays Me not again.
But if I now have paid the utmoft mite,
O let My pangs Thy pity foft excite:
O Father, to My dolours put an end,
Into Thy Hands My Spirit I commend!
Paternal God declared His wrath appeafed,
And with the Offering infinitely pleafed.
His head in adoration He inclined,
And to His Father His dear Soul refign'd.

Bright Michael, with twelve legions, who had
    stay'd
To give, if call'd, afflicted Jesus aid,
A squadron sent to plague apostate ghosts,
Who of destroying Jesus made their boasts;
They lash'd the fiends to hell, with terrors scared,
Where new-forged tortures were for all prepared;
Cursed Invida with her own saws they jag,
And in the furrows of the filthy hag
They her own serpents and her vipers cramm'd,
And to accumulated torments damn'd.

All Nature, when the God of Nature bled,
Was struck with horrid, universal dread,
Despairing Filial God to have survived,
From Whose high Will it origin derived.
The rocks cleft, earth to hell began to quake,
And to increase the fiery brimstone lake,
From its dark, subterraneous stores to throw
Whole mines of flaming sulphur down below;
Infernal ghosts ne'er suffer'd, since they fell,
So hot, so insupportable a hell;
And all the tortured spirits cursed the day
When they sent Judas, Jesus to betray;
The graves flew open, and exposed their store,
And into bodies shook the human ore;
The troubled sea its bed no longer kept,
But o'er its shores its inundations wept;
The temple corner-stones were seen to yield,
And to and fro the labouring fabric reel'd;

The hallow'd loaves were thrown the floor about,
And the seven golden burning lamps went out,
The sacred incense lost its odorous scent,
The awful veil was into pieces rent,
The trembling priests leave holy rites undone,
Affrighted Levites from their stations run,
Harps, psalteries, cymbals, trumpets, on the ground
Lie bruised and broken all the Temple round.
Caiaphas hid his self-upbraiding head,
The impious Council were from Gazith fled;
Black horrors haunted the accursed room,
Where envious sinners hatch'd their Saviour's
    doom;
The evening lamb, which was but newly fired,
As on the Cross the Lamb of God expired,
Grew on the altar, on a sudden, cold,
And from the grate the dying embers roll'd.

  The Pagan soldiers trembled in their stands,
Down dropp'd their weapons from their feeble
    hands,
None ever had recover'd of the fright,
Had not our God restored the solar light.
Aloud the thoughtful, wise centurion cried,
The Mighty Son of God is crucified;
Each envious Jew-spectator smote his breast,
And in his actions plainly Christ confess'd;
They all, convicted at that moving sight,
Denied Messias only out of spite;
Tyrannic sin of empire lay bereft,

The idol ghosts their tottering temples left,
Of their own fatal oracles afraid;
Which, forced by Heaven, unwelcome truth
    display'd.
Eden's bright cherub sheathed his two-edged flame,
Heaven bid him open Paradise proclaim;
Fear the old world into hard labour threw,
It groan'd till 'twas deliver'd of a new.

If heaven and earth, dear Lord, Thy Passion felt,
Ah! how should I with love and sorrow melt!
Thy precious blood 'twas wicked I who spilt,
I grieved, I pierced, I nail'd Thee by my guilt.
Lord, to those very Wounds I gored, I fly,
My hopes of pardon in my outrage lie;
As Thy dear sweetest Mother saw Thy smart,
Thou, when the sword went through her tender
    heart,
With weapon-love didst then anoint the blade,
It gently cured, just as the wound it made;
May I, in penitential tears immersed,
Contemplate Thee, my Jesus, Whom I pierced,
And by sweet sympathy Thy anguish feel,
Deep wound my heart with Love, and wounding,
    heal.

All praise to Jesus! who, lapsed man to free,
Hung on the painful, ignominious Tree.
Glory to Jesus! the whole mount replied,
Offended God, Who for offenders died.

THURSDAY BEFORE EASTER.

The Lord Jesus, the same night in which He was betrayed, took bread; and when He had given thanks, He brake it, and said, Take, eat, this is my body.—1 *Cor.* xi. 23-4.

HOW Godhead to our human flesh was join'd,
    Transcends the reach of an angelic mind.
How God and Man with bread and wine unite,
Is too sublime for bounded human sight:
To boundless Godhead both united are,
God tabernacles here, and temples there.
There undivided God and man exist,
The flesh assumed is ne'er to be dismiss'd;
'Tis transient here, and when a Judas eats
The sacred bread, Christ's Shechinah retreats.
The day and night each other still expel,
Pure God in souls impure can never dwell.
God, to exalt His power, and man debase,
Institutes mean conveyances of grace.
Bless'd water in the font is still the same,
As when unblest it from the river came,
Though worthless in itself, in sacred use
It graces superhuman can produce.
Thus bread and wine, by Jesus set apart,
Presentiate God Incarnate to the heart.
Wise gracious God, sign ectypal[1] ne'er made,

---

[1] *Ectypal* (from ἐκ and τύπος), a copy.

By which the archetype fhould be convey'd;
But every faint in the appointed fign
Partakes of the Original Divine.

  When Peter cried out, finking in the wave,
And Jefus ftretch'd His Hand the faint to fave,
Had Jefus been in Heaven when Peter pray'd,
And fent invifible, yet mighty aid,
He as effectually had Peter freed,
Had been as prefent in the time of need,
As if He had been treading on the main,
And reach'd His Hand His votary to fuftain.
Chrift's virtual Prefence may as Real be,
As if we fhould His Perfon prefent fee.

  Writ Sacred, baptifm, fanctity and prayer,
All to derive God's grace true conduits are:
But His propitious wifdom found a way,
More Love to fhed, more bleffing to convey;
The greateft Love unbounded God could fhow,
Was to refign His Son to bear our woe.
The greateft Love could from the Son proceed,
Was to affume our flefh, and for us bleed.
The Eucharift to fouls both Loves difplays,
Love emulous of infinite to raife;
As if to die had been a love too low,
He on His lovers would Himfelf beftow.
Our Lord Himfelf becomes our heavenly
      meat,
United to us like the food we eat.

The saints, next hypostatic union, none
More noble than the sacramental own.

O wondrous feast! which manna far exceeds,
In which each saint on God Incarnate feeds.
The manna which God's wandering Israel fed
Was mortal food, the eaters all are dead;
But Jesus, our Immortal Food, remains,
And souls to all eternity sustains.

Lord, Who to wash Thy votaries' feet didst
    deign,
Ere feasted with the Lamb unspotted slain;
Set open a full spring in either eye,
Which a capacious laver may supply:
That, bathed all o'er in penitential tear,
I at Thy blissful feast may clean appear.
But tears can never cleanse spiritual stains,
Wash me in drops of Thy own bleeding Veins.
Thy purple Blood can wash a sinner white,
And change dark spots to a celestial bright.

When at Thy Altar, Lord, I prostrate fall,
Thy dolorous crucifixion to recall,
Make my soul fuel to supernal fire,
Into my heart devotion warm inspire.
Shame and contrition vileness to deplore,
Firm resolutions never to sin more;
An humble, pure, and charitable mind,

From all remains of wilful sin refined.
Faith, hope, desire, joy, praise, thanksgiving, zeal,
Languors, and ardours which Thy lovers feel;
All grateful passions which have ever stream'd
From sinners by the Blood of God redeem'd.
Into all love my powers, my spirit turn,
Love which unquenchable may ever burn;
May every thought I of Thy sufferings frame
Sustain, invigorate, increase the flame.
Nourish'd by Thee, I no fatigue shall feel,
And tread Thy steps with persevering zeal;
Or if Thou shorten by the cross my way,
Fill'd with Thy Love, I gladly shall obey.
Before Thy death this Feast Thou didst ordain,
The antidote against internal pain.
Thy saints will imitate Thy solemn care,
And by the Altar for the cross prepare.

GOOD FRIDAY.

A SONG of Jesus I design,
   But stumble at the leading line,
Of Jesus' Passion I would sing,
And for this day's oblation bring;
But cannot the dispute decide
'Twixt Grief and Love, which me divide.

When Jesus' sufferings I review,
And know myself to be the Jew,

Whose sins created all the woe
God-flesh assumed to undergo;
I dread my guilt, and in my eyes
Of tears I feel two fountains rise.

But when sweet Jesus to my sight
Appears in a salvific light,
Where on the Cross He suffers pain,
That I may bliss eternal gain,
O then my heart with love runs o'er,
And is inclined to grieve no more.

While thus my soul is at a bay,
Which of the passions me shall sway,
Mind on a sudden intervenes,
And with sweet temper both serenes;
She promises she'll both permit,
And to keep peace their umpire sit.

Mind bids me grief and love unite,
And then from both a song indite;
For hallow'd grief from love is bred,
Love only grateful tears can shed;
Love for offending Love immense,
Less eyeing vengeance than offence.

To Love entirely then my mind
The conduct of my tears resign'd;
And from the Garden I began
To trace the sufferings of God-man;

GOOD FRIDAY.

I felt into soft tears devout
Love at first entrance bursting out.

I kept it lively in my mind,
That God and man in Jesus join'd,
That Godhead every soul foreknows,
For whom the Manhood suffers woes;
And while His pains my ransom bought,
I and my sins were in His thought.

Mind could no pang of Jesus see,
But still she cried, It is for me;
I the inflammative received,
And all the way both loved and grieved;
God-man for me enduring smart,
Both deluged and enflamed my heart.

I saw Incarnate God at prayer,
With awful, yet enamouring air,
Each tear Paternal God endear'd,
He humbly loved, He sweetly fear'd,
He kneel'd, fell prostrate on the ground,
Aspired with ardency profound.

Complaint of inward grief He made,
I saw dire pangs His soul invade,
With tears He offer'd up strong cries;
Ah then I saw Him agonize,
Ah! I beheld the surface wet
With droppings of His bloody sweat.

GOOD FRIDAY.

He His own load foresaw, had sense
Of sin, and of God's wrath immense,
And pray'd that He the cup might waive,
If a less price lapsed man would save;
Yet, to His Father's Will resign'd,
Content to suffer for mankind.

I loved and grieved at Jesus' pain
I saw Him for my sins sustain;
Yet only eyed the outward part,
And could not reach His dolorous Heart;
His sorrows there none ever knew,
Too infinite for bounded view.

With grief His prayer grew so intense,
Methought His Godhead in suspense;
Withheld consolatory beam,
That agony might be extreme.
Of such suspense what heart can guess
The unconceivable distress?

God sent an angel from the throne,
With sweet supports to ease His moan;
And since He suffer'd in the place
Of Adam's universal race,
We judge His woes proportion'd were
To all the guilt He deign'd to bear.

To God as He resign'd His will,
He rose to meet approaching ill.

I stood the traitor to behold,
Who for vile price his Master sold;
I saw God-man from lips impure
With patience meek a kiss endure.

I saw the arm'd inhuman bands
Stretch towards God-man audacious hands,
His Voice struck all to earth with dread,
He suffering each to raise his head,
They Him when bound to Annas drew,
While from their Lord His votaries flew.

With Jews was leagued infernal power,
Cursed Satan knew the fatal hour,
His legions he review'd, and all
The devils, to revenge their fall,
Blaspheming vow'd, with utmost might,
On God's loved Son to wreak their spite.

My love began fresh tears to shed,
When Jesus was to Caiaphas led,
With the High-priest the Council join'd,
All in His violent death combined,
With envious rage I saw them swell,
All unappeasable as hell.

With buffetings they Him assail'd,
His Face they spit on, and then veil'd,
Bid Him by prophecy disclose
Which was the hand that gave the blows.

Shame mix'd with pain in all His woe,
Ills which from sin coeval flow.

To Pilate next they drag Him bound,
With cruel clamours Him surround:
The Pagan the accused acquits,
And straight to Herod Him transmits;
He and His guards, meek Jesus made
Their scorn, and in mock-white array'd.

To Pilate back they Jesus sent;
He, Jewish malice to prevent,
Proposed that Jesus at the Feast
Might be the criminal released;
But for a murderer they cry,
Barabbas free, let Jesus die!

My Love, my Tear now higher rise,
Incarnate God is in your eyes
Tied to a pillar, naked, stript,
By unrelenting soldiers whipt,
His sacred flesh is wound all o'er,
His blood is streams, 'twas rills before.

Thus bleeding, with redoubled rage,
They choose the common-hall their stage,
They crown Him with a wreath of thorn,
With a mock-purple robe adorn,
For sceptre they provide a reed,
And to insult Him all agreed.

With bended knee, Hail, King! they cried,
Spat on His Face, and mockeries vied,
Then took the reed, and smote His crown,
To make the thorns sink deeper down;
To Jews God-man, thus full of woes,
To move their pity, Pilate shews.

The hell-infuriated crowd
Reiterate, Crucify! aloud,
On our own heads and race the guilt
Shall rest, soon as His Blood is spilt:
And Pilate, by their threats inclined,
The guiltless to their rage consign'd.

My Love, my Tear, your force collect,
You now must on the Cross reflect,
There pain and shame are at full stress,
And for my sins God-man oppress;
See, He begins the dolorous way,
From Pilate's house to Golgotha.

His sacred head with thorn is crown'd,
His bleeding furrows dye the ground,
In His own garments re-array'd,
His ponderous Cross is on Him laid,
With bleeding faint, o'erwhelm'd with woes,
Beneath His load He trembling goes.

Ah! now He sinks, and to sustain
His burden, Simon they constrain,

Love wish'd herself had then been seized,
Her suffering Saviour to have eased;
My Love, my Tear, you now must count
The dolours felt on Calvary mount.

Instead of the accustomed wine,
They offer a mock anodyne,
For wonted myrrh malicious Jews
The most embittering gall infuse;
No anodyne bless'd Jesus knew
But Will Divine, and lips withdrew.

Between two thieves He thither came,
To stigmatize Him with their shame,
Then naked, to augment His woe,
Him on the Cross supine they throw,
Nail Hands and Feet, with gorings pain'd,
Unsluice His blood, till now undrain'd.

The Cross between the thieves they raise;
Soon as the crowd upon Him gaze,
They wag their heads, mock, grin, blaspheme,
With ragings various and extreme;
He, patient, for tormentors pray'd,
With gracious yearnings hate repay'd.

Of thieves, the bad 'gainst Jesus raved,
The good His pity meekly craved,
Bless'd Jesus spake, immensely prone
To ease a penitential moan.

Thy foul the angels shall this day
To Paradise with Me convey.

While Jesus on the Cross was nail'd,
The sun in clouds its splendour veil'd,
At the eclipse of Fontal Light,
Fear'd it should never more be bright,
In shame and pain three hours He hung,
Shot through with darts of venom'd tongue.

My Love, my Tear, you weeping see
The Virgin-Mother near the Tree;
O learn of her to love and weep,
And Jesus in your heart to keep,
Yet even her tender Love and Tear
Reach'd only woes she saw appear.

The length, the breadth, the depth, the height
Of inward woe transcended sight;
Ah, could our elevated eye
Into His dolorous Spirit pry,
A sorrow infinite is there,
No speech angelic can declare.

Mad dogs from the infernal dark,
About the Cross at Jesus bark,
Their foam they in suggestions vent,
And all His inward pangs foment,
And yet their studied utmost spite
No one repining could excite.

GOOD FRIDAY.

My God, My God, I agonize,
Why doſt Thou Me forſake? He cries;
Ne'er ſince the world began was known
Such an immenſe heart-breaking groan;
God-man ne'er made complaint in vain,
'Twas but proportion'd to His pain.

Reflux of Godhead Him relieves,
'Tis but ſhort time bleſs'd Jeſus grieves,
Yet that ſhort time God's mercy ſways,
Man's ranſom to His juſtice pays,
Since God's co-equal undergoes
The quinteſſence of ſinners' woes.

Paternal God's co-boundleſs Son,
For ſinners now His all has done,
His Head He to His Father bends,
His Soul into His Hands commends,
And ſweetly breathing out His laſt,
Into His Father's Boſom paſs'd.

The God of Life gave up the Ghoſt,
Amazed ſtood the angelic hoſt;
Curſed fiends were laſh'd to treble pain,
The Temple-veil was rent in twain,
Earth quaked, back flew the ocean-waves,
Rocks cleft, and open ſtood the graves.

The good centurion Jeſus own'd,
The very crowd His woes bemoan'd;

And of His death all doubt to clear,
His Side was wounded with a ſpear :
That wound the Jewiſh outrage cloſed,
And then He in His grave repoſed.

Soon as I ſaw bleſs'd Jeſus dead,
I found ſad Tear from Love was fled ;
Love, left alone, with joy beheld
His ſhame, His anguiſh now diſpell'd ;
With that ſhe call'd to hymn for aid,
In ſong His Love ſhe re-ſurvey'd.

All praiſe be to Incarnate God,
Who for my ſake the wine-preſs trod,
Who in pure, boundleſs Love inclined
To give His life for lapſed mankind,
Who miſeries immenſe endured,
That I might live from all ſecured.

May I, like bleſſed Paul, to know
Dear Jeſus, my choice hours beſtow,
The Croſs is the ſole book I need,
In that all-ſaving truths I read,
God's attributes all harmonized,
Evanid[1] wealth, pomp, joys, deſpiſed.

Man's heinous guilt apparent made,
For which the Blood of God was paid,
Sin's curſed attendants, pain and ſhame,
With horrors of infernal flame,

[1] Vain, apt to decay.

Death and the terrors of the grave,
From which God-man could only save.

All graces which adorn the mind,
An ardent love, a will refign'd,
A lamb-like meeknefs, confcience clean,
A patience humble and ferene,
Obedience conftant and fincere,
Undaunted courage, filial fear;

Large charity, a temper fweet,
All men like brethren prone to treat,
Devotion fix'd, a zeal right aim'd,
Self-holocauft, all paffions tamed;
I with all thefe, and numerous more,
From Jefus' Crofs myfelf may ftore.

Lord, in Thy Crofs is all my truft,
I'll crucify all fenfual guft,
And if Thou call'ft me to the ftake,
Help me to fuffer for Thy fake,
Thy Crofs I'll daily keep in eye,
And learn from that to love and die.

EASTER EVEN.

GOD-MAN, Who on the dolorous Tree
    Didft facrifice Thyfelf for me,
For me! O wonder! What am I,
That great God-man fhould for me die?

I who 'gainst Love immense rebel,
A slave to sin, and claim'd by hell.

But Thou hast my deliverance wrought,
Thou hast me out of slavery bought,
Thou boundless vengeance hast allay'd,
By price inestimable paid;
I am by purchase wholly Thine,
And justly can style nothing mine.

Ah, wo is me! I, Lord, am prone
To rob Thee hourly of Thine own,
For sensual joys I oft purvey,
Which steal from Thee my heart away,
Thou canst no sacrilege endure,
My heart, O help me to secure!

God-man, while here to live He deign'd,
In self-oblation still remain'd:
Centred in Jesus I should live,
Myself entirely to Him give,
Himself He to redeem me gave,
Which makes me His devoted slave.

His slave? O no, in pity He
From ghostly bondage set me free,
By His own Blood He me redeem'd,
That I should be His friend esteem'd.
Strange Love to slaves, which thought transcends,
God bleeds to raise them to His friends!

I with my Friend ſhould ſympathiſe,
And live to Thee in ſacrifice,
I will remember what I coſt,
Thou, Lord, ſhouldſt all my powers exhauſt,
My faith ſhould keep my Friend in ſight,
His Will ſhould be my ſole delight.

The more ſouls love, the more they ſtrive
To their friend's likeneſs to arrive;
My ſoul, Lord, Thy Veronique¹ make;
That I may Thy reſemblance take,
That Will may be in both the ſame,
And both may have one heavenly aim.

EASTER-DAY.

SAY, bleſſed angels, ſay,
　　How could you ſilent be to-day?
Your hymn the ſhepherds waked that morn,
　　When great God-man was born,

---

¹ It is an ancient tradition that when our Saviour was on His way to Calvary, bearing His croſs, He paſſed by the door of a compaſſionate woman, who, beholding the drops of agony on His brow, wiped His face with a napkin, or as others ſay, with her veil, and the features of Chriſt remained miraculouſly impreſſed upon the linen. To this image was given the name of Vera Icon—the *true* image—ſubſequently, the name given to the image was inſenſibly transferred to the woman of whom the legend is related.—JAMESON's *Sacred and Legendary Art* (1848), vol. ii. p. 269.

But when He rose again,
They heard no Eucharistic strain.

You saw God-man expire,
Did you His rising not admire?
How when His soul at parting breath
    Enter'd the realm of death,
    He conquering forced His way,
And re-inspired His buried clay.

Had you His rise admired,
Hymn is by admiration fired;
But you profoundly were amazed
    When you upon Him gazed,
    And while amazement reigns,
It all poetic force restrains.

Your intellectual eyes
Saw Heaven and earth from nothing rise,
You then admired the noble sight,
    And hymn'd God's boundless might;
    Yourselves from nothing raised,
In your first moment Godhead praised.

When you saw Jesus dead,
The strangeness then was mix'd with dread,
The King of Terrors had surprised,
    God-man when sacrificed,
    You ghosts apostate quell'd,
Yet with amaze that Death beheld.

At Jesus' dying groan,
The graves by earthquake open thrown,
All the tremendous horrors shew'd,
    In frightful death's abode,
    You with amazement saw
God-man the tyrant over-awe.

    Amaze not long could last,
But into admiration pass'd;
The wonder calmly you conceived,
    And grace of hymn retrieved;
    And hymning still remain
The Lamb triumphant, Who was slain.

    To a sublimer height
That I may faith and love excite,
I Calvary this morn intend,
    As pilgrim to ascend,
    To see the hallow'd ground,
For Jesus' sepulchre renown'd.

    Impulsed with zeal, my mind
Soon reach'd the mountain I design'd;
Two angels there I could behold,
    Who first the rising told,
    Came down on radiant wing
Their Easter annual hymn to sing.

    I heard them with delight,
And as they spread their wings for flight,

In Jesus' Name besought their stay,
    To perfect my survey:
    The angel, they replied,
Who guards the mount, will be your guide.

    My fervour to foment,
The Guardian mildly gave consent,
And, lest my sight should be oppress'd,
    He damp'd his glorious vest;
    I then to every place
Could every leading footstep trace.

    Within, said he, the womb
Of this hard rock was Jesus' tomb,
That ponderous stone which on it lay
    The angel moved away,
    Descending in pure white,
With look like awful lightning bright.

    The guards his presence fear'd,
And like dead men all pale appear'd,
The solid earth's foundation shook,
    Down as his flight he took,
    In open'd graves the just
Felt life rekindling in their dust.

    Clothed in celestial ray,
There Heaven's two envoys fix'd their stay,
Each on the stone possess'd his seat,
    At Jesu's head and feet,

EASTER-DAY.

    To watch 'gainſt Jew and hell,
And to good ſouls glad tidings tell.

    The female ſaints took care
Embalming odours to prepare,
To Jeſus they firſt honour gave,
    They ſaw the empty grave,
    And Magdalen took flight,
To tell His votaries the ſight.

    Loved John, and Peter ran
To ſearch the grave where lay God-man,
The ſhroud and napkin they admired,
    Yet in ſuſpenſe retired,
    Diffidence veil'd their eyes,
Slow to believe their Lord ſhould riſe.

    Soft Mary there remain'd,
That ſhe had loſt her Lord complain'd
To the two angels with ſad tears,
    While her dear Lord appears,
    At Whoſe reviving beams
Sweet tears of joy flow'd down in ſtreams.

    Of all the truths reveal'd,
The riſing is moſt firmly ſeal'd,
Heaven took peculiar care that none
    Who think, ſhould it diſown,
    That Love Divine to fire,
The motive might remain entire.

The angels from the Throne,
Sent to the monumental stone;
The saints who, risen from the dead,
The truth o'er Salem spread;
The earthquake which exposed
The graves, and scatter'd dust reclosed;

The prophecies of old;
Types which the promised Seed enfold;
Our Lord's predictions now fulfill'd;
The lie by Jews instill'd;
The guards who truth confess'd,
The Resurrection co-attest.

From death bless'd Jesus rear'd,
Ten several times to saints appear'd,
Was undeniably made known
To votaries when alone,
Oft when in numbers join'd,
Who view'd Him with considerate mind.

Five hundred you might count,
Who saw Him on the hallow'd mount;
He forty days with saints discoursed,
Truths heavenly reinforced,
With them He drank and eat,
By miracle created, meat.

When present to their view,
His Voice they heard, His Shape they knew,

His Hands, and Feet, and wounded Side,
    They felt and nicely eyed,
    Infallibly assured
'Twas Jesus, Who the Cross endured.

    Full power bless'd Jesus gain'd,
By which o'er Heaven and earth He reign'd;
The power which Heaven on Him bestow'd,
    From Him to votaries flow'd;
    All sent with aid Divine,
To teach the Faith of Godhead Trine.

    To them He promised might,
To put infernal ghosts to flight,
The force of all disease to break,
    In various tongues to speak,
    Drink poisons most acute,
Or crush the most envenom'd brute.

    That, in cleft tongues of fire,
The Holy Ghost should them inspire;
His influence should with them remain
    When He should bliss obtain;
    All punctually fulfill'd
When they began the Church to build.

    Succeeding saints, who weigh'd
Those motives when together laid,
To Jesus with firm faith adhered,
    And love which nothing fear'd.

Thus God to saints abounds,
And faith in constellation founds.

Spite Pagan, magic skill,
The devils from their minds of ill,
Fierce tyrants, who long rack'd their brains
For quintessential pains,
Though they the saints assail'd,
The Resurrection still prevail'd.

This, when the angel said,
In wonted splendour re-array'd,
He straight invisible retired,
Left me with truth inspired:
I gracious God adored,
Who faith with such bright motives stored.

God-man be ever praised,
Who, when from death Himself He raised,
That He our joy might not delay,
Rose early the third day;
And yet entomb'd so long,
Gave of His death conviction strong.

God-man be loved, Who rose
Victorious o'er infernal foes,
Who death, and sin, and hell disarm'd,
That lovers might unharm'd
Live, of their bliss secure,
And gladly short-lived woes endure.

From fin which fouls deftroys,
By deadnefs to celeftial joys,
May I, with penitential cries,
  To a new life arife,
  And reft when I revive,
Dead to the world, to Heaven alive.

MONDAY IN EASTER WEEK.

Yea, and certain women alfo of our company made us aftonifhed, who were early at the fepulchre; and when they found not His Body, they came, faying, that they had alfo feen a vifion of angels, which faid that He was alive.
S. Luke xxiv. 22, 23.

WHEN Jefus Truth celeftial taught,
  And miracles propitious wrought,
And humble, in a Life Divine,
Difplay'd the Love of Godhead Trine,
That penitents might pardon gain,
And with God-man in glory reign,

The tender fex to Him adhered,
His awful goodnefs fome revered,
Some for the loaves made up His train,
Some cure for ailments to obtain;
But none till Magdalen appear'd
To have from guilt her confcience clear'd.

She early to bless'd Jesus came,
Led by the odour of His Name.
All souls, with sin's hard bondage tired,
A Jesus ardently desired,
And soon as she of Jesus heard,
Jesus was to her heart endear'd.

But oh! how could a guilty breast,
While by seven devils 'twas possess'd,
Give entrance to the Godhead pure,
Or God that odious sight endure?
Jesus first drave the fiends away,
And cleansed her spirit with His ray.

Great God, though outraged by our sins,
In pity yet our change begins,
O wondrous Love, 'twas that which broke
The sinful Mary's grievous yoke,
She instantly impatient grew,
To keep sweet Jesus in her view.

From the first moment of her turn,
The Love divine began to burn;
A sinner who her sin bewails
Weighs sin and pardon in just scales;
Dear Jesus' Name them both involves,
And hearts to love and tear dissolves.

When souls in love with Jesus fall,
They consecrate to Him their all:

Mary a box of ointment brought,
Which for a liberal sum she bought,
Yet 'twas too mean, in her esteem,
For Him, Who should the world redeem.

Entering where Simon made his treat,
She with her tears wash'd Jesus' Feet,
Then kiss'd them, to give Love its share,
And wiped them with her loosen'd hair;
Then on His Head pour'd rich perfume,
Which sweetly scented all the room.

O heart, by Jesus highly prized,
Soften'd by Love, in tears baptized!
From sins habitual, numerous, great,
Your Absolution was complete,
Jesus Himself to speak it deign'd,
From thence you lead a life unstain'd.

When Jesus journey'd to and fro,
Seed heavenly o'er the land to sow,
The female votaries, by you led,
Still follow'd His instructive tread;
You from your stores His wants relieved,
And for the ills He suffer'd grieved.

But when you through the dolorous way
Follow'd God-man to Golgotha,
Your love, your tear, seem'd then at height,
At that sad, wondrous, tender sight,

Yet both increafed each ftep you trod,
After diftrefs'd Incarnate God.

Out of your broken heart there came
A flood of tears, a fervent flame,
The flood ran down, the flame afpired,
One moiften'd, and the other fired,
Yet they in mutual aids combined,
And in one centre Jefus join'd.

Each dolour which you wept to fee,
Your love cried out, Ah! 'tis for me,
You in His veft beheld the ftains
Of His late agonizing pains,
Frefh blood, from gorings of His crown,
And from His furrows trickling down.

You faw Him with the Crofs opprefs'd,
How on Mount Calvary diftrefs'd,
You on the Crofs beheld Him laid,
The wounds which by the nails were made,
Saw Blood from His wide nailings ftream,
And heard fpectators Him blafpheme.

His dolorous cry you heard Him make,
My God, why doft Thou Me forfake?
With gall you faw His potion mix'd,
And with a fpear His Side transfix'd,
To His blefs'd Mother you ftood near,
And vied with her in love and tear.

You saw His Soul its manſion quit,
The Lord of Life to death ſubmit,
Recounting then the boundleſs pain
You ſaw God-man for you ſuſtain,
You ſaw the guilt of ſin diſplay'd,
When dying God our ranſom paid.

As at dear Jeſus' Croſs you ſtood,
Weeping from either eye a flood,
'Twas then your tendereſt love and tear
Fill'd all the expanſion of its ſphere,
While your compaſſionating eyes
Saw love unbounded agonize.

Of Jeſus' Love a lively ſenſe,
Mournful, endearing, and intenſe,
To martyr's height raiſed love and tear,
Love which like Jeſus caſt out fear;
In grace your progreſs was much more
Than e'er it was in ſin before.

Eve's guilty daughters, who ſhall hear
The bliſs you gain'd by love and tear,
Will of their ſins take ſtrict review,
They'll ſtrive to love and weep like you,
You! next to His own Mother bleſs'd,
Beloved by God Incarnate beſt.

With female ſaints, by break of day,
You your laſt honours came to pay,

For richeſt gums you ſpent your gold,
In them you would have Him enroll'd,
By the void grave you weeping ſtay'd,
To learn the place where He was laid.

God with a viſion graced your ſight,
You ſaw two angels robed in light,
An angel you aſſurance gave,
That Jeſus had unbarr'd the grave,
Jeſus, the more you to endear,
Would firſt to your bleſs'd eyes appear.

You were His envoy to infuſe
Into the apoſtles the glad news,
His deareſt Mother never knew
Her Son aroſe, till told by you.
Souls purified in God's mild eye
Thus with pure ſouls, in favours vie.

O may we learn, for life miſpent,
Of weeping Mary, to repent!
Heaven her for our example ſet,
Her progreſs we ſhould ne'er forget,
We, if like her in love and tear,
Shall be alike to Jeſus dear.

TUESDAY IN EASTER WEEK.

The Resurrection.

Thus it is written, and thus it behoved Christ to suffer, and to rise from the dead the third day.—*Luke* xxiv. 46.

BLESS'D Jesus, on the Cross in boundless pain,
In boundless joy, when Thou didst rise again,
One of Thy joyful rays be pleased to dart,
Headed with Love Divine, into my heart,
That ardent love and joy my soul may raise,
To sing Thy Rising in exalted lays.

Our Lord His dissolution had commenced,
And Deity His Soul re-influenced,
Infernal malice now had reach'd its height,
And God had to the land restored the light,
When the chief priests the Governor bespeak,
That some the malefactors' legs should break.
By Pilate's order, with a ponderous stroke,
The two thieves' bones were by the soldiers broke,
To hasten death, lest hanging on the tree
Upon the feast, it might polluted be.
But seeing Jesus dead, they pass'd Him by,
God watch'd Him with a providential eye,
That all the prophecy fulfill'd might own,

Messias should not have a broken bone.
One thrust his spear into His tender Side,
And from His Pericardium streaming eyed
Both Blood and Water, and from thence we know
From His Heart-love, Rites Sacramental flow;
The wound was mortal, and the spiteful Jews
With a feign'd death could not the world abuse;
The wound predicted in the Sacred Book,—
They on Messias, Whom they pierced, shall look.

 The pious Joseph then to Pilate goes,
Begs he of Jesus' Body might dispose:
Pilate consents, and in the marble womb
Of a hard rock, where was a new-dug tomb
For his own burial in his garden made,
Our Lord took rest, where never man was laid,
Lest, when He rose, it might suggested be,
Some other there entomb'd arose, not He;
Or that He rose not by His Power Divine,
But contact of some saint's or prophet's shrine.
Good Nicodemus, to adorn his hearse,
Brought odours o'er His Body to disperse,
All was enwrapp'd in a fine linen fold,
And a huge stone upon the entrance roll'd.

 Meanwhile His separate Soul to Hades flew,
The receptacles of the dead to view,
O'er ghastly death His triumph to proclaim,
And make all Tophet tremble at His Name.
A bright angelic squadron on the wing

Attended on their death-subduing King,
With a bright Cross of rays transversed made,
And His inscription at the head display'd,
In great resplendent characters, like those
Which God's celestial Book of Life compose.
Our Lord began His awful radiant march,
Descending first to the infernal arch,
Damn'd ghosts at His dread sight began to quake,
Flouncing for shelter in the burning lake;
He their malicious tyranny restrain'd,
And orders gave they should be all rechain'd.
The prison next where souls polluted dwell,
Infested daily by near neighbouring hell,
Where they too late impenitent bewail,
Reserved for judgment in that dolorous jail,
He enters, with strange terror each was dash'd,
And with fresh stings of guilty conscience lash'd.

Thence He to Paradise ascends direct,
Where holy souls with languor Him expect,
There saints are in the interim at rest,
Till, judgment pass'd, they are completely bless'd;
There each good soul remains in widow'd state,
In longings till remarried to its mate;
Thither our Lord the Thief benignly brought,
Who to the saints the Crucifixion taught.
The holy souls their gracious Lord revered,
And He with sweet supports their languors cheer'd,
Advanced their joys to a more rapturous height,
And placed them nearer to the blissful sight.

Some He for present resurrection chose,
His train at His own Rising to compose,
Whose tombs then open by the earthquake lay,
Ordain'd a while to re-assume their clay.
The third day's dawn gave Him His rising call,
He pour'd out heavenly favours on them all.
Down then He flew with His selected train,
That He and they might glad re-union gain.

The envious Jews once more to Pilate came,
His jealousy thus striving to inflame;
We oft have heard that great Deceiver say,
That He would re-inspire His buried clay;
A guard we for the sepulchre implore,
Which day and night may strictly watch the door,
Lest His admirers some new fraud impose,
And then affirm He from His grave arose.
At their request straight Pilate guards assign'd,
And watchful duty to them all enjoin'd:
The Jews, lest votaries should His Body steal,
See the watch set, and stone sepulchral seal,
Wisdom divine Judaic malice steer'd,
And they, the truth they strove to smother, clear'd.

Bless'd Jesus' Flesh and Spirit re-unite,
He rose from death by His own boundless might;
His Blood re-circling made His Pulses beat,
All vital channels felt rekindled heat.
The seventh day's Jewish Sabbath breathed its last,

And into defuetude eternal pafs'd,
The firft day's hallow'd gleams were then begun,
Illumined by God's co-eternal Son;
When a new earthquake gave the awful fign
Of God Incarnate rifing from His fhrine.

   In the firft, earth and air at every pore
Tranfpiring thunders globe terraqueous tore,
The frighted fea its channel then forfook,
Foundations of the globe terreftrial fhook,
The pillars on which arch'd heavens rely,
Were on their feveral bafes fcrew'd awry:
But in the fecond, by propitious force,
All things recover'd their connatural courfe;
Back to their magazine the waters roll'd,
Fix'd were foundations which the earth uphold,
The pillars fcrew'd aright which heaven fuftain'd,
The world, with Jefus, refurrection gain'd.
His foes alone had of the omen dread,
And fear'd His glorious Rifing from the dead:
The guard who watch'd the tomb, in horrid
      fright,
To the chief priefts took inftantaneous flight,
They told the wondrous truth, while envious
      Jews,
(Convinced, but not converted at the news,)
Bribed high the foldiers, charging them to fay,
His votaries ftole Him, while they flept, away:
And if the Governor fhould doubt the tale,
They would for their impunity prevail.

The soldiers took the bribe, and could not hold,
But all abroad both truth and fiction told.

 Explosions which the second earthquake gave,
By Heaven directed, open'd Jesus' grave;
They raised the stone erect, while Jesus rose,
Which straight fell down, the sepulchre to close,
Till from high Heaven a mighty Angel flown,
Roll'd quite away the monumental stone,
That saints who thither came their tears to shed
Might see plain marks of rising from the dead.
The tender sex got of the men the starts,
They first the tribute paid of thankful hearts;
They, ere the sun could gain the morning point,
Haste Jesus with rich odours to anoint.
The guard was fled, the stone away was roll'd,
And on the stone an Angel they behold,
His face like unafflicting lightning bright,
His vesture than the new-fall'n snow more white,
The guard he struck into amazing fears,
But the soft votaries he benignly cheers;
'Tis Jesus whom ye seek, be not afraid,
Come see the empty tomb where He was laid,
The living 'mongst the dead ye seek in vain,
He oft foretold that He should rise again;
'Tis now fulfill'd, haste to His votaries make,
That they may of the happy news partake;
Two other Angels, each in radiant vest,
The same propitious wonder co-attest.

The news, too good in haste to be believed,
Was with suspicions at the first received;
Loved John, and Peter gave them greatest heed,
Both ran to reach the sepulchre with speed,
With Magdalen they both the tomb survey,
Minutely all the circumstances weigh,
The grave they enter, linen shroud they view,
And the impression which His Body drew;
The napkin which around His Head was tied,
Wrapt up, they in another place descried,
They both believe, yet doubts were intermix'd,
Till fresh illuminations faith refix'd.
They both returning, Magdalen remain'd,
Showers from her eyes into the tomb she rain'd,
At head and feet where Jesus lay she saw
Two radiant Angels sit with humble awe:
Why weepest thou, they mildly her bespeak,
Ah me! she said, I here loved Jesus seek,
But they have moved Him from His burial-place,
And I, alas! their motions cannot trace.
Our Lord with that to her glad view appears,
And changed afflicting into joyful tears.
Jesus on love and tears sets value high,
And first with His dear sight, bless'd Mary's eye.
To His great Father in the garden shade,
Jesus first-fruits of resurrection paid,
In hymns divine and eucharistic joys,
And next a glorious Angel He employs,
To carry to His Mother the glad news,
Which o'er her soul high rapture should diffuse.

The saints departed who with Jesus rose,
To Salem came the wonder to disclose:
Jews them beheld with a surprise profound,
Who rose, when no last trump was heard to sound,
Known by their bodies, they with saints conversed,
Each heart they with the Love of Jesus pierced.
To female saints Himself He early show'd,
Whose tears like Mary's had His tomb o'erflow'd;
To James, to Peter, to the saints who talk'd
Of Jesus, as they to Emmaus walk'd,
To His disciples in assembly join'd;
When Thomas stay'd by accident behind,
Peace to you all, was His benign salute;
Their want of faith to chide, and to confute,
He shew'd His wounded Hands, and Feet, and
      Side,
That by their sense His Body might be tried.
He food demanded, and before them eat,
Beyond all doubt conviction to complete;
Peace to you, Jesus said, I now decree,
To send you, as My Father first sent Me:
Then breathing, adds, the Holy Ghost receive,
To tender you, when I My votaries leave.
Heaven will the sins, you here absolve, remit,
And no bold sinners, whom you bind, acquit;
When Thomas present was, He them reviews,
His solemn benedictions He renews;
His hands into the Wounds of spear and nails,
Whilst Thomas thrusts, past doubting he bewails;
My Lord, my God, he passionately cried,

The same now risen, Who was crucified.
Our Lord made visit to His friends again,
As on Tiberias' sea they fish'd in vain:
A wondrous draught made risen Jesus known,
By Whom a greater miracle was shown;
For as to land the mighty shoal they drew,
A fire, broil'd fish, and loaves, they had in view;
Our Lord with them at the same table fed,
Or by the angels, or creation spread.
For Peter's trine denial, there a trine
Profession, He required of Love divine;
Bade him His lambs and sheep with zeal to feed,
Predicting, he by martyrdom should bleed;
To heavenly solitude He then withdrew,
Where angels to congratulate Him flew.

Weak, conquer'd death, on Jesus I rely,
And all your whole artillery defy;
You of dire terrors are no longer king,
By Jesus disenvenom'd is your sting;
Our Jesus' Rising, has unbarr'd the grave,
From your insulting horrors saints to save;
Your force, which you by sin accursed gain'd,
Is now by His all gracious might restrain'd;
You may the body for a while surprise,
But from its fall, it shall to glory rise.
May I, Lord, by repentance sin bewail,
Sin, which arm'd death, o'er sinners to prevail,
And early rising from a life impure,
My rising to eternal bliss secure.

All praife to Jefus! Who from death arofe,
And triumph'd over our infernal foes.
Glory to Jefus! o'er the mountain rolls,
Who rifing, opens Heaven to faithful fouls.

FIRST SUNDAY AFTER EASTER.

Jefus on Tabor.

St. John xx. 19-23.

BLESS'D Jefus from His radiant cloud defcends,
Thus fweetly greeting His furrounding friends:
Peace to you all; peace which fhall never fail,
Peace which o'er worldly trouble fhall prevail;
Peace at your death, peace in your wills refign'd,
Peace with your God, eternal, unconfined.
Over all heaven and earth, all power divine,
Is now become, by refurrection, Mine:
This of My Crofs is the immortal gain,
I now renew My mediatory reign.
Renew; for foon as man his God forfook,
I his redemption freely undertook.
All faints, from Abel, to the pious Thief,
By My devoted Blood, had full relief.
What they of old beheld in fhadows dim,
You fee completed, and devoutly hymn.

You, who My chofen miffionaries are,
Muft to the world all-faving truth declare.

Mercy no more to Jewry is confined,
Go out with zeal, disciple all mankind;
In name of Father, Son, and Holy Ghost,
Baptize, co-hymn'd by the celestial host;
Teach saving truth to Gentile and to Jew,
Teach faithfully all truths I taught to you.
The gracious Paraclete shall in short time
Your spirits fill, enlighten, and sublime.
The truths derived from the Eternal Source,
You shall with wondrous miracles enforce.
You, in My Name, shall devils dispossess,
And in all languages your thoughts express;
Unharm'd, the deadliest serpents shall take up,
And safely drink of an empoison'd cup;
Your hands you on the dying sick shall lay,
Restore firm health, and drive disease away.
I'll at your humble prayers your wants supply,
When suffering for My sake on Me rely,
I'll influentially with you abide,
My Spirit always shall with you reside;
I'll give my angels charge your souls to aid,
That you may ne'er be conquer'd or dismay'd.
The world awhile your persons may oppress,
My comforts shall endear your worst distress.
Be valiant for the truth, no labour spare,
You are My Father's, and My tender care.

   With that, their spirits, which till then were
      closed,
He open'd, and for heavenly truth disposed;

Their minds were from that moment unperplex'd,
They clearly underſtood the ſacred text.
Then their Illuminator they adore,
Amazed they ſhould not ſee bright truth before.
Their vows of firm obedience all renew,
And Jeſus to His ſolitude withdrew.

    All praiſe to Jeſus! Who from death aroſe,
And for our faith that ſtrong foundation choſe.
Riſing from death was an appropriate ſign
Of power moſt inconteſtably divine:
A ſign which men could by their Senſe diſcern,
And we by uniform Tradition learn.
Five hundred ſaints, who in the mount remain'd,
Of virtue and veracity unſtain'd,
Who heard His voice, His Wounds could feel and
    ſee,
Aſſured that Jeſus could no phantom be;
Truths at the ſpring could by their ſenſes know,
Which down by a traduced ſenſation flow.
Whether at Jordan's fountain-head I ſup,
Or at his diſemboguing fill my cup,
I quench my thirſt alike, and his whole courſe
Is but continuation of the ſource.
My faith on this Tradition, Lord, relies,
As firm as if I ſaw Thee with my eyes.
But faith will ſtronger grow by ghoſtly ſenſe
Of emanations from Thy Love immenſe;
Of that dear Love let me the influence feel,
And with my blood Thy ſacred truth I'll ſeal.

SECOND SUNDAY AFTER EASTER.

*I am the Good Shepherd : the Good Shepherd giveth His
life for the sheep.—St. John* x. 11.

WHENE'ER my voice of Jesus sings,
My fingers meet th' exilient strings,
Which leap up into chords, to show
What sweets harmonious, from Him flow.
Discordant souls He puts in tune,
To sing the praise of God Triune.

Of Jesus I a song intend,
Whose Loves, all other loves transcend;
While I of Jesus sing, my sheep
At that dear Name will silence keep,
They'll meekly listen to my air,
And all the while their food forbear.

Guide me, my strings, and every line
Shall with your leading chords combine,
He's the Great Shepherd of the plain,
And He deserves the noblest strain :
And while my song to Him takes flight,
My love shall give it flame and height.

Shepherds no fitter theme can find
Than Jesus to employ their mind,
He's the Good Shepherd, justly styled,
And governs with an empire mild;

He on His flock casts tender eyes,
His boundless Love all wants supplies.

His flock He in rich pasture feeds,
To crystal streams the thirsty leads,
He watches with kind wakeful care,
Against thief, lion, wolf, or bear,
Provides agreeable retreats,
In freezing cold, or scorching heats.

The teeming ewes He gently drives,
His bosom dying lambs revives;
Supports the faint, the sick restores,
Sets broken bones, heals all their sores;
He every sheep distinctly knows,
And sympathises with their woes.

But now, my guiding strings, methinks
You languish, and your vigour sinks;
Ah, 'tis no wonder you can well
What I must sing of next, foretel;
Yet keep your movements just alive,
The softest chords you can, contrive.

Tears best with those soft chords will suit,
My tears shall drop while love is mute;
I'll write in the sad tears I shed,
What I of Jesus would have said,
The Sov'reign Shepherd, Who from on high
Came down for His dear sheep to die.

AFTER EASTER.

My strings, now change your softer vein,
In chords with sorrow mix disdain;
My tears shall with your chords consent,
That I may all past sins lament,
And water the surrounding shade,
That I His Love so ill repaid.

'Twas that Good Shepherd I forsook,
The ready way to death I took;
I strove His tender calls to shun,
And into endless dangers run;
His boundless Love would me pursue,
Which I despised, and faster flew.

But now, my strings, your chords prepare
To sound a soul-enamouring air;
Sweet Jesus sought me all about,
Ne'er left till He had found me out;
The stray He on His shoulders laid,
And gently to His fold convey'd.

Angelic quires my welcome sung,
And I recover'd my lost tongue;
My tongue, which stopp'd with grief before,
Shall never now lie silent more;
I'll sing His praises day and night,
And love shall every song indite.

THIRD SUNDAY AFTER EASTER.

Submit yourfelves to every ordinance of man for the Lord's fake, whether it be to the king, as fupreme: or unto governors, as unto them that are fent by him, for the punifhment of evildoers, and for the praife of them that do well.—1 *Peter* ii. 13, 14.

THE king who with juft title reigns,
  The magiftrates whom he ordains,
All fathers, mothers, mafters, to whofe care
  Others fubjected are,
 All paftors who the flocks of Jefus feed,
  To be our parents God decreed.

 God gives to them a power in truft,
  They to their ftations fhould be juft,
They for God's Glory all things fhould contrive,
  From Whom they power derive,
 Should exemplary be, benign, and mild,
  To treat inferiors as a child.

 Inferiors, who fubjection owe,
  Muft juftice in fubmiffion fhew,
Love, honour, reverence, efteem, obey,
  For their fuperiors pray,
 Be patient when rebuked, their pofts attend,
  Prone to pleafe, tender to offend.

 Juft are all men, who human race
  With a fraternal love embrace,

Do wrong to none, and all with sweetness treat,
  Free from revengeful heat,
Who to all others measure just the same
  Which they themselves from others claim.

O happy age, would men unite
In giving all degrees their right,
Men's jarring souls would co-harmonious be,
  From war and rapine free,
Few would be their accounts, death their release,
  When with the world and God at peace.

FOURTH SUNDAY AFTER EASTER.

Nevertheless I tell you the truth, it is expedient for you that I go away: for if I go not away, the Comforter will not come unto you; but if I depart, I will send Him unto you.—*John* xvi. 7.

ETERNAL Dove, by Jesus sent
 Love heavenly to foment,
Since we of Jesus are bereft,
 Thou, Comforter, art left,
And Thou dost in Thy saints abide,
Their souls to strengthen, comfort, guide.

I would invite Thee to my heart,
 Thence never to depart,
Thou source of hymn and Love Divine,
 To both doth souls incline,

But know Thou never canſt endure
To temple in a heart impure.

My heart, bleſs'd Paraclete, refine,
    That it may Thee enſhrine,
Thy tender Wings o'er me extend,
    Make me to Thee propend,
From the kind heat Thou wilt diſpenſe,
I ſhall ſpiritual life commence.

Thou, boundleſs Love, doſt love excite
    Where'er Thou takeſt Thy flight,
To raiſe a penitential ſhower
    Thou haſt the gracious power,
My eyes, when kiſs'd by Thy ſoft Wings,
Will guſh in never-ceaſing ſprings.

In tears I'll bathe, then bathe again,
    My eyes I ne'er ſhall drain,
To ſin expoſed while I live here,
    Sin will ſupply my tear,
Or ſhould my fountains chance to ſtop,
One gentle ray will make them drop.

Thou didſt Thy Plumes on Mary ſpread,
    And glorious influence ſhed,
With Hymn and Love Thou didſt her ſtore,
    Ere great God-man ſhe bore,
No mortal ſin could her invade,
For Hymn and Love ſhe chiefly pray'd.

AFTER EASTER.

I Hymn and Love of Thee implore,
    And beg one blessing more,
Tears of Love filial, to bemoan
    That I to sin am prone,
Soft tears and sin are so allied
They ne'er can separate abide.

When I my vial full have wept,
    And God shall it accept,
O let Thy Wings their virtue dart
    From eyelids to my heart,
O soul-intenerating Dove,
Melt me entirely into Love.

Love will afresh my eyelids fill,
    In rivers to distil,
That on the world I love should spend,
    And Love immense offend,
I Jesus in my eye shall keep,
Love will with consolation weep.

While I dissolve in filial tear,
    Thy Wings my soul will cheer,
Celestial joys will me o'erflow,
    And make a Heaven below,
And Thou my spirit wilt sublime
To love, joy, weep, at the same time.

FIFTH SUNDAY AFTER EASTER.

Pure religion and undefiled before God and the Father is this, To visit the fatherless and widows in their affliction, and to keep himself unspotted from the world.

James i. 27.

OF Jesus' brethren to take care
    You never should or purse or labour spare,
Your very life you must not dear esteem
    Bless'd Jesus' brethren to redeem,
Your purse, your pains, your life, are of no weight
When you the Cross of God Incarnate rate.

    All kindness to His brethren shown,
As done to Himself He'll most benignly own,
With Jesus' Love all saints who overflow,
    Joyful on Him their all bestow,
Cold water He accepts, and every mite
With boundless treasure pays in endless light.

    Fear not the stench nice sense may meet,
Or loathsome objects tenderly to treat,
You'll find the fumes which bless'd Arabia sheds
    Less sweet than prisons or sick beds,
Where Jesus in His poor grieved brethren cries
For sympathy and opportune supplies.

    Alms for the poor, aids for distress'd,
For hungry food, for naked limbs a vest,

Salves for all wounds, medicines for each difeafe,
    Cordials for faint, for painful eafe,
Relief for prifoners, ranfom for the flaves,
Shrouds for the dead, for the unburied graves.

    Urania's[1] love would you obtain,
Learn Jefus' Love, and how to love again,
When Jefus in His brethren you perceive,
    Jefus Himfelf in them relieve,
Count that day loft when in your alms and prayers
Dear Jefus wants His confecrated fhares.

ASCENSION-DAY, OR HOLY THURSDAY.

MY faith and hope, your powers unite,
    While I a hymn indite,
You are twin-graces, fledged this day,
    And warm'd by the fame ray,
And you, my love, make up the Trine,
This day you reach'd maturity Divine.

    You faith and hope, till Jefus fhined,
        Were embryos of the mind,
Lodged, or in dark prophetic fchemes
    Where truth gave languid gleams,

---

[1] *Urania.* Wifdom. See Paradife Loft, Book 1, "Defcend from Heaven, Urania," &c. And In Memoriam xxxvii. "Urania fpeaks with darken'd brow."

Or with terrestrial promise fed,
In which supernal hardly could be read.

   When Jesus here diffused His Light
      Faith was absorb'd by sight,
   Assurance superseded hope,
      Love gain'd a freer scope,
   Till our Redemption was complete
Man scarce had full inflammatory heat.

   On Olivet's fair lofty head,
      His votaries Jesus led,
   That they His glory should behold,
      And to the world unfold,
   And His past loves, with hands uprear'd,
By blessing valedictory endear'd.

   As the celestial fountain stopt,
      Which heavenly sweetness dropt,
   A cloud descended, one of those
      God for His chariot chose,
   Which opening Jesus to surround,
With gentle force remounted from the ground.

   Bless'd Moses, seized with sacred awe,
      Received of God the Law,
   Thick cloud the Mount then overspread,
      Which Israel struck with dread,
   And while he there his station fix'd,
The cloud with a devouring fire was mix'd.

The cloud in which God-man was rear'd,
    Benign and bright appear'd,
Like what saints saw on Tabor stream,
    Enlighten'd by His beam,
God speaking from effulgence clear,
This is My Son beloved, Whom all must hear.

The horse and chariots were of flame, -
    Which for Elias came,
The whirlwind hurrying them through air,
    Fann'd them to frightful glare;
He pass'd through an ethereal glade,
Steer'd and supported by God's gracious aid.

But when to Heaven bless'd Jesus flew,
    Cloud only was in view,
He, to accelerate His speed,
    Of chariot had no need;
Incarnate God, by His own might,
Both rose from death, and took His heavenly flight.

The saints the cloud, with steady eyes,
    Traced as it pass'd the skies,
But soon it reach'd celestial height
    Transcending human sight,
And, as it swift to glory soar'd,
Incarnate God devoutly they adored.

Ere their ejaculation closed,
    Our Lord in bliss reposed;

Bless'd Jesus re-assumed His Crown,
    And at God's Right sat down;
Think with what wondrous speed He pass'd,
In a few moments, the expanded vast.

Should a swift eagle heavenwards spring,
    With an unwearied wing,
And swifter make through Heaven his way
    Than when he flew for prey,
Scarce in a million of years
He'd shoot the gulf of the supernal spheres.

When God is present in a place
    He passes through no space,
By Will, not motion, He from nought
    Things into being wrought;
God-man in bliss His Person will'd,
Which in a minute He Himself fulfill'd.

Good souls would tire who heavenward fly
    Ere they could reach the sky,
Or numerous painful ages spend
    Ere they could Heaven ascend,
If they on wing were bound to keep
All their long passage through supernal deep.

A seraph, though on twice six wings
    His message down he brings,
And quicken'd with warm, heavenly zeal,
    His message to reveal;

Yet 'midſt ethereal wave would fail,
If he on unaſſiſted wings ſhould fail.

   God wills juſt ſouls ſhould mount on high,
      Wills angels down ſhould fly,
   Almighty Will impreſſes force,
      For each appointed courſe.
   The ſaints by that at bliſs arrive,
And ſwiftly up the waves unfathom'd dive.

   With near an inſtantaneous flight,
      Fly rays of morning light;
   A million-fold they ſwifter go
      Than arrows from a bow;
   A myriad-fold an angel flies,
Swifter than morning ſplendour gilds the ſkies.

   The heavenly orbs flew open wide,
      When they their Maker eyed;
   The ſtars left off their morning lay
      To ſing that glorious day;
   On either hand they back retired
To clear the road in which God-man aſpired.

   The angels to the heavenly gate
      Flew, on God-man to wait;
   The ſaints outflew the radiant hoſt,
      They took the nobler poſt,
   And, to attend Him to His Throne,
Each guardian left that day his charge alone.

All Heaven to a new song agreed,
   For great God-man decreed;
But a sweet emulation rose
   Who should the song compose;
The angels urged God's Will, that they
Should to His First-Begotten worship pay.

Saints urged, God-man His Blood resign'd
   For none but lapsed mankind;
Place then to saints the angels gave,
   Whom Jesus died to save;
Yet, since for penitent souls they joy'd,
With them they would in song be co-employ'd.

Saints on the Lamb, for sinners slain,
   Sang a new heavenly strain,
With them join'd all angelic quires
   With their harmonious lyres;
Heaven never song more grateful heard,
A fuller concert ne'er in bliss appear'd.

My guardian, who then bore his part,
   Trajected to my heart,
That he the saints and angels eyed,
   How they in singing vied,
And, though he both admired, confess'd
Saints the more sweet enamourments express'd.

They call bless'd Jesus' Loves to mind,
   All for their bliss design'd,

Take super-effluent delight
　　In His endearing sight,
And their new anthems to complete,
To the Lamb slain doxologies repeat.

When Jesus had withdrawn His Light,
　　Two angels, robed in white,
Bespake the saints in such amaze,
　　Why upwards do you gaze?
God-man, Whom you ascending saw,
At His return shall strike the world with awe.

When the last trumpet sounds aloud,
　　In flaming fire and cloud,
He to the Judgment shall descend,
　　The dead shall Him attend,
He'll then pronounce to all their doom,
The wicked damn, the just to bliss assume.

The saints who Jesus saw when pain'd,
　　Joy'd that He bliss had gain'd,
That Manhood at God's Right was placed,
　　With highest honour graced,
That session endless rest implied,
With the eternal Word co-glorified.

In hymns they all resolved to sing
　　Their dear redeeming King,
Their course to Salem then they bent,
　　Exulting as they went,

There charged to ſtay, till on them all,
The Holy Ghoſt ſhould in full ſplendour fall.

There in God's ſacred Houſe they dwelt,
   His gracious Preſence felt,
To perpetuity of praiſe
   Devoting all their days,
And waiting for the happy hour,
When the Eternal Dove ſhould them empower.

Our Heavenly King in glory reigns,
   Infernal ghoſts reſtrains,
All to His Throne have free acceſs,
   To open their diſtreſs,
From thence He cheers each ſoul who prays,
With mighty, ſweet, benign, enamouring rays.

From thence His goodneſs overflows,
   And heavenly gifts beſtows,
From thence He ſends the ſpotleſs Dove,
   The Source of Holy Love,
And in His own aſcent declares
The bliſs of ſaints who are with Him co-heirs.

Our great High-prieſt there intercedes,
   For ſinners pardon pleads,
Preſents to His dread Father's Eyes
   His own dear Sacrifice,
And gracious God by that atoned,
Forgives each ſin, as ſoon as 'tis bemoan'd.

To Jesus, though He disappears,
   My steady faith adheres,
My hope on Jesus now unseen,
   Shall as my anchor lean,
I Jesu's blessing shall receive,
Since though I see not, firmly I believe.

My love, since Jesus' Love you see
   Rise to such high degree,
Your ardours to no measure bind,
   Expatiate unconfined,
Call faith and hope their aids to bring,
Of Love Incarnate the ascent to sing.

All praise to Jesus now above,
   Below, diffusing Love,
Who mansions for the saints prepares,
   Makes them His tender cares,
Who with His Church unseen abides,
And full supplies for all her wants provides.

May we our souls to Jesus rear,
   While in this vale of tear,
Long to our heavenly home to go,
   While strangers here below;
A heavenly mind can never miss,
To sit like Jesus enthronized in bliss.

SUNDAY AFTER ASCENSION-DAY.

Jesus Present.

WHEN our redemption was complete,
 Thou, Jesus, didst to Heaven retreat,
  And on the Throne Divine
  Make up the Godhead Trine,
There Heaven Thy glorious Body shall retain,
Till Thou at Judgment shalt the world arraign.

 Yet with Thy saints 'tis Thy delight
 To stay, converse, and to unite,
  The Church in humble prayers
  Thy gracious presence shares,
Thou at our hearts, when they are closed, dost knock,
And entering dwell, if we the door unlock.

 How Thou, Who wilt not Heaven forsake,
 Canst in my heart Thy mansion make,
  Is by experience taught,
  Though it transcends my thought.
I feel Thee knock, my heart fly open wide,
Enter dear Jesus, and with me abide.

 My Jesus now my spirit fills,
 His Love in suavities distils,
  Preventions, tractions sweet,
  Devout Christ-hymning heat;

Kind checks, and calls benign, and gracious might,
And coruscations of the joys in light.

   With these and with a thousand more,
    Thou, Lord, art pleased my mind to store,
       Thy Love long-knocking stay'd,
       While I my bliss delay'd,
Thou of my heart, dear Jesus, hast the key,
Why didst not Thou unlock for entrance free?

   Free entrance is from love alone,
    My heart was then obdurate grown,
       And till it softer grew
       Declined Thy awful view:
Break it, my Lord, wide open to remain,
Never against Thee to be shut again.

   Thou while below wert yet on high,
    By omnipresent Deity,
       And Thou dost condescend
       Sweet hours with saints to spend.
O lovely Jesu, keep my love on fire,
Thou from Thy lovers never dost retire.

   My Jesu, while I Thee enjoy,
    I'll on Thy Love my powers employ,
       Thy Love will mine excite,
       I'll hymns of Thee indite,
By meditation I'll prolong Thy stay,
And Thou shalt bless me ere Thou goest away.

Away Thou canst not, Jesu, go,
Or to Thy lovers stranger grow,
    Thou mayst effulgence shroud
    Awhile in some dark cloud,
But still Thy gracious, Thy all-seeing Eye,
Inspects Thy saints, all blessings to supply.

When, Lord, Thou present wert below,
Saints felt a virtue from Thee flow,
    Which at a distance cured
    Diseases long endured;
Lord, when from me Thou wilt Thyself conceal,
Let virtue from Thee stream my soul to heal.

If up to Heaven Thou wilt ascend,
Though Heaven I cannot open rend,
    Though I want wings to soar
    Where seraphs Thee adore,
I'll draw Thee down from Heaven by violent prayer,
To visit me, and re-assume my care.

To Heaven when my petitions flown,
Wait for admittance at the Throne,
    I'll to the Altar fly,
    There offer up my cry;
My Jesus, I am sure is present there,
And I in His sweet influence shall share.

Lord, when Thou to Thy Throne wilt rise,
I offer Thee this compromise,

The Paraclete depute,
Who shall for Thee commute,
He'll love, devotion, consolations shed,
And with fresh grace of hymn inspire my head.

He'll wing my prayer with sigh and groan,
More swiftly to approach the Throne,
Than sages thought of old
Celestial orbs were roll'd;
And never leave the Throne till from on high,
It shall as fast with blessings pray'd for, fly.

Glory to Jesus at God's Right,
Enthroned in majestatic light,
Yet to converse is prone,
With saints below alone.
Live, Lord, with me, and when Thou wilt return,
Take my soul with Thee, and my dust in-urn.

WHIT SUNDAY.

O FOUNTAIN of all Grace Divine,
Third of the co-eternal Trine,
We on Thy sacred day
To Thee devoutly pray,
To Thy full praise to tune our hearts,
That we with saints above may bear our parts.

For Thou to all the faints above,
Art Author of both hymn and love,
  Thou doft exalt their fight
  To beatific light,
Eternal hymn, love moft intenfe,
Rife from clear view of Lovelinefs immenfe.

On chaos, dark, inactive, rude,
Thou with creating force didft brood,
  Thou art to every thing
  Of life and motion Spring,
And when the world was made anew,
From Thee all ghoftly life and motion drew.

In fin we are by nature dead,
And can no ftep to glory tread,
  By Thee we born again,
  Are freed from native ftain,
We at the font from death arife,
To live to God perpetual facrifice.

Blefs'd Jefus to His promife true,
The Holy Ghoft, when He withdrew,
  Sent from His Throne on high,
  His prefence to fupply,
His Church to form, erect, control,
And be His Body's Univerfal Soul.

God-man, when He His blifs regain'd,
The great inflammative remain'd,

But sin stark coldness wrought,
  Froze up celestial thought,
Till thaw'd by inward heavenly Fire,
The kindled flame to Jesus should aspire.

Next to the Love God-man display'd,
When on the Cross our Victim made;
  He none to us below,
  More infinite could show,
Than when essential Love He chose,
In whose soft care His Church He would repose.

Essential Love from Glory came
To saints, in cloven tongues of flame,
  And resting on each head,
  All gifts, all graces shed,
Sublimed them to celestial Light,
And warm'd their love to a seraphic height.

High wisdom the straight course to steer,
Of mysteries a knowledge clear,
  Faith which bless'd Jesus eyed,
  And tortures all defied,
Power which disease should put to flight,
Of miracles a full commission'd might.

Prophetic prescience, God-like view,
Of spirits to discern the true,
  All tongues which men confound,
  To speak and to expound,

That they united truth might spread,
As their division had cursed idols bred.

Aid to the saints high truths to write,
And to the Church traduce their sight,
And priesthood to ordain,
Who should those truths explain,
That every soul, with rule and guide
To perfect heavenly Love, might be supplied.

These gifts essential Love bestow'd,
When Jesu's votaries He o'erflow'd,
Gifts which divinely shined
On teachable mankind,
And of the mysteries they taught
An irresistible conviction wrought.

When Fontal Love o'erflow'd the whole,
He stream'd on every faithful soul,
Love was the leading grace
Shed on the heaven-born race,
Love which to God devotes our hearts,
And to all other graces force imparts.

Love of God loving joy excites,
In pleasing the Beloved delights,
Sweet peace serenes the mind,
To boundless Love resign'd,
Minds which the joys of Love serene,
From filthy passions keep a conscience clean.

WHIT SUNDAY.

A temper sweet, long-suffering, mild,
Still yielding to be reconciled,
   Prone blessings to disperse,
   To all deceit averse,
In provocations wrath restrain'd,
All appetites by moderation rein'd.

These fruits from Love each soul derives,
Who Fontal Love to copy strives,
   Love's influential ray
   Makes evangelic day,
Love, souls enlightens and enflames,
Love, founds to Grace and Heaven our filial claims.

Essential Love enlivens, leads,
With sighs, groans, ardours intercedes,
   Our frailties He relieves,
   Our slidings He retrieves,
Devotion fervent He instils,
And turns to God the pondus[1] of our wills.

That heavenly Paraclete, a saint
Supports and comforts sad or faint,
   From sin the spirit clears,
   Casts out tormenting fears,
With conscience co-attests our zeal,
And of our bliss is both the pledge and seal.

Of loves which from the spirit stream,
None more illustrious saints esteem,

[1] *Pondus*, weight, burden.

None love more vigorous darts,
More elevates their hearts,
Than when their souls Love's temples are,
And Love vouchsafes His gracious presence there.

Of heavenly gifts though Love has store,
'Tis Love, Love only I implore;
Flow out Thou boundless Source,
With full enamouring force,
Till Thou hast deluged all my breast,
My prayers, my sighs shall never give Thee rest.

Thou art Oil, Water, Wind, and Fire,
How can these different powers conspire?
Yet they harmonious be,
May they combine in me,
Dispel all sensual clouds like wind,
When it grows languid, agitate my mind.

With Oil of gladness me restore,
Diffusing sweetness through each pore,
Do Thou my Spring remain,
To purge each daily stain,
To quench my thirst for Love Divine,
And be Thou Fire to lighten, warm, refine.

Essential Love, just is their doom,
Who Thee to grieve or damp presume,
Who Thy sweet force oppose,
With fiends impure to close,

Even hell itself with hate extreme
Shall torture all who Love immense blaspheme.

When Jesus bade the Baptist lave
Upon His Head clear Jordan's wave,
    And to the bank retired,
    His soul in prayer aspired,
And Heaven its gates all open threw,
Of great God-man to have transporting view.

Paternal God proclaim'd His Love,
Down flew the co-essential Dove,
    And, hovering o'er His Head,
    His beams celestial spread,
Which on His human nature stay'd,
And boundless Love co-breathed His conduct
    sway'd.

From this idea we derive
The grace which keeps our souls alive,
    We on God's Love rely,
    His gracious promise eye,
And when we for the Spirit pray
We ne'er are with denial sent away.

Ten days from great God-man's Ascent,
His votaries in the Temple spent,
    Ere to their prayers devout
    Essential Love flow'd out,
Love who, endearing His delays,
Can acquiescence with sweet languor raise.

May we, Thou God of Love, in prayer
Perſiſt, till in Thy Love we ſhare;
  Thou canſt no filth endure,
  Doſt dwell in ſpirits pure,
O may we, waſh'd in tears contrite,
To temple in our ſouls Thy Love invite.

From Thee the grace of hymn proceeds,
Its ſtreams Thy fontal effluence feeds,
  All love, all praiſe to Thee,
  Since we Thy temples be,
Within Thy hallow'd Temple's bound,
Heaven-emulating hymns ſhall daily found.

MONDAY IN WHITSUN-WEEK.

All Bleſſings by Jeſus.

For God ſent not His Son into the world to condemn the world, but that the world through Him might be ſaved.—*John* iii. 17.

FROM Adam all, to thoſe who ſtay
  Alive at Judgment-day,
Who hear the awful trumpet found
  Ere reaching underground,
Heaven, by the promiſed Seed obtain,
And freedom from or guilt or ſtain.

Great God averse to lapsed mankind,
   Born to cursed sin inclined,
Till by God Filial reconciled,
   Had all from Heaven exiled,
Just God might have no pity shown,
And barr'd approaches to His Throne.

When Jesus Filial God appear'd,
   God's clouds of wrath were clear'd,
The source of pity, till then stopt,
   With sweetest mercy dropt,
And rivers by degrees gush'd out
Of blessings on all souls devout.

Saints, who approach the Throne by prayer,
   Found glad acceptance there,
God Filial could His sufferings plead,
   Which He for man decreed,
All things are present to God's Eye,
The Father then saw Jesus die.

In promise only saints of old
   Our Jesus could behold,
We see perform'd what was decreed,
   Blessings which thought exceed;
Paternal God no good bestows
But what through Jesus on us flows.

Thou, Filial God, the world hast made,
   And earth's foundations laid,

Thy Power to creatures Being gave,
  Confined the ocean's wave,
Caſt Heaven by Thy ideal mould,
And all the orbs harmonious roll'd.

Thou in the new creation art
  The Former of the heart,
Grace, pardon, love, life, ghoſtly light,
  Joy, conqueſt, bliſsful fight,
All bleſſings of the gracious Dove
Deſcend through Thee from Fontal Love.

My Lord, our Mediator none
  Could be, but Thou alone,
Nothing to mediate could excite
  But pure Love infinite,
And mediation to complete,
In union God and man muſt meet.

Praiſe to the Father, Who was pleaſed
  To have His wrath appeaſed,
Who Filial Deity reſign'd
  To die for lapſed mankind;
Infinite God that we might live,
Godhead co-infinite would give.

Godhead co-infinite when paid,
  Full ſatisfaction made,
Godhead could not be paid to ſave,
  Till ſubject to the grave,

Godhead must stoop to mortal dust,
His mediation to adjust.

O Love, O Wisdom without bound,
   Which such a medium found!
O who can Filial God offend,
   Who thus would condescend?
O what can God to saints deny,
Who gives God-man for them to die?

Yet woe is me, how oft denied
   Is Jesus crucified!
Our hearts on joys destructive set,
   Love infinite forget;
Hell-pains by all are justly felt,
Whom Love unbounded cannot melt.

Love's Source, which all our vacuums fills,
   Which through God-man distils,
When God is outraged straight is dried;
   Sweet Jesus' Love defied,
Makes souls beyond the devils pain'd,
Who ne'er a Saviour's Love disdain'd.

My Jesus, I'll to Thee adhere,
   Than all the world more dear,
On all Thy loves I'll daily muse,
   Till they fresh hymns infuse,
Or should my soul be in arrears,
I'll add soft penitential tears.

On Thee in co-eternal beams
　　Co-equal Godhead ſtreams,
Lord, out of Thy co-boundleſs ſtore,
　　I love-ſupplies implore,
On me from Fontal Godhead ſhine,
Be always ſtreaming Love Divine.

TUESDAY IN WHITSUN-WEEK.

Then laid they their hands on them, and they received the Holy Ghoſt.—*Aɛts* viii. 17.

OH, I ſhall ne'er forget the happy hour
　　When of the gracious Dove I felt the power;
　I in a moment was no more
　The odious thing I was before,
　　All my propenſions heavenwards ſtream'd,
　I felt enamourments of ſouls redeem'd,
　To my own conſcience I was reconciled,
I joy'd that glorious God would own me for His child.

　I the perpetual motion learn'd from Love,
　I felt my powers in circulations move,
　　Love from the Source of Love deſcends,
　　My love to God, Who fired it, tends,

And love, soon as it mounts on high,
Brings down of Heavenly Love a fresh supply,
When love returns, I send it back for more,
Incessantly I spend, and yet increase my store.

God in all lights most amiable appear'd,
Endearing most, and most to be endear'd,
   In Him alone my boundless mind
   Commensurable bliss can find,
   I felt a love my soul possess,
Congratulating God His Loveliness,
Love incommunicable and intense,
Striving with all its force to stretch to Love immense.

To please my Love was my chief care and aim,
My tender zeal to honour His great Name,
   To do Love's Will was my delight,
   The thought of God would love excite,
   Yet love oft felt damps, wanderings, cold,
Which, though involuntary, I condoled,
And on remembrance of my sinful years,
The joys of pardon mix'd with penitential tears.

Ah, did the world the consolations know
Which from the tears of sweet contrition flow,
   With fervent prayer they'd day and night
   Implore from God a heart contrite,
   And learn as the first tear distill'd
From those high joys which then their spirits fill'd,

What joys there are above, where tears are
    dried,
When tears shed here below so rapturously glide.

  As the fair trees which odorous Gilead crown,
  Secure from harm, drop tears balsamic down,
    Perfuming all the mountain's head,
    And pleasure take their sweets to shed,
    Thus when I learn'd of Love to weep,
  Though free from dread my tears no bounds
    would keep,
  Their trickling gave me soft enamouring ease,
O gracious force of Love, which makes our sor-
    rows please!

  My heart was turn'd, dilated, raised, refined,
  By the soft breathings of a heavenly wind,
    I felt a thousand love-constraints,
    Yet my free-will made no complaints,
    My inclination took the part
  Of Love, co-operating with my heart,
  My tendencies and temper Love well knew,
And with soft cords my soul con-naturally drew.

  The charming ways Love to inflame me used,
  Additional inflammatives infused,
    As the soft wax absorbs the seal,
    My heart I could thus melting feel,
    All Love's impressions to receive,
  Love's lovely image striving to retrieve,

God loves Himſelf, the more God ſees in me
Of His moſt lovely Self, the dearer ſhall I be.

   I cannot love, but I muſt live in pain,
   Till of my love I the fruition gain,
     My cloſet I frequent, for there
     I with my Love converſe by prayer,
     The Sacred Books my ſpirits cheer,
   There I the Voice of my Beloved hear;
   Lord, in Thy courts with ſaints I Thee adore,
There in full meaſure Love communicates its
     ſtore.

   My ſoul Thy Altar with moſt zeal frequents,
   Where to our love, God-man Himſelf preſents,
     I, when I Thee, bleſs'd Jeſus, meet,
     In Thy poor brethren waſh Thy Feet,
     Where'er Thy Love diffuſes rays,
   There I ambitious am to ſpend my days,
   My meditation oft Thy Love revolves,
And ſtays till to high ſea it of freſh Love diſſolves.

   But, Lord, Thy amiableneſs, below
   We but obſcurely, but remotely know,
     Your wings, kind angel, to me lend,
     To Heaven I'll inſtantly aſcend,
     The ſight of lovely God above
   My ſpirit will transform to God-like Love,
   But God here wills my ſtay, God's Will is
     mine,
Lovers to the Beloved wholly their wills reſign.

Shouldst Thou, dear Lord, protracted life decree,
Indulge me languors till my soul is free,
   They who assuming to love most,
   Of love disinterested boast,
   Imperfectly Love apprehend,
All native lovers to fruition tend
To love God all-sufficient, and abstract
Propension is a thing impossible to act.

My God, no dangers, difficulties, woes,
My love shall terrify, tire, discompose,
   I am all heart, and all desire,
   In Thee I centre, yet aspire,
   My spirit fain would sally out,
At Love's unbounded Source to quench my drought,
I love, would fain love more, O when shall I
Fall sick of Love Divine, and of that sickness die!

Die! O dear Lord, I must that word revoke,
Love never feels of death the ireful stroke,
   Love may shake off this lumpish clay
   Wont souls immortal down to weigh,
   But when it into freedom springs,
   It mounts to glory on exilient wings;
   To Fontal Love and life it joyful flies,
Enjoys most life when here it in appearance dies

TRINITY SUNDAY.

GREAT God Triune, enthroned above,
Thou Trine co-effluential Love,
Of all the powers thou haſt impreſt,
Our love can comprehend Thee beſt.

Immenſely Thou co-lovely art,
To love Thee with ſoul, mind and heart,
Our bliſs, our duty is, both join
To make us love the Loves Divine.

The ſacrifice for Loves immenſe
Is to re-love with love intenſe,
Though knowledge ſoon may ſoar too high,
Yet Love without reſtraint may fly.

Thy Loves to us in exile here,
At diſtance and in clouds appear;
Remote and diſtant as they be,
We Trine irradiations ſee.

Paternal God, God Filial gave,
Our loſt rebellious race to ſave;
And God co-breathed lapſed man refined,
To re-imprint His God-like mind.

Should mighty God, by power divine,
Will three coeval ſuns to ſhine,

From the trine fountain there would stream
All o'er expanse, triunal beam.

Trine beams to us would one appear,
And undistinguish'd gild the sphere;
But God by His omniscient eye,
Distinctly could the three descry.

Great God thus Unity displays,
In sweet co-penetrating rays,
And co-benignities divine
Gush out on us from Godhead Trine.

Thus coalesce in sacred lays
A trinity, love, joy, and praise,
All co-derived from God the Source,
Mix and reciprocate their force.

In this coeval three, the bless'd
Duration spend, and never rest;
Triunal loves all three excite,
In saints they co-exert their might.

Pure love will joy coeval raise,
That love and joy coeval praise,
Saints strange co-inexistence find,
In those three graces of the mind.

The greater height these graces reach,
The clearer they the mystery teach;
Saints best in their own souls may read
The illustration of their creed.

TRINITY SUNDAY.

Three worlds should the Almighty will,
His Godhead all alike would fill;
To all the three He might dispense
Distinct, coeval influence.

New men He might create in this,
In that raise souls to heavenly bliss,
And in the third diffuse His grace
On an impure, degenerate race.

One God thus to three worlds below
Would in three different acts outflow,
At the same moment there would be
Triunal co-infinity.

Should there exist a boundless space,
Great God, unlimited to place,
Would o'er the vast effulgence shed
With an indivisible spread.

God's Presence is Himself; for none
Unbounded is but God alone;
Alike communicable be
God's Presence and His Deity.

God a pure Act, all men define,
And 'tis con-natural to assign
To an eternal boundless Might,
Communication infinite.

The mode transcending human thought,
Is by no revelation taught;

The thing, in its true light revered,
Is from all contradiction clear'd.

We firmly God Triune believe,
Admire what we can ne'er conceive;
The less we can conceive, the more
We Love immense, Triune adore.

Saints' love in Heaven has reach'd its height,
Who have of God Triune the sight;
We here with infinite desire
Towards blissful view and Love aspire.

Lord, when Thou Adam didst create
In his primeval God-like state,
Soon as he could be said to be,
He was a coetaneous Three.

Life, thought, and breath in him combined,
All three distinct, yet not disjoin'd,
All three though they coeval are,
Yet order and relation share.

Life is the first in order styled,
Thought is of life coeval child:
Both life and thought by breath subsist,
Three thus related, co-exist.

In likeness of the Godhead Trine,
Since to form man was Heaven's design;
We guess, from man's coeval three,
At God's adored Triunity.

God is essential Life, and gives
Its life to every thing that lives;
God is essential Thought, and knows
All that His attributes enclose.

Self-happy Life and Thought excite
A co-eternal, Self-delight;
God feels Himself in thought immense,
And breathes self-complacential sense.

Eternal Word, God's Image bright,
Is Source of intellectual Light;
The hovering of the gracious Dove
Creates in saints a joyous Love.

Co-infinite Life, Thought, and Joy,
Distinct co-une great God employ;
If infinite, then God must be,
And Godhead is, a boundless Three.

Paul, who had in his rapturous flight
Of Heaven pre-beatific sight,
That bliss remember'd, thought, desired,
Three acts at once in him conspired.

Remembrance, ever thought implies,
From both desires coeval rise;
All three in spirits co-unite,
Illumined by celestial Light.

An angel when for guardian chose,
In three coeval acts outflows;

TRINITY SUNDAY.

Remembers, thinks, defires the joys,
Which earth immenfely over-poife.

Thus Godhead feems three Acts diftinct,
In unity effential link'd;
God's Word as Perfons them difplays,
We to Three Perfons offer praife.

God's Word! for it is God alone
Makes His myfterious effence known;
Our feeble thought can ne'er explain
A common infect, weed, or grain.

One felf-originated mind,
Immutable, and unconfined,
Is myftery as great, as high,
As Trine, Eternal Deity.

Let curiofity then ftrive,
In God Triune in vain to dive,
O may I feel the influence trine
Of Life, and Thought, and Joy Divine.

I by experience more fhall know,
Than fpeculation e'er can fhow;
And by trine grace enflamed, fhall fing
Trine Hymn to the Triunal King.

FIRST SUNDAY AFTER TRINITY.

And it came to pass that the beggar died, and was carried by the angels into Abraham's bosom.
Luke xvi. 22.

YOU Friend of God, for God's dear sake,
   Show me the gulf, that's fix'd between
The upper Hades and the sub-terrene;
He yielding, Thought obtain'd a vista clear,
To lower Hades, from the upper sphere;
There Dives for one watery drop still cried,
          Yet still denied.
  You, said Thought, when to Pain confined,
Had a regard for those you left behind;
From distributions, which unequal seem,
Of temporal things, which worldlings most
    esteem,
Say, is great God unjust, when He bestows
Wealth on the wicked, and loads saints with
    woes?
Most just, said Dives, men who dare dispute
God's justice, when in life, in hell themselves
    confute;
 I, when in life, you know, fed every day
Deliciously, wore garments rich and gay;
  My slaves search'd all Engaddi's vines,
          To choose the richest wines;

I gratified each sense to the utmost heights,
Wallow'd in gold, purvey'd for all delights;
The world my presence honour'd and admired,
   O, I had all my lust desired,
   Yet all could ne'er me happy make!
   O, 'tis a damnable mistake,
   To think on earth true bliss to gain,
Where Solomon found all that glitter'd vain.

   Like me, the wicked live in fear
               At Judgment to appear;
   Th' uncertainty of vital breath,
               The certainty of death;
               Sharp pains, acute disease,
When wealth gives neither cure, nor ease;
The cries to Heaven of indigents oppress'd,
Horrors of conscience, which corrode the breast;
   Vexation which on wealth attends,
   Insidious flatteries, and false friends;
               Of carnal sweets
               The disappointing cheats;
   The terrors of exchanging all
   For endless torments, at death's call,
All wicked mortals more or less infest,
That like the troubled sea they feel no rest;
They here their hell foretaste, and none can say,
   That sinners live one happy day;
Such terrors to the deep the worldlings sink,
               Whene'er they think;
Or if they think not, greater risks they run,

Their reprobation is in life begun;
Pride harden'd me the needy to pafs by,
    Dogs were more merciful than I.

Fool as I was, I thought my eafe and health,
Honour, profperity, command, and wealth,
The bleffings of kind Heaven, that Heaven had
    chofe
Me for a favourite, and fecured from woes;
             But now, too late, I find
Heaven only for my trial them defign'd;
My portion, while I lived, I mifemploy'd,
And what I fhould have merely ufed, enjoy'd;
What were my idols once, me now forfake,
They no cool drop give in this burning lake.
The fool who to himfelf, from plenteous ftore,
Promifed long life, and ne'er to forrow more;
    Into a neighbouring furnace flung,
Begging, like me, one drop to cool his tongue;
Though fool in life, true wifdom learnt in hell,
    And the like mournful truth can tell.
My luxury would fpare no time to look
             Into the Sacred Book;
Ah! had I caft on that, confiderate eyes,
One line of Solomon had made me wife;
Wealth fuell'd fin, and had it been withheld,
    In thefe fierce flames I ne'er had yell'd;
I, to my fad experience, feel too late
The woes of what the world ftyles happy ftate;
View Lazarus in blifs, and me in flame,

And if you can, God's juſtice blame;
On earth men live on purpoſe to be tried,
Death beſt God's juſt allotments will decide.

Thought, next to Lazarus addreſs'd:
When in the world you lived diſtreſs'd,
With painful ſores, and want of bread,
And wanting place to lay your head,
Expoſed to cold, to nakedneſs, to all
That men could miſerable call,
Did you, for your afflicting lot,
On God's ſtrict juſtice caſt a blot?
O no, ſaid he, I ſtill God's juſtice clear'd,
God all my woes endear'd;
I had no merit at God's Throne to plead,
God ſaw 'twas beſt for me to live in need;
A heaven-erected mind,
Good conſcience, and a will reſign'd;
Woes which enervate ſin,
And raiſe a calm within;
Death which would free me in ſhort time,
From poſſibility of crime,
The lively ſenſe
Of Jeſu's Love immenſe,
Aſſurance of God's promiſes fulfill'd,
On which glad hope of Heaven the faithful
build;
One glance of God's paternal, tender eye,
One ſhort foretaſte of bliſs on high,
Create unutterable joys,

Which worldly woe a thoufand times o'erpoife;
No faint below men fhould unhappy ftyle,
Were his wants great, and his condition vile;
　His wants, which God for medicine fends,
For which one pulfe above makes infinite amends.

SECOND SUNDAY AFTER TRINITY.

God is Love.

Hereby perceive we the love of God, becaufe He laid down His life for us: and we ought to lay down our lives for the brethren.—1 *John* iii. 16.

THE loved difciple, full of Love Divine,
　Would in one word the Infinite define;
Thou, Lord, art Love, Love only can exprefs
All that Thou art, all that Thou doft poffefs;
Of Thy own Self the amiable fight
Raifes eternal, unconfined delight;
Thy Love felf-complacential relifh gives,
It is by Love the Source of Being lives;
Thou art Ideal, Fontal Love, in Thee
Being and Love co-une the bleffed fee;
In Thee triunal rays co-equal fhine,
Love, Lover, and Beloved, in Thee combine.

　By various names we Thy perfections call,
But pure, unfathom'd Love exhaufts them all;
By Love all things were made and are fuftain'd,

Love, all things to allure man's love ordain'd;
Love, vengeance from lapsed human race suspends,
Love, our salvation, when provoked, intends;
Love, Lord, Thy infinite perfections join'd,
Into all forms of love to save mankind;
Enlightening wisdom, and supporting might,
Grace to forgive, compassion to invite;
Thy bounty in rewards which thought exceed,
Munificence to promise all we need;
Truth to perform, paternal, tender care,
A patient mildness long to wait, and spare;
A justice to chastise Love's hateful foes;
Jealousy cursed rivals to oppose;
Benignity to hear a sinner's cry;
Unbounded all-sufficience to supply;
They all are Love, Love only is their aim,
My verse shall love and hymn Thee by that name.

All-charming Love, thou dost my love prevent,
Thou sweetly dost constrain me to repent;
I never shed true penitential tear,
Till I began Love boundless to revere;
The thought that I should Love immense offend,
Began my heart to chide, grieve, soften, rend;
Love, shining in, gave with one beam a stroke,
My heart it into numerous atoms broke;
And in a tear each atom melting lay,
As of past outrages I took survey;
Love would not let my heart lie long in pain,

The beam that brake it made it whole again;
All over wash'd in penitential dew,
Cleansed from all wilful stains and form'd anew;
My soul it into Love's own temple framed,
To Love devoted, and by Love inflamed.

Thee, mighty Love, I praise, invoke, adore,
O may I daily love Thee more and more!
Thou, when Thou dost attract a lover's will,
Infusest strong antipathy to ill;
No greater grief can damned souls invade,
Than that they boundless Love with hate repaid;
Thou, Lord, art Love, that Name canst never quit,
And yet, one sin, Thou never wilt remit;
The sin, which Thy eternal Dove blasphemes,
And from the God-detesting spirit streams;
They justly shall God's endless hate endure,
Who the sole Author of His Love abjure.

My love, the heart, where it was kindled, leaves,
And to Thy Love inseparably cleaves,
O keep me there, my soul to Love unite,
Keep omnipresent Love still in my sight;
That I in acts of love my age may spend,
No whispers of concupiscence attend;
In that dear union I myself would lose,
Would into Love Immense my soul transfuse;
In Love I should entirely acquiesce,
Drown'd in abyssal Love, feel no excess.

To Thee, O Love, my spirit I resign,
O keep me incommunicably Thine;
Thy Love I would appropriate to my heart,
Yet, for Thy sake, wish all mankind a part;
I wish that all would love Thee more than I,
Or strive with me, who should in Love outvie;
With all my powers stretch'd to their utmost
    might,
I'll love myself and love in them excite;
But till I my Beloved in Heaven behold,
Love will feel interruptions damp and cold;
They'll be my constant crucifixions here,
And make me long for Heaven, Love's native
    sphere;
Yet still my love shall strive Thy Love to please,
Though love in absence never is at ease;
Fruition only gives a lover rest,
I languish of my Love to be possess'd.

Eternal Father! 'twas Thy Love alone
Gave Thy loved Son Thy anger to atone.
Eternal Son! Love drew Thee from on high,
To be incarnate and for sinners die;
Eternal Spirit! Thee pure Love inclined,
To build Thy temple in a lover's mind;
O Love Triune! celestial Love inspire,
Help me to love as much as I desire;
The very seraphims would grieve in bliss,
To think their love's too little, too remiss;
But that Thou their capacities dost fill,

And limitation is Thy Heavenly Will;
But Love will strive from limits to get free,
And that sweet strife will everlasting be.

Into Thy image, Love transform my mind,
May I, like Thee, become Love unconfined;
I sing, I joy, with all the saints above,
And I congratulate that Thou art Love;
My meditation on Thy Love is sweet,
On that I feast in my devout retreat;
On Love my contemplation loves to stay,
And opens to receive Thy lovely ray;
With my Beloved, I with delight converse,
And song of my enamourment rehearse.

The Blessed Three in man's formation join'd,
All Three co-breathed is God's enamour'd mind;
All Three to re-enkindle the quench'd fire,
In co-immense philanthropy conspire;
From God Triune my powers triune distil,
My intellect, my memory, and will;
I to Triunal Love devote all three,
They, in that Love, shall co-united be;
My intellect shall sail God's Love about,
Find lands unknown, of Love unbounded, out;
Each voyage in infinity I take,
Will of God's Love some new discoveries make;
My memory shall faithful journals keep,
Of blessings gain'd in that unfathom'd deep;

Into my will when I unlade my ſtore,
Inſatiate Love will ſend me back for more.

   Give me a love, Lord, full of zealous flames,
Which at infinity of loving aims;
Which all things dares, which all things under-
      goes,
And ſin excepted, no affliction knows;
Give me a love which Thou wilt re-exhauſt,
Beſt found, when moſt in Love's vaſt ocean loſt;
Give me a love which feels no reſt beneath,
Which with impatience after Thee ſhall breathe;
Give me a love which Love celeſtial may
With re-ejaculated Love repay;
Give me a love which martyrdom endears,
Love on the Croſs moſt Jeſus-like appears;
And when my love its utmoſt height acquires,
I'll fill its wants in infinite deſires.

THIRD SUNDAY AFTER TRINITY.

   Likewiſe I ſay unto you, there is joy in the preſence of the angels of God, over one ſinner that repenteth.—*Luke* xv. 7.

   YOU bleſſed angels at the Throne
     Sing when a ſinner makes his moan;
Have you no ſong to ſing above
When penitents begin to love,

In which you blissful love and joy
To hymn the God of Love employ?
O if you have, teach it my heart,
That I with you may sing my part.

But when with you my part I've sung,
I yet shall want a nobler tongue;
God's Love to souls you cannot reach,
It far transcends angelic speech;
The seraphs sing the loftiest tune,
And nearest are to God Triune,
Yet never could a hymn compose
Which to the height of saints arose.

Can you conceive the Love Divine
Essential to the Godhead Trine?
The boundless Love the Father shews
To Filial God, Who from Him flows?
The boundless Love the Son repays
For His communicated rays,
A Love like this God deigns to bear
To all who His chaste lovers are.

To be beloved to this degree
Is nearest to infinity;
You angels, though confirm'd in bliss,
Feel you a Love sublime as this?
Say, ye celestial orders nine,
Should your poetic powers combine,
Say, can ye all a hymn indite
Of such a Love to reach the height?

You in the Heavenly Temple wait,
You hymn God's majeſtatic ſtate,
You keep with God a diſtance due,
And cannot bear too bright a view;
God in His lovers' hearts appears,
There He His Throne and Temple rears,
And here they bliſsfully unite
With God by Love, as you by ſight.

Since ſongs of ſeraphs fall too low,
The praiſes which to God I owe,
Teach me, Eternal Dove, to ſing,
Of ſacred ſong Thou boundleſs Spring;
All I derive from Thy ſweet aid
Shall be in hymn to Thee repaid;
Thus, Lord, between Thy Love and me
Shall dear reciprocations be.

FOURTH SUNDAY AFTER TRINITY.

And not only they, but ourſelves alſo, which have the firſt fruits of the Spirit, even we ourſelves groan within ourſelves, waiting for the adoption, to wit, the redemption of our body.—*Romans* viii. 23.

MY God, ſince I in exile here,
Live from the beatific ſphere,
And Thou above
Haſt the ſole title to my love,

I muſt my envoys ſend,
Who ſhall on Thy dread Throne attend,
And there relate
Of my devoted love the various ſtate.

My prayers I ſend up every day,
They meet with frequent juſt delay,
Yet oft deſire
Will in a pulſe to Heaven aſpire,
And in a pulſe re-fly;
But that which ſooneſt mounts on high,
I all my days
Have found to be ejaculated praiſe.

Faſt as a thought, praiſe ſoars direct,
God His own praiſe will not reject,
While praiſe I ſing,
No ſeraph has a ſwifter wing,
When it has made its flights,
It brings a taſte of Heaven's delights,
My gains below
I more to praiſe than ſupplication owe.

Since darted praiſes had ſuch force,
And mounted with ſo ſwift a courſe,
I thought to try
To ſend a ſolemn embaſſy,
And while I prayers deſign'd,
For common envoys of my mind,
Turn'd round my eye
To chooſe ſome fit plenipotentiary.

Of sacred hymn I straight made choice,
With organ equipaged, and voice;
  Soon as my Hymn
Reach'd the supernal ocean's brim,
  The angels, who before
Stood ready on the heavenly shore,
  Their friend embraced,
And its high entrance with their chariots graced.

My Hymn its public entrance made
With an angelic cavalcade,
  It pass'd along
Through an immense God-hymning throng,
  While the celestial choir
To welcome sacred Hymn conspire,
  Which sung on earth,
Yet from Divine Extraction took its birth.

Soon as my Hymn had reach'd the Throne,
Adoring low the Three in One,
  The glorious Three
Acceptance gracious co-decree,
  Its failings overlook,
The well-meant song benignly took,
  It brought rich store
Of Love, and I straight sent it back for more.

Since that, I every night and morn
A new ambassador adorn,
  A hymn prepare,
To lie my daily ledger there,

It at the Throne remains,
Still facrificing grateful ftrains,
With languors ftrong,
Till I in Heaven fhall perfect every fong.

FIFTH SUNDAY AFTER TRINITY.

Life.

For he that will love life, and fee good days, let him refrain his tongue from evil, and his lips that they fpeak no guile. Let him efchew evil, and do good; let him feek peace, and enfue it.—1 *Peter* iii. 10, 11.

O LIFE, what art thou? oft I try
To paint thee to my ghoftly eye,
I all evanid things furvey,
But them when I againft thee weigh,
A vapour, flower, a fleep, a dream,
Preponderating turn the beam.

A vapour ere diffolved in air,
A flower ere ceafing to look fair,
A fleep, a dream, ere they expire,
Some fhort duration ftill require;
But Life fleets rather than abides,
Away in half a fecond flides.

Methinks, when Death I call to mind,
Life might be eafily defined;

Death's a privation of our all,
Life then we should fruition call:
Yet nothing we to Life allow,
But the fruition of this Now.

Thought Life infers; to dust we sink
That moment when we cease to think:
From thought to thought my life runs on,
'Tis irretrievably soon gone:
Thought, ere I can enjoy it, flies,
Till a new thought fresh life supplies.

O fool, of short-lived goods possess'd,
In mere incertainties to rest,
From your full barns and bags of gold,
To dream of slowly growing old;
Can you bribe Death with all your store,
To respite you one moment more?

Ah! who can this short life ensure,
That it beyond this thought shall dure?
Of millions Death the end has wrought,
Just in the middle of a thought.
This life of mine each moment lies
In danger of a like surprise.

Surprise! Ah me, that word I dread,
To drop down on a sudden dead,
And be by fiends to judgment haled,
Ere prayers for mercy have prevail'd;

No wretch but quakes, when we relate
The horrors of so dire a fate.

Tell me, my soul, is there no art
To arm against Death's sudden dart?
Has gracious Heaven contrived no way
Of lengthening here our mortal stay,
Or on this momentaneous stage
In a short time to live an age?

'Tis sin which shortens vital day,
And when we feel our breath decay,
Convictions then come rushing in,
That Life has been but death in sin;
On time misspent we ne'er reflect,
Till we are damn'd for its neglect.

The infants, from the font who fly
Unsullied to the joys on high,
Live longer than obdurate men,
Who sin to threescore years and ten:
Old sinners ne'er true life obtain,
Till ghostly babes and born again.

Were I Immortal Life to spend,
In all the woes which sin attend,
In dangers, sickness, troubles, pain,
Which we in wretched life sustain;
I Death would court, this life not prize,
And immortality despise.

Souls who to endless joys aspire,
This life endure, but Death desire:
The shortest life they deem the best,
The soonest freed from sin and bless'd;
No weary pilgrim but revives
When he at wish'd-for home arrives.

Saints live eternally above
In beatific joy, hymn, love,
At Life's unbounded Source they drink,
Of God they never cease to think.
We those dear moments only live,
Which we to God devoutly give.

Lord, may I never lose Thy sight,
May I in Thy sole Love delight;
I am, live, move in Thee alone,
God-man will for my sins atone;
While I by trebled zeal and tears
Strive to retrieve my careless years.

SIXTH SUNDAY AFTER TRINITY.

Jesus our All in All.

Therefore we are buried with Him by baptism into death: that like as Christ was raised up from the dead by the glory of the Father, even so we also should walk in newness of life.—*Romans* vi. 4.

MY Jesus, since Thy Love Divine
Indulges me to call Thee mine,
Assist me while I cast accounts,
To what a sum my stock amounts,
A fulness I in Thee possess,
Beyond the reach of human guess.

The wealth which dazzles worldly eyes,
Which in gold mines or diamonds lies,
Is vain, short-lived, and gaudy dirt,
Can heal no wound or mortal hurt;
Can cure no sickness, ease no smart,
And sticks with thorns the miser's heart.

To souls born blind, their cheerful sight,
The radiance of salvific light,
Love, which the pondus of the will
Shall weigh to good, averse to ill,
Wild passions tamed, a soul serene,
From wilful guilt a conscience clean.

Patience or ease in sharpest pain,
All loss for Jesus turn'd to gain;

Afflictions to the soul endear'd,
All clouds of God's displeasure clear'd,
In martyrdom support and joy,
The force of torture to destroy.

In weakness vigour to oppose,
And conquer our infernal foes,
A yoke benign, a burthen light,
Omnipotent and gracious might,
A price inestimable paid,
The blood of God our ransom made.

To penitents full pardon seal'd,
Truth, graced with miracles reveal'd;
Acceptance to our worthless prayers,
A freedom from distracting cares,
In trouble consolations sweet;
God's presence in devout retreat.

In error's labyrinths when we stray
Guides to direct the heavenward way,
To frailties a compassion mild,
Wisdom to keep us unbeguiled,
A purity from native stain,
Souls new-inspired, and born again.

The curse original suppress'd,
And all our earthly portion bless'd,
Love providential which contrives
For saints the blessings of both lives,

To be God's sons, and when we die
Co-heirs with Filial God on high.

God Filial pleased to condescend
To be our all-sufficient Friend,
And though exalted to His Throne
That dear relation still to own,
And send the boundless Source of grace,
The Spirit, to supply His place.

Our rising from death's dismal shade
In bodies glorified array'd,
In Heaven eternally to share
In all the joys and glories there,
Which seraphs who that bliss imbibe,
Want comprehension to describe.

These blessings and unnumber'd more,
For all our needs a boundless store,
To the bless'd lot of lovers fall,
Jesus to them is All in all,
Saints here who Jesus make their choice,
Ne'er cease to triumph and rejoice.

Jesus, shouldst Thou forsake my heart,
With Thee I with my All should part,
And should my All abandon me,
Love would annihilated be,
But Thee and Love to keep I'll strive,
I cannot my lost All survive.

SEVENTH SUNDAY AFTER TRINITY.

I speak after the manner of men, because of the infirmity of your flesh: for as ye have yielded your members servants to uncleanness, and to iniquity, unto iniquity; even so now yield your members servants to righteousness, unto holiness.—*Romans* vi. 19.

LET others sail the world about,
    To find strange countries out,
A land unknown I have within,
    Inhabited by sin,
Which from my intellectual view
    Long time itself withdrew.

My thought had often made essay,
    Its limits to survey,
But still it found out something new,
    Which ne'er before I knew,
And though I launch'd my thought again,
    Its voyage made in vain.

It glides away like floating isles,
    My anchor it beguiles,
Worse monsters there excite my dread,
    Than Afric ever bred,
Proud Babel's ruins never bore
    Such a misshapen store.

To God I then myself applied,
    That He my course would guide;

Kind Heaven a compaſs to me gave,
    To ſteer me in the wave,
And coaſting round the moving ſands,
    My thought upon it lands.

It was my heart I ſearch'd, unknown
    To all but God alone;
It was by God's all-gracious aid
    I my diſcoveries made,
His law my needle, in ſtraight line,
    Turn'd to the Pole Divine.

With that I o'er the region ſtray'd,
    It was of labyrinths made,
And I when diſengaged from one,
    Into another run.
When their amuſements me aggrieved,
    My needle me relieved.

Equivocation, mints of wile,
    All ſhapes of baneful guile,
Of all impieties the ſprings,
    The ſerpent's bites and ſtings,
Reſerve, lie, ſalvo, and excuſe,
    The conſcience to ſeduce.

Luſts ſiding with the powers of hell,
    Which 'gainſt great God rebel,
Strong averſations to God's law,
    All theſe and more I ſaw,

I could much sooner count my hairs,
    Than all its mazy snares.

Long time these furies had declined
    The empire of my mind,
A thousand stratagems had tried
    Themselves from me to hide;
But I the rebels vow'd to chain,
    My empire to regain.

When of the foe I had this sight,
    I then began the fight;
And I by succours from on high
    Made my heart prostrate lie,
I placed my spirit on the throne,
    Forced all its rule to own.

But traitorous lusts me still waylaid,
    Conceal'd in ambuscade,
They storm'd my mind with new-spun cheats,
    Till lash'd to their retreats;
And if I chance my watch to slack,
    My soul they re-attack.

To gracious God I made my prayer,
    Mistrusting my own care,
The Guardian of my heart to be,
    Which was too hard for me,
He deign'd my offering to accept,
    He safe my spirit kept.

God will its frauds to me impart,
    Sole Searcher of the heart,
It shall no more on me impose,
    Or with the tempter close.
The more its powers to Thee incline,
    Lord, 'twill the more be Thine.

EIGHTH SUNDAY AFTER TRINITY.

Brethren, we are debtors, not to the flesh, to live after the flesh. For if ye live after the flesh, ye shall die: but if ye through the Spirit do mortify the deeds of the body, ye shall live.—*Romans* viii. 12, 13.

O FOOLISH heart, which often strays,
    And for destructive lusts purveys,
You numerous experiments have tried,
    Yet still return dissatisfied,
      Why seek you thus in vain,
    For what you never can obtain?

All worldly joys which glittering seem,
    And at a distance raise esteem,
Soon as they have admittance to your arms,
    Betray their meretricious charms,
      The cheat apparent grows,
    You only court eternal woes.

EIGHTH SUNDAY

Egypt, with various idols ſtored,
Such idle fancies ne'er adored,
When to their onions they their worſhip paid,
　Their hunger was by them allay'd;
　　But all things you purſue,
　Allay not hunger, but raiſe new.

Would you one minute make eſſay
Yourſelf againſt the world to weigh,
You then would ſoon perceive the world confined,
　And the immenſeneſs of your mind,
　　'Twixt an immenſe and bound,
　Think what proportion can be found.

It is not narrowneſs alone
Should make you this low world diſown,
Since it for ſin was curſed, it is impure,
　Saints its empoiſon'd baits abjure,
　　And where it once intrudes,
　It damns, as well as fouls deludes.

Fix, O my heart, your ghoſtly eye
On God's immenſe benignity,
God is the only Object which can fill
　The ſphere of your capacious will,
　　While you to God aſpire,
　You all poſſeſs you can deſire.

In God is all-ſufficient ſtore,
My heart, O never wander more:

O that I had a cherub's numerous eyes,
   To guard me from a re-furprife!
      Lord, to my fuccour hafte,
   To Thy dear Love, O keep me chafte.

NINTH SUNDAY AFTER TRINITY.

I fay unto you, Make to yourfelves friends of the mammon of unrighteoufnefs, that, when ye fail, they may receive you into everlafting habitations.—*Luke* xvi. 9.

MORE blefs'd to give than to receive,
   We, taught by Heaven, believe:
That, copies Deity immenfe,
   This, fprings from indigence.
To that the faint with zeal propends,
Which infinitely this tranfcends.

To covetoufnefs I am inclined,
   When that I call to mind,
I would at every foreign fhore,
   Freight boundlefs precious ore;
I Dives' mighty treafures crave,
The fool's full barns I fain would have.

Like Solomon I would abound,
   With gains more precious crown'd,
Yet wealth, ore, treafure, barns and gem,
   I wholly fhould contemn;

Had I not Solomon's large heart,
Gold to the needy to impart.

O happy riches, which o'erflow
    To all in want or woe!
Which have no wings to fly away,
    But with the liberal ſtay,
Of friends and wealth, they ſtore provide
In Heaven immenſely multiplied.

Happy rich man! did he but know
    How riches to beſtow,
Who truſts not in his plenteous ſtores,
    Or idol wealth adores;
God's goodneſs who to copy ſtrives,
And gains the bleſſings of both lives.

My God, we indigent below
    Have nothing to beſtow;
Our all is from Thy gracious Throne,
    We nought can ſtyle our own,
And when to Thee we offerings bring,
The drops are of Thy boundleſs ſpring.

But, O benignity divine!
    When offering what is Thine,
Thou doſt as ours Thy own accept,
    For which rewards are kept,
We all our days receivers live,
Of what we to the donor give.

A dying giver of God's own,
    The living poor bemoan;
He advocates in Heaven will find,
    To plead for him combined,
Jesus' poor brethren will contend,
Who shall most shew himself his friend.

Soon as by Heaven's appointment led,
    Death shall approach his bed,
His Guardian will to th' happy sphere
    Traject his death is near;
And ere one minute drops, the news
O'er happy Hades will diffuse.

The poor who bliss before had gain'd,
    Whom he in life sustain'd,
At the trajected thought will meet,
    And falling at God's Feet,
With ardour for him intercede,
And for joys supereffluent plead.

The hungry will recall his bread,
    On which they daily fed,
The thirsty, the refreshing bowls,
    With which he cheer'd their souls;
The stranger wandering in the street,
    His free, his hospitable treat.

The naked, clothes which them secured
    From cold they had endured;

The sick, the visits they received,
    And how by them relieved,
The prisoners, helps and succours kind
He shew'd them when in chains confined.

The debtors, how their debts he paid,
    By losses when decay'd;
The Christians, slaves to Pagans sold,
    Whom he redeem'd with gold;
Widows and fatherless, supplied
By him, when by the world denied.

His foes for whom Christ-like he pray'd
    And good for ill repaid,
Damn'd souls to whom he warnings gave
    And tried all means to save,
Shall self-confused before the Throne
His charities to either own.

The guardians whom Heaven deign'd to send,
    The happy poor to tend;
Devoutly will the same declare,
    Enforcing all their prayer,
And his own Angel will recount
Vast sums to which his alms amount.

None to search chronicles shall need,
    For a past noble deed;
As the great King by Esther gain'd
    For Mordecai ordain'd:

Each grain of charitable gold
Is in the Book of Life enroll'd.

There the poor's prayers recorded lie,
  And all his fuccours by;
There the poor's praifes patent ftand
  For fuccours from his hand;
And him the favourite of Heaven's King,
Guardians and happy poor will fing.

Blefs'd Jefus folemnly will own
  Love to His brethren fhewn,
And guardians of the poor he fed
  Defpatch'd to his death-bed,
His beatific flight will aid,
With an angelic cavalcade.

Jefus the Judge will at His Right
  Allot him manfions bright,
Among the blefs'd with a high place,
  His bounteous lover grace;
Heaven fhall in Hymn the truth atteft,
To give, than to receive, more bleft.

May I to Jefus' brethren fpare
  In all His gifts a fhare,
And not defer till I go hence
  My portion to difpenfe,
A death-bed alms extorted feems,
A life of alms God moft efteems.

TENTH SUNDAY AFTER TRINITY.

Jesus' Love Preserved.

No man can say that Jesus is the Lord, but by the Holy Ghost.—1 *Cor.* xii. 3.

MY Jesus, Thou all lovely art,
And shouldst be loved with all the heart;
But woe is me, my heart is prone,
Thee, for cursed trifles to disown;
O with a Love Thy votary bless,
Proportion'd to Thy loveliness!

Our want, Thou, Jesu, didst foreknow,
And didst proportion'd Love bestow;
At Thy ascent Thou in Thy place
Didst leave the boundless Source of Grace.
We at the Source of Love abide,
Where wants of Love are all supplied.

O blessing, next to that dear Love,
Which drew God Filial from above!
Oh God co-breathed, who Love art styled,
Delighting in souls undefiled!
Towards God my whole propension turn,
Love heavenly cannot downwards burn.

Great Third of the co-glorious Trine,
O may my spirit Thee enshrine,

O consecrate my mortal frame
Into a temple to Thy Name!
O be Thou of my soul the Soul,
And all rebellious powers control!

O Love Immense, within me dwell,
All loves but Thy own Love expel!
Within my heart Thy piercing eye
Will all absconded lusts descry;
Thy goodness, which all thought exceeds,
Will bring supplies for all my needs.

My soul with Truth's bright radiance fill,
Keep me resign'd to God's sole Will;
Whene'er I stray, be Thou my Guide,
Fix me, inclining to backslide;
Quicken me when I stupid grow,
Deep consolations, when in woe.

O purify my soul from stain,
All tendencies towards ill restrain;
My soul with warm devotion fire,
Which may with sighs and groans aspire;
Invigorate me when afraid,
When weak, vouchsafe me heavenly aid.

Truth sacred in my memory keep,
For sin create contrition deep;
All filial grace in me excite,
Be Witness that I walk upright.

Seal pardon for transgressions past,
Support me when I breathe my last.

Be Monitor Thy law to heed,
Be Advocate my cause to plead,
By Thee may I be born again,
By Thee celestial glory gain;
To me be Water, Oil, Fire, Wind,
To cleanse, oint, warm, and wing my mind.

Into my soul good thoughts inject,
Inculcate them till I reflect;
Consideration thence will grow,
Affections from considering flow;
Affections to resolves arise,
And for eternals make us wise.

Such graces, O co-effluent Dove,
Are the effluxes of Thy Love;
No mortal can their numbers tell,
They all arithmetic excel;
And yet, though numberless they are,
Each saint in all enjoys a share.

I objects see; yet in my brain
How vision's made, cannot explain;
My soul the Spirit working feels
While modes of working He conceals;
When God makes in our souls abode,
'Tis curiosity to search the mode.

O Love co-breathed, I Love implore,
O give me Love, I need no more;
Gifts are for souls heroic meet,
Reserved for heights or sufferings great;
But void of Love I cannot live,
In that Thou wilt all graces give.

Jesu! I'll love, I'll hymn Thy Name,
From Thee co-effluent Godhead came;
Love shed by Him, through Thee shall rise,
Paternal Godhead's sacrifice,
Of Love the co-eternal Three
Are thus the Spring, the Stream, the Sea.

ELEVENTH SUNDAY AFTER TRINITY.

Jesus our Priest.

For I delivered unto you first of all, that which I also received, how that Christ died for our sins, according to the Scriptures.—1 *Cor.* xv. 3.

WHEN Adam sinn'd, and all his line
Lost the similitude Divine,
Angels who saw proud ghosts rebel
And hurl'd unpitied down to hell,
Expected when Almighty ire
Should thunder-strike our guilty sire.

Should general flame this world confume,
As great as at the day of doom,
An holocauft for fontal fin,
Big with a vicious race within,
'Twould be too little to atone
God's wrath for His infulted Throne.

But when God Filial offer made
To be in human flefh array'd,
To die for man, from blifsful fight
They drew of Saviour in juft light
Ideas clear, and to their lyres
Sang Filial God in all their quires.

O Love, too boundlefs to be fhewn
By any but great God alone!
O Love offended, which fuftains
The bold offender's curfe and pains!
O Love which could no motive have,
But mere benignity to fave!

O Sacrifice from blemifh free,
Worthy the God of Purity!
O Sacrifice, like God, immenfe,
Atoning by equivalence!
O Sacrifice too dear to fail
With God Paternal to prevail!

We angels thought ourfelves fupreme
To fpotlefs man in God's efteem;

But God shows Love to Adam stain'd,
Which sinful angels ne'er obtain'd;
God's Love we to lapsed man adore,
And Justice, which gave angels o'er.

Death only can atone for guilt,
Angels no blood had to be spilt;
Had God angelic form assumed,
To death He never could be doom'd;
Pure mercy, man condemn'd to die,
That Jesus might his doom supply.

God Filial we admire, decreed
A Sacrifice for man to bleed;
But for a priest we look intent,
Who shall the Sacrifice present;
O there is none but God's own Son,
Both Priest and Sacrifice are one.

Thus angels sang, who but began
To see Love future of God-man:
Soon as Redemption was complete
Their hymns had more ecstatic heat,
God-man His Throne then re-possess'd,
And to His Father thus address'd:

Great Father, to soft pity prone,
I Myself offer at Thy Throne,
I for lapsed man My Blood have shed,
Transferr'd his guilt on My own Head,

And My Blood spilt before Thee plead,
That man may be from vengeance freed.

Thy tender Bowels yearn'd on Me,
When I hung tortured on the Tree;
May those dear Bowels yearn on all,
Who seek recovery from their fall;
Thy attributes full glory gain
In Me, Thy Son co-equal, slain.

My Sacrifice before Thy Eyes,
Eternally, to melt Thee lies,
Forgive all sins, no grace refuse
To votaries who My Name shall use;
May all who have to Thee recourse,
Of My Atonement feel the force.

Rays more benign than ever shined,
Since the first rise of human-kind,
From God's Paternal Sweetness stream'd
On His dear Son Who man redeem'd,
God melting, like His Son all o'er,
Gave all He heard His Son implore.

O Love, which at the Throne remains,
Which all inflammatives contains,
Which gives to all a free access,
Compassion shews to all distress!
O Love, in which all joys conspire,
Which fill and terminate desire!

O sin, God's hatred for which, none
But Filial God could God atone!
Past sins which grieve me, Lord, forgive,
Thy priest and sacrifice I'll live,
Till I, like Thee, in Heaven above
Re-offer and complete my love.

TWELFTH SUNDAY AFTER TRINITY.

Likeness to Jesus.

If the ministration of death, written and engraven in stones was glorious; so that the children of Israel could not stedfastly behold the face of Moses for the glory of his countenance, which glory was to be done away; How shall not the ministration of the Spirit be rather glorious?

2 Cor. iii. 7-8.

MOSES on high twice twenty days,
Ingulf'd in majestatic rays,
And had ideas bright
In elevated sight,
Of all the sacred things which God ordain'd
Should in His tabernacle be contain'd.

See, said Jehovah, all things made,
Like to the patterns you survey'd;
The numerous precepts he
Kept stored in memory,

And all things by those heavenly patterns drew,
Presented on the mountain to his view.

   My Jesus, when in bless'd retreat,
   I Thee in meditation meet,
      Thou dost exalt my eye,
      Thy beauties to descry,
Each grace which in Thee shines, devotion fires,
I to abide with Thee am all desires.

   My soul, which should Thy temple be,
   From all pollution should be free;
      But though now wash'd in tear,
      My treacherous heart I fear,
Warp'd to the world, may make it too impure,
For purest God the building to endure.

   Ah should it warp, I'd weep it clear,
   A temple then to thee I'll rear,
      Adorn'd with every grace
      I in Thy footsteps trace;
O keep Thy graces lively in my mind,
That all my powers by Thee may be refined.

   Thou sweetly dost my soul enjoin
   To copy out each grace divine;
      Lovers at likeness aim,
      That two may be the same:
Thou infinitely amiable art,
I by Thy model long to form my heart.

Thou, God's loved Son, hast God appeased,
God is immensely in Thee pleased;
    May I, like Thee, be styled
    Paternal Godhead's child:
The more I like to the loved Son appear,
The more I shall be to the Father dear.

My Jesus, when Thou goest away,
All Thy ideas soon decay,
    I want a longer time
    To treat of things sublime;
I forty years too short a space esteem,
To live absorb'd in Thy transporting beam.

Dear Jesus, long, long with me stay,
When of my heart I take survey,
    Thy dread, all-seeing eye,
    Into each thought will pry,
Shouldst Thou one moment leave my heart alone,
It to my search may leave reserves unknown.

Thy Love, sweet Jesus, Thee inclined
To stoop to frailties of mankind,
    Thou, pitying our lapsed state,
    Dost of our debt abate,
Thou dost no hard severities impose,
Short tears begin our joys, and end our woes.

Jesus, when Thou from me wilt part,
Deep grave Thy image on my heart,

> O confcience, keep awake,
> Care of the image take,
> And from its likenefs, when my life declines,
> Check me, and rectify my devious lines.
>
> Loved and adored be Thy great Name,
> My Jefus, Who doft fouls reframe,
> To a true God-like height,
> Tranfcending Adam's flight,
> Ere the curfed tempter his confent o'erpower'd,
> And lovely virgin innocence deflower'd.

THIRTEENTH SUNDAY AFTER TRINITY.

Which now of thefe three, thinkeft thou, was neighbour unto him that fell among the thieves?—Luke x. 36.

> SEE there a Jew from th' hallow'd town
> To Jericho is going down,
> Unguarded as he goes that way,
> To bloody thieves becomes a prey;
> They rob, ftrip, wound, and bruife him fore,
> There he lies weltering in his gore;
> A Prieft and Levite fee his ftate,
> But fearing like difaftrous fate,
> Left him half dead, and gafping lie,
> And pafs in hafte their brother by;
> But a Samaritan, a name
> To Jews moft hateful and infame,

When he sees where the Jew was cast,
Who bleeding seem'd to breathe his last,
Soft pity pierces deep his breast,
He there draws near his foe distress'd,
With wine and oil, which by his care
For his own health provided were,
He tries the helpless to relieve,
And in the hopeless, life retrieve,
His sores he searches with kind hand,
Cleanses with wine from dirt and sand,
Pours oil to ease and heal each wound,
Which there is with soft swathing bound;
To save the Jew he freely chose
Himself to danger to expose;
There on the envious naked Jew
He his own upper garment threw,
On his own beast the wretch he lays,
And to a distant inn conveys,
To walk afoot to tend him deigns,
And with kind arms his bulk sustains;
There of the inn defrays the scores,
Charged them to tend his painful sores,
There promises the rest to pay
Soon as he should return that way.

    This parable by Jesus was design'd
By picture to inform and please the mind,
To copy the Philanthropy Divine,
Who on the worst of sinners deigns to shine;
Each saint the story to herself applies,
By Jesus taught, go, and do thou likewise.

FOURTEENTH SUNDAY AFTER TRINITY.

And when He saw them, He said unto them, Go shew yourselves unto the priests. And it came to pass, that as they went, they were cleansed.—*Luke* xvii. 14.

BLESS'D Jesus, Thy propitious Heart
   Would sympathise with every smart;
  When wretches to Thee cried,
    No help was e'er denied,
Thy wondrous goodness was display'd,
In giving super-human aid:

I bring an object to Thy sight,
Will glorify Thy gracious might,
  A confluence of needs
    Here for Thy pity pleads,
I of Thy miracles implore
A mighty confluential store.

Lord, 'tis my heart, let Thy mild Eyes
Vouchsafe commensurate supplies,
  To heavenly truths my mind
    Is by the lapse, born blind,
My ears to Thy sweet calls are closed,
My tongue to praise Thee indisposed.

By baneful lusts I am possess'd,
Tempestuous passions me infest,

I'm impotence all o'er,
Inveterate is my fore,
With leprofy I am befpread,
Love in habitual guilt lies dead.

My Lord, my God, to Thee I pray,
Unpitied fend me not away,
My malady control,
Command me to be whole;
Thy word will me to health reftore,
Speak but one word, I afk no more.

My eyes Thy Love will then fee clear,
My ears Thy gracious call will hear,
My filent tongue will fpeak,
And into praifes break,
Of lufts I fhall be difpoffefs'd,
Sweet peace will then becalm my breaft.

Thy powerful aids will me fuftain,
Of weaknefs I'll no more complain,
My rocky heart will melt,
When it Thy Love has felt,
No leprous fpots will me furprife,
My love from ghoftly death will rife.

Thou didft our frailties undergo,
That Thou mightft foft compaffion fhew,
Thy tender Heart condoles
With all afflicted fouls;

Oh! for Thy dolorous Passion's sake,
Haste to my restoration make.

Thou in one single act divine
A heap of miracles wilt join,
   In complicate disease
    Give complicated ease,
And when Thou shalt my heart restore,
With all my powers I'll Thee adore.

Among the saints I'll concerts raise,
To sing Thee complicated praise,
   My heart by Thee refined,
    Shall live to Thee resign'd,
I loves for Loves will strive to pay,
New Hymns I'll offer every day.

Thy Love kept Thy own Mother pure,
And from infernal force secure,
   No lust her soul could harm,
    Supported by Thy Arm,
She in the world lived disembroil'd,
And God's bright Image kept unsoil'd.

She always ghostly health enjoy'd;
My soul is with disease annoy'd,
   Do Thou my spirit heal,
    Do Thou my pardon seal:
Oft a deliverance more endears
Than an immunity from fears.

FIFTEENTH SUNDAY AFTER TRINITY.

The Sermon on the Mount.

S. *Matthew* vi.

O JESU! with Thy Spirit fill my breast,
　Design'd by Thee on faithful souls to rest;
May He Thy words to my remembrance bring,
That I Thy own divine discourse may sing.

　Incarnate Word upon a mount appear'd,
That He might by the multitude be heard;
And to the twelve, and crowd, who thither flock'd,
The treasures of true wisdom thus unlock'd.

　Bless'd are the poor in spirit, vile and low
In their own eyes, who their own frailties know,
Who on God's grace, not their own merit lean,
And like the leper, style themselves unclean;
The humblest here are highest in God's sight,
Theirs is the glorious realm of endless light.

　Bless'd are all they who mourn, whose sighs their own
And others' sins with bitterness bemoan;
Ne'er in this vale of woe from sorrow free,
Where they their God so oft offended see;
They sow in tears, and from each tear they weep
They shall a thousand-fold of comforts reap.

Bleſs'd are the meek, of temper gentle, ſweet,
Who unimbitter'd, the injurious treat;
They ſhall the earth inherit, and exhauſt
That right to things below, which Adam loſt.
Though others wealth unſanctified retain,
God's bleſſing ſhall on what they have remain;
With God, themſelves, the world, they live in peace,
Anticipating joys which never ceaſe.

Bleſs'd are all they who thirſt and hunger feel
For righteouſneſs, who with unwearied zeal
Strive righteous God's bright image to regain,
And purge themſelves from their congenial ſtain;
All their propenſions ſhall their aims acquire,
Till fill'd with God, they feel no more deſire.

Bleſs'd are the merciful, whoſe melting eyes
With others' griefs benignly ſympathiſe;
Who uncondoled paſs no one's ſorrow by,
No danger, pain, or want, without ſupply;
They mercy ſhall obtain, and all their woes
God for their good ſhall graciouſly diſpoſe;
They ſhall the joys of pardon taſte below,
Their alms ſhall in full ſtreams of bliſs reflow.

Bleſs'd are the pure in heart, who have refined
Each thought, each inclination of the mind,
Who to no foul ſuggeſtions harbour give,
Amidſt pollutions, unpolluted live;

Who keep God's temples holy, and take care
That no abominations enter there;
They shall of God have beatific sight,
Who only in pure votaries takes delight.

 Bless'd are peace-makers, they who sweetly
   strive,
Fraternal, mutual dearness to revive,
Who are themselves true lovers of mankind,
And wish that all to love were co-inclined;
They shall be call'd God's children, in them best
The God of Peace His likeness sees express'd.

 Bless'd are all they, who persecuted are,
Who martyrdom for Love of Jesus bear:
The greater torments they for Heaven endure,
The more they shall their happiness secure;
The heavenly kingdom is more firmly theirs,
Of higher bliss and brighter mansions heirs,
They future joys more fully shall foretaste,
And to their glory make the greater haste.

 Woe to the rich! who fading riches crave,
They here their short-lived consolations have;
Woe to the full, who their own gusto feed,
They'll be abandon'd to unpitied need;
Woe to all those who laugh, and pleasures heap,
They in eternal misery shall weep;
Woe to all those who court evanid fame,
They shall sink down to everlasting shame.

You, whom I to apostolate exalt,
To the dark, tasteless world, are light and salt;
You Heavenly relishes from Me derive,
You must the taste of truth in souls revive;
You must disseminate the Love Divine,
Placed in conspicuous orbs must brightly shine;
That all who feel your Heaven-enkindled rays,
May God, the Author of your graces, praise.

I come the law and prophets to fulfil,
I mental curb, as well as outward ill;
All who henceforth a claim to Heaven pretend,
In saintship must the strictest Jew transcend.

Thou shalt not kill, was the old legal style;
I all forbid their neighbour to revile;
Even odious names shall irritate God's ire,
And run the danger of infernal fire:
Their Altar offerings God esteems defiled,
Who to their brethren live unreconciled.

The law will no adultery endure,
I no one wanton look or thought impure;
You all lust's sinful cravings must deny,
Though dearer than your own right hand or
      eye.
The marriage-knot which you so oft untied,
Henceforth shall indissoluble abide;
Perjurious oaths you only sinful call,
I, in converse, permit no oaths at all.

You eye for eye, and tooth for tooth require,
And to retaliate injuries defire;
But charity muft now revenge affuage;
In no vexatious fuits of law engage;
You for peace' fake, muft from full rights recede,
And never for too rigorous juftice plead;
With private force no outrages repel,
On earth with condefcending fweetnefs dwell;
To needy neighbours freely give, or lend,
To guide ungrateful pilgrims condefcend.

'Twas the old maxim of the Jewifh ftate,
To love our neighbours, and our foes to hate;
I love fincere to enemies enjoin,
Do good to them, who ill to you defign;
Blefs them who curfe you, daily pray for thofe
Who to rude perfecutions you expofe;
'Tis God's unbounded goodnefs to ordain,
For bad as well as good, His fun and rain;
You, like your Father, merciful muft be,
And copy His immenfe benignity.

Give liberal alms of all that God gives you,
Give fecretly, and fhun vain-glorious view;
God's piercing Eye the lowly heart regards,
To fecret alms gives vifible rewards.

Your clofet with devotion oft frequent,
There fervent, humble, fecret prayer prefent.
No prayer by multitude of words efteem,

But by the filial love from which they ſtream;
Vain, ſenſeleſs repetitions caſt away,
And by this form with firm reliance pray:

 Our Father, throned in Heaven, Thy Name
  be praiſed,
Thy kingdom over all the world be raiſed;
May all Thy ſubjects here, Thy ſovereign Will,
Like angels, with alacrity fulfil;
Send bread and due ſupports, by which we live;
Remit our ſins, as we our foes forgive;
Let no temptations us allure or blind,
Guard from all ill our body and our mind;
Thine is the Heavenly Kingdom, Glory, Might,
Thou to diſpoſe of all things haſt the right.

 If you forgive not wrongs men offer you,
In vain you ſhall to God for pardon ſue;
Your ſins, by faſting, conquer or chaſtiſe,
Obſerved by none but God's all-ſeeing Eyes;
More ſecret 'tis, the more it God will pleaſe,
He'll hear you and your troubled ſpirit eaſe;
Place not your bliſs on earth, all treaſures there
To ruſt, moths, thieves, and death, ſubjected are;
Make Heaven your treaſure, that can ne'er decay,
And where your treaſure is, your heart will ſtay.
The eye imparts to all the body light,
Let pure intention guide your ghoſtly ſight;
From a dim eye the body cloud contracts,
Intentions ſenſual defecrate your acts.

None can a servant of two lords abide,
And equal duties to them both divide,
None God and Mammon can at once obey,
They human wills antarctically sway.
For clothes and food take no immoderate cares,
God, lilies clothes, and food for fowls prepares;
God tenders you much more than fowls or
    flowers,
And blessings down in their due season showers,
Seek Heaven in the first place, live saint below,
And God will these as overplus bestow.

Judge not, lest God you with like rigour treat,
You must expect the measure which you mete;
Censure no motes within your brother's eye,
While in your own you will not beams descry;
With care your own spiritual state attend,
Condemn not others, but yourself amend;
Distribute wisely pearls of Truth Divine,
Waste none on souls brutised like dogs or swine.

Ask and you shall receive, seek and you'll find,
Knock and Heaven opens to a humble mind;
For fish and bread, what hearts so hard are grown,
As to give children scorpions or a stone?
If earthly sires thus tender are, much more
Is God, when sons His aid benign implore.
Do that to all you'd have all do to you,
The rule which prophets and the law pursue.
Take heed to choose the narrow path and gate,

Found but by few, who reach the bleſſed ſtate;
Through the wide gate and ſin's broad beaten way
Moſt of mankind to endleſs ruin ſtray.

Falſe prophets ſhun, and their inſidious lies,
Wolves inwardly, though clad in ſheep's diſguiſe;
The kinds of trees their native product ſhow,
Thus by ill aims you may deceivers know;
They cry, Lord, Lord! yet God's commands reject,
They not God's glory, but their own reſpect,
They'll boaſt prophetic gifts, and go about
To work ſtrange things, and devils to caſt out;
Their frauds they'll act in God's moſt ſacred Name,
But God will the preſtigious cheats diſclaim;
They'll either Faith deny, or Church divide,
Betray rapacity, luſt, rage, or pride.

They who attend the truths I now inſtil,
And by ſincere obedience them fulfil,
Are like to the wiſe man, who, 'gainſt the ſhock
Of tempeſt, built his houſe upon a rock:
The ſaint all ſtorms which hell can raiſe, defies,
And on the Rock of Ages firm relies.
But all who hear, and ſaving truths withſtand,
Are like the fool who built upon the ſand,—
One blaſt threw down the fabric to the ground;
Thus ghoſtly fools their future bliſs confound.

All praife to Jefus, Who His gracious law
Taught to His fubjects with endearing awe.
Glory to Jefus was the mountain's clofe,
Who would for laws beatitudes impofe.

SIXTEENTH SUNDAY AFTER TRINITY

Love taught by Jefus.

That ye being rooted and grounded in love, may be able to comprehend with all faints, what is the breadth, and length, and depth, and height; and to know the love of Chrift, which paffeth knowledge.—*Eph.* iii. 17-19.

THOSE days I often call to mind,
When God Himfelf in flefh enfhrined;
Had I beheld the radiant ftar,
Which eaftern fages led from far;
Or had the news fome angel told,
Sent to the fwains who watch'd their fold;

God-man had fo enflamed my foul,
That, had I dwell'd at either pole,
Entrench'd in ice, immured in fnow,
With boifterous winds tofs'd to and fro,
While from that fphere the fun took flight,
And left me in long difmal night;

O'er rocks of fnow I would have trod,
Walk'd o'er the frozen fea unfhod,
The force of winds impetuous ftemm'd,
Fiends ranging in the dark contemn'd,
All rigours of the cold fuftain'd,
Till of God-man the fight I gain'd.

Soon as I near God-man had drawn,
I fhould have known Him at firft dawn,
Benignities would from Him glide,
Which 'twas impoffible to hide,
The faireft, fweeteft of mankind,
In whom all lovely graces fhined.

I fome endearments fhould have fpied,
Which angels might not have defcried,
Of His philanthropy fome beams
On finners flowing in full ftreams,
And falling proftrate on the ground,
Adored, loved, joy'd with awe profound.

I fhould have been all eye, all ear,
My Saviour to behold and hear,
I fhould have watch'd till I difcern'd,
That His foft pity on me yearn'd;
That yearning would have been the fign,
To break my mind to Love Divine.

My Lord, my God, I fhould have cried,
To Heaven the finner's only Guide.

AFTER TRINITY.

O for Thy Infinite Love's sake,
Tell me the way my soul must take,
Most happy to abide with Thee,
In mansions of eternity!

Ah me! forth from the fire of lie,
Abroad deluding spirits fly,
Disguised like angels of pure light,
To fascinate and cheat my sight,
A thousand different ways they shew,
All leading to eternal woe.

I live in dread, left I to bliss
The single narrow way should miss;
But conscience here my spirit check'd,
And bid me on myself reflect,
You daily may God-man behold,
And to His Love your mind unfold.

Dear Jesus' Gospel would you heed,
You the same question there may read,
With His infallible reply,
On that you safely may rely,
The reprimand I just confess'd,
And read with care the volume bless'd.

Jesus there taught the scribe that Love,
Love only gain'd the joys above,
Love the command, primeval, great,
Connatural, transporting, sweet,

On which all law divine depends,
Which all our holocausts transcends.

When, that my way was Love, I heard,
A duty which my soul endear'd,
Benignly condescending, mild,
The task not of a slave, but child,
I humble thanks to Jesus paid,
Who Love the way to glory made.

My way to Heaven when taught me clear,
I thither vow'd my bark to steer,
But native lusts like adverse wind,
To sensual joys blew back my mind,
I long indulged them to prevail,
And wanted now a prosperous gale.

All winds which on the ocean blow,
Out of God's airy treasure flow,
And in His Sacred Book is store
Of aids to reach the heavenly shore,
Repentance I there learn'd had force,
To turn and keep my heaven-ward course.

My Jesus' Love was in my eye,
Who to excite my love would die:
I grieved I should His Love offend,
Yet joy'd He would my bliss intend,
That grief, that joy with gentle stroke,
My heart, till then reluctant, broke.

From that dear ſtroke my ſoul I felt,
Into a ſoft contrition melt,
Grief for my ſins my eyelids drain'd,
Joy for a Saviour me ſuſtain'd,
I thus ſupported while diſtreſs'd,
To Jeſus diſembogued my breaſt.

Whene'er I chill'd, ſank, wander'd, tired,
The Sacred Book zeal re-inſpired,
My faith kept Jeſus in my view,
His voice in every line I knew,
He ſtep by ſtep my ſpirit led,
And ſmooth'd the ways which I ſhould tread.

SEVENTEENTH SUNDAY AFTER TRINITY.

Unity.

One Lord, one faith, one baptiſm, one God and
Father of all.—*Eph.* iv. 5, 6.

OFT has my mind took flight,
   For proſpects of Love infinite;
  It forward ſtill aſpired,
  It moſt agreeably was tired;
   And when it came to port,
I ſent it back to make a freſh effort.

In every flight it made,
Soon as it could its freight unlade;
  This always back it brought,
Which I keep treasured in my thought;
  One God I must adore,
And 'tis impossible there should be more.

Mind daily saw on high,
Bright ministerial angels fly;
  Among them, one of those
Who wait on children, out it chose,
  Who still God's Face behold,
And fittest seem'd the Godhead to unfold.

You, said my Mind, have sight
Of God in beatific light;
  Sits He not there alone,
Or had He partner in His throne?
  Alone, he made reply,
There is no partner in infinity.

Were Godhead more than one,
It up to numberless might run;
  Fecundity divine,
'Tis Godhead only could confine;
  And wheresoe'er it stops,
All Godhead ceases as to bounds it drops.

Were Infinites but two,
And we to pay them worship due;

AFTER TRINITY.

  We neither could revere,
 And neither boundlefs would appear;
  Would greater be combined,
We lefs and more in infinite fhould find.

  Embroilments ne'er would ceafe,
 Should rivals fhare the realm of peace;
  We fiercer war fhould wage,
 Than that againft apoftate rage;
  Gods then would fight maintain,
If more omnipotents than one fhould reign.

  We on one God depend,
 He our Beginning is and End;
  Beyond His boundlefs ray
 We happy fpirits cannot ftray;
  In One we acquiefce,
And all in the One Infinite poffefs.

  Though near the Throne we wait,
 We cannot what we fee relate;
  All the angelic choir
 Adorable I AM admire;
  While we compofe new ftrains,
God pure indivifible One remains.

  Our loves on God diffufe,
 His attributes for hymn we choofe;
  Though One, they various feem,
 We vary, as our views, our Theme;

Men ruder gueſſes make,
When views from their compounded ſelves they
　　　　　take.

　　　One God, ſaid he, one Love
　　　There is among the bleſs'd above;
　　　　High praiſe to God he ſang,
　　　Juſt as from me he ſprang;
　　　　And then began the hymn
Which angels ſing, when the expanſe they ſwim.

　　　Thou, Lord, didſt Thy great Name
　　　With Thy dread Unity proclaim,
　　　　When of ſoul, might, and mind,
　　　Love undivided was enjoin'd;
　　　　Love ever one ſhould be,
Since out of God it naught can lovely ſee.

　　　The bleſs'd for hymn will none
　　　But Thee, Great One, for ſubject own;
　　　　And ſince to Thee below
　　　We like peculiar offerings owe,
　　　　I proſtrate at Thy Feet,
Acceptance of my humble ſong entreat.

　　　Praiſe to great One, may I
　　　In love be ever unity;
　　　　Thou uncompounded art,
　　　From ſenſual joys, Lord, cleanſe my heart;
　　　　May it abide unmix'd,
On Love Triune indiviſibly fix'd.

EIGHTEENTH SUNDAY AFTER TRINITY.

*Thou shalt love the Lord thy God with all thy heart,
and with all thy soul, and with all thy mind.*
St. Matthew xxii. 37.

FALSE world, I'll you no more endure,
   Vexatious, transient, vain, impure,
     Too long your friendship feign'd
     My ghostly vitals baned;
You nothing are but universal snare,
I 'gainst your charms antipathy declare.

   My heart to God would fain reflow,
   But I am still detain'd below,
     Ah! is there no retreat,
     Secure from worldly cheat?
If such a one dear guardian you can find,
O thither me transport, there lodge my mind!

   Your wings between us two divide,
   Each through expanse on one shall glide:
     The doves, their wings to spare,
     On one can swim in air;
Our unwing'd arms shall round each other lie,
And our wing'd arms shall row us in the sky.

   Long we may range, our wings may tire,
   And yet not compass my desire;
     While God here wills my stay,
     His grace my powers shall sway:

Grace in a pest-house can my health ensure,
Or sick with noxious steams, my spirit cure.

   Jesus, whose mind on Heaven was fix'd,
   Lived with terrestrial joys unmix'd,
     He still to Heaven aspired,
     To solitudes retired,
He in the world, lived from the world; His aim
Was to do good, and worldly minds reclaim.

   Thus Christ-like charity and prayer
   Should all my vacant minutes share,
     My busy part I'll spend,
     My calling to attend,
When I the poor in my excursions meet,
They Jesus' brethren are, I'll wash their feet.

   With ghostly alms, I'll souls relieve,
   Instruct, reprove, exhort, retrieve,
     With God my heart shall close,
     And when I die, repose:
Should any worldly taint to me adhere,
I'll wash it off in oratory tear.

   Watch, reading, meditation, prayer,
   And hymn, of saints the employments are;
     While these we mind,
     Hell can no entrance find:
O wondrous goodness of the law divine,
Preservative and duty to combine!

NINETEENTH SUNDAY AFTER TRINITY.

Having the underſtanding darkened, being alienated from the life of God through the ignorance that is in them, becauſe of the blindneſs of their heart.—*Eph.* iv. 18.

    OF all the monſters which appear'd,
        Since God the world from nothing rear'd,
    None ſhould ſo odious be eſteem'd,
        As ſinners, by God-man redeem'd,
Who outrage for that boundleſs Love repay,
To make themſelves to helliſh ſpite a prey.

    E'er ſince God-man for ſinners bled,
        God His dear Love diffuſedly ſhed,
    Of all He the ſalvation wills,
        Due grace He into all inſtils;
God reconciled to ſinners, Love became
Of Deity atoned, the proper name.

    God who of Love the title choſe,
        Averſion to our ruin ſhews,
    Love pities, and complains, and grieves,
        Whene'er repulſes He receives,
A thouſand ſolemn proteſtations makes,
He no delight in our damnation takes.

    Love long for our converſion ſtays,
        Gently upbraiding our delays;

Love for each soul which torment feels,
  Can make unnumber'd just appeals:
Ah! what can Love do more to rescue one,
Who Love contemn'd, and chose to be undone?

Love, when provoked, to wrath is slow,
  Unwilling to inflict a woe;
  His anger He'll long time suspend,
  To try if sinners will amend:
God even in wrath is of a temper meek,
Remembering He is Love, and man is weak.

Love, when a daring guilt provokes,
  Shortens, and moderates His strokes,
  On this side of eternal pains,
  God's wrath, allays of Love retains;
And when they harden'd down to Tophet fall,
Love wishes they had hearken'd to His call.

Say, all lapsed Adam's offspring, say,
  When love of sin to heart you lay;
  When men with devils you compare,
  Who have in dying God no share:
Say, if your stretch'd imaginations find
More horrid monsters than foul humankind.

Dark intellect, perverted will,
  All powers, all passions warp'd to ill;
  The likeness diabolic placed,
  Where God's bright image was effaced:

A hell-fired tongue, a heart of senseless stone,
Are the foul shapes by which the monster's known.

   I such a monster, Lord, remain'd,
   While I 'gainst Love cursed war maintain'd;
   Thy Love, Lord, first proposed a peace,
   First made hostilities to cease:
Thy pure free Love created me anew,
Till from a monster I a lover grew.

   Mind was enlighten'd, passions tamed,
   My powers re-hallow'd, will inflamed;
   I felt Thy image re-impress'd,
   Well-govern'd tongue, a tender breast:
I ever will that Love immense adore,
Who when I monster turn'd, would me restore.

TWENTIETH SUNDAY AFTER TRINITY.

Speaking to yourselves in psalms, and hymns, and spiritual songs; singing and making melody in your heart to the Lord.—Eph. v. 19.

OF all the gifts which Heaven design'd
   To hallow and adorn the mind,
Sweet poetry has suffer'd most
By bards from the infernal coast,
Who in her beauteous visage spit
The putrefaction of their wit.

The gift of God, by God infufed,
Should be for God, the Donor, ufed;
From God primevally it ftreams,
And fhould in hymn reflect His beams,
And every fong it ftrives to fing
Should have the flavour of its Spring.

Great God, the Altar to fupply,
Bright fire commanded from on high,
The heavenly fire Jehovah fent,
Was only on His Altar fpent,
And all poetic heaven-born flame
Should be devoted to God's Name.

Great God intends His gifts divine
Should have an influential fhine,
God is of love and joy the Source,
His gifts fhould have a God-like force,
And gifted poets fhould excite
Pure heavenly love, and pure delight.

When bards againft great God confpire,
And kindle fervour at ftrange fire,
When they are warm'd by Pagan heat,
Their borrow'd phrafes they repeat,
Mean and inglorious aims purfue,
And find the Pagans them outdo.

Would they to God devote their wit,
And borrow lights from Sacred Writ,

Their fancies nobler tracks would find,
With brighter thoughts enrich the mind,
They then would take supernal flights,
Verse would retrieve its native heights.

Souls raised to a celestial stand
With freedom might their powers expand,
Of things divine they would discourse,
From the eternal boundless Source,
The subjects would their souls sublime,
And keep wit ever in its prime.

True poets are a saint-like race,
And with the gift receive the grace,
Of their own songs the virtue feel,
Warm'd with an heaven-enkindled zeal,
And warm'd itself, a sacred Muse
Like ardours may with ease infuse.

A poet should have heat and light,
Of all things a capacious sight,
Serenity with rapture join'd,
Aims noble, eloquence refined,
Strong, modest, sweetness to endear,
Expressions lively, lofty, clear.

High thoughts, an admirable theme,
For decency a chaste esteem,
Of harmony a perfect skill,
Just characters of good and ill,

And all concentred, fouls to pleafe,
Inftruct, inflame, melt, calm, and eafe.

Such graces can nowhere be found,
Unlefs on confecrated ground,
Where poets fix on God their thought,
By facred infpiration taught,
Where each poetic votary fings
In heavenly ftrains of heavenly things.

Prophets and poets were of old
Made of the fame celeftial mould,
O that the prophets now would ftrive
That hallow'd union to revive,
They'd facred poetry affert,
And the degenerate bards convert.

Bards, who will ftruggle ere they quit
Their bold and falfe pretence to wit,
They'll for a while make hideous cries
At priefts, who them would exorcife,
But Chriftian poets would gain ground,
And Antichriftians' ravings drown'd.

TWENTY-FIRST SUNDAY AFTER TRINITY.

Brethren, be strong in the Lord, and in the power of His might.—Eph. vi. 10.

THRICE happy man whose soul is staid
On God's unseen, but certain aid,
Beneath his shadow he'll retreat,
And never fear afflicting heat.

I am by sweet experience sure
My God a Refuge is secure,
He is my Fort against my foes,
In God I trust in all my woes.

My soul, He'll save thee from the snares
Which hellish spite for thee prepares;
When noisome pestilence shall reign,
Infection he'll from thee restrain.

His gracious Plumes shall thee enclose,
Thy trust shall in His Wings repose,
His truth shall arms defensive yield,
It shall thy buckler be and shield.

Thou shalt no terrors fear by night,
No arrows which are shot in light,
No dangers which in darkness rise,
Or at noon-day shall thee surprise.

Amidſt ten thouſand round thee ſlain
Thou unaſſaulted ſhalt remain,
And ſee, when ſinners outrage God
The juſt dire vengeance of His rod.

My ſoul, thou doſt on God rely,
And haſt thy ſhelter from on high,
No evil ſhall approach thy bed,
Thou no judicial plague ſhalt dread.

God will command on angels lay
To guide and guard thee night and day,
They'll thee uphold in tender arm,
And no rude ſtone thy foot ſhall harm.

Thou ſhalt on fierceſt lions tread,
Shalt bruiſe the aſp's and dragon's head,
With the old ſerpent doom'd to hell
Their venom damp, their fury quell.

Hear what God utters from above,—
Since he has fix'd on Me his love,
Has known, and has obey'd My Will,
I'll place him out of reach of ill.

Whene'er he prays his prayers I'll hear,
I'll in his trouble ſtill be near,
Not only him from guilt redeem,
But raiſe him in the world's eſteem.

He long shall happy live below,
My blessings here shall overflow,
When languishing for Heaven he dies,
Eternal joys shall glad his eyes.

TWENTY-SECOND SUNDAY AFTER TRINITY.

Prayer for Love.

And this I pray, that your love may abound.—*Phil.* i. 9.

MY prayers for Love to Heaven directly fly,
The God of Love cannot these prayers deny,
The God of Love these prayers inspires,
He first the incense fires,
Which, as it heavenward burns,
What Love sent down, to Love returns,
God is both Loveliness and Love immense,
And loves to be re-loved with love the most intense.

All-gracious God, I cried, make no delay,
Vouchsafe me one inflammatory ray;
And straight a ray of Love Divine
Deign'd on my soul to shine,
I knew from whence it came,
It kindled in me heavenly flame,
I felt it gently over-shine my breast,
But its sweet mighty force can never be express'd.

Down on my spirit flew the spotless Dove,
Pluck'd from His splendid Wings a beam of Love,
   My heart with that bright beam He fill'd,
    Which heavenly Love instill'd;
    My heart was at one stroke
   Of that soft beam in pieces broke,
I long for its obdurateness was grieved,
And wonder'd how the rock could by a beam be cleaved.

When His all-glorious Wings the Spirit spread
O'er chaos, and enlivening influence shed,
   As He descended His bright rays
    Made ante-solar days,
    Light on the mass appear'd
   Ere into creature it was rear'd;
Thus on my heart when down the Spirit flew,
Light heavenly on it fell ere 'twas a creature new.

When Jesus to the man born blind gave eyes,
He all the creatures saw with strange surprise;
   Thus Love's diffused enamouring light
    Gave an amazing sight,
    I clearly saw my heart,
   Pry'd nicely into every part,
Concupiscence had made it so impure,
Unspotted Love Divine could not its sight endure.

  Sin now in a true light itself displays,
  And diabolic ugliness betrays;

AFTER TRINITY.

O I have lived till now ſtark blind,
　　Stranger to my own mind,
　　Ah, I too late begin
　To ſee the ſinfulneſs of ſin,
My deepeſt wound is that I ſhould miſpend
My ſtrength ſo much, ſo long, Love boundleſs
　　　to offend.

When I confront my ſins, and Love Divine,
The infinite free Love of Godhead Trine
　　Has ſuch ſweet force, that it endears
　　　The bittereſt of my tears,
　　　Hearts humble and contrite
　　In lamentations feel delight,
Each tear alleviates their afflicting moan,
And glad advances makes, Love outraged to atone.

All worldly luſts I from my heart expell'd,
And the loved ſin which furiouſly rebell'd,
　　I then implored Love's gracious might,
　　　Love ardent to excite;
　　　Soon as my heart was clear'd,
　　Love in His temple re-appear'd,
　My broken heart Love fill'd, and Love re-
　　　cloſed;
And in His temple there Love Infinite repoſed.

TWENTY-THIRD SUNDAY AFTER TRINITY.

Heaven Firſt Sought.

For our converſation is in Heaven, from whence alſo we look for the Saviour, the Lord Jeſus Chriſt.—*Phil.* iii. 20.

WHETHER I will or no, I find
    Myſelf to happineſs inclined,
What happineſs I then deſire,
    I next inquire.

I all my inclinations weigh,
What would content them, bid them ſay,
But ſee, they no enough will own,
    Inſatiate grown.

Pride, luſt, and avarice ſtill would crave,
Should they ten worlds for portion have,
Intoxicated though with ſtore,
    They'd thirſt for more.

I then conſult each learned ſect,
Who authors numberleſs collect,
They who all ſciences purſue
    Enough ne'er knew.

In Solomon, of all mankind,
    Wealth, honour, pleaſure, wiſdom join'd;

He felt the quinteffential heights
    Of all delights.

He ftrove with an unbridled will
Of fenfual joys to take his fill,
Yet to his forrow, found his gain
    Vexatious, vain.

Our God in that great King defign'd,
To unbeguile each worldly mind,
And teach that higheft joys below
    Expire in woe.

'There's no true fatisfaction here,
'Tis only in the Heavenly fphere;
Souls who to perfect joys afpire
    Quite lofe defire.

In death enough faints fhall not have,
Though flefh lies fenfelefs in the grave;
And he their fpirits fhall difmifs
    To enter blifs.

Enough no feparate fouls obtain,
Till bodies glorified they gain,
They'll live in languifhing defire
    For blifs entire.

Jefus, to fix our choice aright,
Bids us firft feek the realm of light,
And to His Righteoufnefs Divine
    To co-incline.

None but the righteous are difpofed
For joys in endlefs light difclofed;
Polluted fouls the region pure
    Would not endure.

Left the vain world fhould us allure,
He deigns Heaven's feekers to affure,
That God their portion juft decreed
    For earthly need.

Thus love unbounded overflows,
Both Heaven and earth on faints beftows:
What can the Infinite give more,
    Or man implore?

If Heaven ye worldlings firft would choofe,
And not enjoy this world, but ufe;
'Twill pleafe you, to fubjection brought,
    More than firft fought.

My Jefus, had I fought Thee firft,
I ne'er had felt afflicting thirft;
But this vain world from heavenly view
    My fpirit drew.

Lord, to that fovereign blifs I tend,
Which all-fufficient has no end,
Perfections which belong to none
    But Thee alone.

Meanwhile I on my God rely,
The wants, He wills me, to fupply;

My juſt enough He only knows,
    For want or woes.

In God's enough, my ſoul ſhall reſt,
Though here I am but partly bleſs'd,
Saints of the Croſs have ſtill alloy
    To temper joy.

Enough we have for earthly need,
Heaven's joys our foretaſtes far exceed,
Enough, my God, is where Thou art,
    There lodge my heart.

TWENTY-FOURTH SUNDAY AFTER TRINITY.

Heaven.

For the hope which is laid up for you in Heaven.
Coloſſians i. 5.

NOR eye, ear, thought, can take the height
    To which my ſong is taking flight,
    Yet raiſed an humble wing,
    My gueſs of Heaven I'll ſing;
'Tis Love's reward, and Love is fired
By gueſſing at the bliſs deſired.

Gueſs then at ſaints' eternal lot,
By due conſidering what 'tis not,

No mifery, want, or care,
No death, no darknefs there,
No troubles, ftorms, fighs, groans, or tears,
No injury, pains, ficknefs, fears.

There fouls no difappointments meet,
No vanities the choice to cheat,
   Nothing that can defile,
   No hypocrite, no guile,
No need of prayer, or what implies,
Or abfence or vacuities.

There no ill confcience gnaws the breaft,
No tempters holy fouls infeft,
   No curfe, no weeds, no toil,
   No errors to embroil.
No luftful thought can enter in,
Or poffibility of fin.

From all vexations here below,
The region of fin, death and woe.
   Song, to your utmoft ftrefs
   Now elevate your guefs,
Sing what in facred lines you read,
Of blifs for pious fouls decreed.

They dwell in pure ecftatic light,
Of God Triune have blifsful fight,
   Of Fontal Love, who gave
   God Filial, man to fave;

Of Jesus' Love, who death sustain'd,
By which the saints their glory gain'd;

Of Love co-breathed the boundless Source,
From which saints' love derives its force,
    Within the gracious shine
    Of the co-glorious Trine,
The saints in happy mansions rest,
Of all they can desire possess'd.

Saints' bodies there the sun outvie
Temper'd to feel the joys on high,
    Bright body and pure mind,
    In rapture unconfined,
Capacities expand, till fit
Deluge of Godhead to admit.

In all-sufficient bliss they joy,
Duration in sweet hymns employ;
    With angels they converse,
    Their loves and joys rehearse,
Taste suavities of Love immense,
Of all delights full confluence.

With God's own Son they reign co-heirs,
Each saint with Him in glory shares,
    Like Godhead, happy, pure,
    Against all change secure,
In boundless joys they sabbatise,
Which Love Triune will eternise.

By boundlefs Love, for fouls refined,
Are joys unfpeakable defign'd,
    When I thofe joys imbibe,
    I then may them defcribe;
Joys to full pitch will hymn excite,
When from fenfation I endite.

TWENTY-FIFTH SUNDAY AFTER TRINITY.

Jefus our King.

Behold, the days come, faith the Lord, that I will raife unto David a righteous Branch, and a King fhall reign, and profper, and fhall execute judgment and juftice in the earth.—*Jeremiah* xxiii. 5.

BLESS'D Spirit, aid me, while I fing
Our humble, our Almighty King.
    Curfed pride man firft debafed,
    And from fweet Eden chafed;
Man proudly likenefs to great God defired,
And loft all God-like grace which God infpired.

Man all to God as creature owes,
And his entire dependence knows,
    As finner he's God's hate,
    And muft his doom await.
Sinner and proud, a contradiction feems,
    Yet in fall'n man concentre both extremes.

Jefus the fovereign fin to quell,
Which men and devils fank to hell,

AFTER TRINITY.

  Lowly and meek appear'd,
  To God the more endear'd,
He taught how sweet humility and height
In souls would co-harmoniously unite.

  God sent an angel to proclaim
  Both His Conception and His Name,
   Yet a poor Maid He chose,
   Whose womb should Him enclose;
Our new-born King in a poor manger lay,
Which a bright star ennobled with its ray.

  God-man, who deign'd to live below,
  Endured all the insults of woe,
   Rejected, scorn'd, reviled,
   And diabolic styled;
Yet all the while wrought miracles divine,
And in the humble man made Godhead shine.

  When on the Cross He tortured hung,
  Blasphemed by every hell-fired tongue,
   Twelve legions were at hand,
   To fly at His command;
The king of terrors, and the hellish host,
Fled trembling soon as He gave up the Ghost.

  God-man would in His earthly state,
  By condescensions, pride abate;
   The King adored on high,
   Would for His rebels die;

And now enthroned, benignly intercedes
For full supplies to humble votaries' needs.

   Descending from His glorious sphere,
    Our humble King began to rear
      His mediatory realm,
      And set Himself at helm;
His realm antarctic to all worldly aim,
Where none but humble souls can entrance claim.

   Pure self-denial, and the Cross,
    To count all things for Jesus loss,
      Of saints the badges are,
      Who live His royal care;
They in Heaven inchoate, have foretastes sweet
Of joys above, which in full confluence meet.

   God-man to Jews His realm restrain'd,
    Till He His heavenly Throne regain'd;
      Now o'er the world He reigns,
      Allots rewards and pains,
Gives laws, support, deliverance, shelter, aid,
To humble souls by His kind sceptre sway'd.

   The Lamb of God is King of kings,
    He Death disarms of all its stings:
      And when a tyrant raves,
      The Lamb, the Shepherd saves;
He the seven-headed, ten-horn'd beast o'erpowers,
Who all the world who worship him, devours.

Angelic hofts the Lamb obey,
Kings at His Feet their fceptres lay,
    The Lamb all Tophet awes,
    Souls refcues from its jaws;
When men, when devils, the Lamb's realm affail,
Our mighty King, the Lamb, will ftill prevail.

Blefs'd faints, whom the meek Lamb of God
Rules with a gracious, gentle rod;
    I'll on the Lamb repofe,
    Follow where'er He goes;
And when I flip, to the mild Lamb addrefs,
Ready to pardon, foon as I confefs.

Praife to the Lamb enthroned, whofe Love
Sent in His ftead the heavenly Dove;
    O blefling paft compare,
    In which the humble fhare!
They in fweet reft, joy, peace fecure abide,
Who have the Lamb their King, the Dove their
    Guide.

But when the Lamb His realm lays down,
And God Triune refumes the Crown,
    When faints abfolved from fin,
    Eternal joys begin;
May I with them adore the Godhead Trine,
And have my fill of all that is divine.

ST. ANDREW'S DAY.

BLESS'D Andrew! in your call we trace
The conduct of preventing grace,
While we recount the happy steps you trod,
To be the favourite of Incarnate God.

You to hard toil and care inured,
A common fisher's life endured,
On Galilean waves, you night and day,
Expofed to cold, heat, storm and billows, lay.

Long had the Galilean name
Been reprobated and infame,
Till God convinced the Jews' contemptuous eyes,
That good might out of Galilee arife.

Heaven, which God-man's fore-runner fent
To move Judæa to repent,
With gracious force meek Andrew's heart dif-
    pofed
To tafte the truths God's harbinger difclofed.

The awful tidings reach'd his ear,
Of God's blefs'd kingdom drawing near,
And he ambitious grew himfelf to mould,
That he might in that kingdom be enroll'd.

His fins he then with care furvey'd,
And every aggravation weigh'd,

Oft with his tears he ballaſted his boat,
As on Tiberian lake it was afloat.

   While for his ſins his heart would bleed,
     He of a Saviour ſaw the need;
And God, Who always tenders hearts contrite,
Took care to bleſs him with his Saviour's ſight.

   One day, which Jeſus well foreknew,
     He paſs'd in John and Andrew's view,
And John cried out, Behold the Lamb of God,
Who ſinners ſaves from Heaven's avenging rod!

   Meek Andrew, and his humble mate,
     Wont on the Baptiſt's lips to wait,
Joy'd at that dear diſcovery, grew intent
To follow Jeſus whereſoe'er He went.

   Sweet longings in their hearts they felt,
     To ſee the ſpot where Jeſus dwelt,
And He vouchſafed the votaries to invite
To lodge in His bleſs'd manſion all the night.

   O favour not to be expreſs'd,
     To be of God Incarnate gueſt!
Their hearts were at each word with rapture fill'd,
While from His Lips ſalvific truths diſtill'd.

   Meek Andrew, by loved Jeſus. fired,
     To copy Jeſus' love aſpired,
His brother Peter out with zeal he ſought,
And to obtain like bliſs to Jeſus brought.

Both then returning to their trade,
 Heaven more their care than fiſhing made;
Till Jeſus gave them apoſtolic call,
And both to follow Jeſus, left their all.

 From toil marine good Andrew freed,
  To fiſh for human ſouls decreed,
Vaſt Scythia was his lot, where 'twas his aim,
Men fierce as fiends they worſhipp'd, to reclaim.

 Pains, labours, perſecutions dire,
  All that could fright, torment, or tire,
He meekly bore from Pagan and from Jew,
As evangelic nets he o'er them threw.

 In ſpite of hell, he mighty ſhoals
  Caught in his net, of Scythian ſouls;
O'er Grecia next, to pride and idols bred,
His ghoſtly nets with like ſucceſs he ſpread.

 He truth, with heavenly vigour taught,
  Confirm'd by miracles he wrought;
Ne'er ceaſed his labours, till with age oppreſs'd,
God ſaw it time to give him endleſs reſt.

 He traverſed the Achaian land,
  At Patras made a ghoſtly ſtand,
Whoſe altars yearly reek'd with virgin gore,
When they convened, Diana to adore.

 Their idol-temples down he caſt,
  Forced oracles to breathe their laſt;

Till Pagan zeal, with hellish fury fumed,
The Saint to die upon a saltire doom'd.

   With cords his hands and feet they tied,
     That long he might in pain abide;
Unnail'd he strength retain'd, and from their spite
Advantage took to shed celestial light.

   Two days he on the cross, aloud
     Preach'd Jesus to the listening crowd,
Conversions numerous made, while thus he hung,
Till he in transport his own requiem sung.

   All praise to God, who lifts on high
     Souls who are lowliest in His eye;
Who humble Andrew for great things design'd,
And first to penitential tears inclined.

   From penitent to saint he rose;
     From saint he was apostle chose;
The martyr's crown he, when apostle, gain'd,
And ever since with blessed Jesus reign'd.

   My God, may I with faith behold
     The Lamb of God for sinners fold;
In Holy writ, hymn, meditation, prayer,
And Eucharist may I His Presence share.

   When Jesus calls, with ready mind
     May I leave all the world behind;
May I, like Andrew, never once look back,
But forward tread in my Redeemer's track!

May I with Jefus fix my ftay,
And languifh when He goes away;
Till, Andrew-like, I others fhall enflame,
Prepared to die a martyr for His Name.

ST. THOMAS THE APOSTLE.

WHEN Jefus notice gave
Of Lazarus fleeping in his grave,
And that to wake His friend,
His courfe fhould towards Judæa tend,
His votaries to diffuade Him ftraight combined,
Since there the Jews His ftoning had defign'd.

Blefs'd Thomas, who well knew
The rage of the malicious Jew,
Who in like fate refolved
His votaries all fhould be involved;
To run the danger with his Lord was bent,
Rather than hinder His benign intent.

This was his brave reply,
O let us go and with Him die;
Him we for Mafter chofe,
And of our lives let Him difpofe;
The radiant gates of Heaven are open fet,
Thrice happy thofe that early entrance get.

Bleſs'd ſaint, by Jeſus taught
Of things below to value nought,
　　With love, which caſts out fear,
　To your Redeemer to adhere;
May I, like you, the world and life deſpiſe,
And live to God perpetual ſacrifice!

　　Our Lord, with melting Heart,
　Had warn'd His friends He ſhould depart
　　To Fontal God, and they
　Were told, the Croſs ſhould be the way;
That when He made His re-aſcent, He there
Celeſtial manſions would for them prepare.

　　Bleſs'd Thomas, deeply grieved
　Of Jeſus' ſight to be bereaved,
　　Begg'd, that the way He went,
　He would more clearly repreſent;
He who before with Jeſus would have died,
Would tread all paths where Jeſus was the Guide.

　　Our Lord was pleaſed to ſay,
　I am the Truth, the Life, the Way,
　　None can accepted be
　With my dread Father, but by Me:
Me, Whom you know with God Paternal One,
The Father ſhines in His co-equal Son.

　　May I, dear Lord, reſign
　My faith to all Thy Truth Divine;

Make it my daily aim,
Conform to Thine, my life to frame,
That I, with Thomas, may that realm obtain,
Where saints with Thee in mansions bright remain.

When Jesus death subdued,
And His desponding friends review'd,
 The saint, then absent, heard
That Jesus had to them appear'd,
Yet doubted of the thing he most desired,
And free sensation for his faith required.

Our Lord saw joy devout
At the good news, had caused the doubt,
 And His next view contrived,
When doubting Thomas was arrived.
He Who our human frailties deign'd to bear,
Of souls sincere, though weak, has tender care.

Our Lord the Saint enjoin'd
By sense to satisfy his mind;
 With trembling he drew nigh,
Into his Saviour's Wounds to pry,
Search'd His gored Hands, and Feet, and gaping Side,
And loud, my Lord, my God! in rapture cried.

My Lord, Thy Love be praised,
Thou by the doubt which Thomas raised,
 Our doubting didst prevent,

We without fight give firm affent,
With joy Thy benediction we receive,
They bleffed are, who fee not, yet believe.

    All glory be to Thee,
  Thou Who didft heretics forefee,
      With lying ghofts would ftrive
  Thee of Thy Godhead to deprive;
Didft fix fuch faith on Thy Apoftle's breaft,
Which fhould to death Thy Deity atteft.

    That faving-truth his zeal
  To Gentiles labour'd to reveal;
      Round the vaft Parthian coaft
  He vanquifh'd the infernal hoft;
Preach'd Æthiopia and all India o'er,
And made them Jefus, his Lord God, adore.

    The idols then enraged,
  Their votaries in his fall engaged;
      They on a crofs decreed
  He, Jefus-like, fhould hang and bleed;
And as he hung, they pierced him with a fpear,
And gave his foul to blifs a paffage clear.

    When martyr's crown he gain'd,
  Thy Love, my Lord, his foul fuftain'd;
      Thou 'midft his dying woe,
  His Lord, his God, Thyfelf didft fhew;
He Who, blefs'd Saint, was Lord and God to thee,
My Lord, my God, O may He ever be.

CONVERSION OF ST. PAUL.

OF all the conquests which Thy grace
   E'er gain'd, dear Lord, o'er Adam's race,
I none more glorious can recall
        Than that of Saul.

He, reeking with bless'd Stephen's gore,
Had still a raging thirst for more;
His very temper seem'd on fire
        With hell-bred ire.

That ire, by Pharisaic pride,
Which censured, hated, scorn'd, decried,
All but themselves, more fiercely burn'd,
        To madness turn'd.

He threaten'd, grieved, imprison'd, bound,
And doom'd to death all saints he found,
Compell'd the timorous to blaspheme,
        With rage extreme.

No tyrant 'gainst the Christian name
Could kindle more devouring flame;
He evangelic truth denied,
        And Christ defied.

Sent by the priests to bring the saints
To Salem from remote restrains;

He strove to execute with speed
>   The ills decreed.

But gracious God stopp'd his career;
Light, than meridian beams more clear,
Round him, and all who with him join'd,
>   At mid-day shined.

The light, which dazzled all their eyes,
Struck them to earth, with strange surprise;
Saul heard plain words, while on the ground,
>   They, only found.

Why, Saul, should I thy fury feel?
'Tis hard to kick 'gainst pointed steel.
Who art Thou, Lord, soon as he cried,
>   The voice replied:—

I Jesus am, grieved with each woe,
Which My dear brethren undergo;
Arise, I thee from embryo chose,
>   Truth to disclose.

He rising, the o'erpowering light,
By Heaven's appointment, damp'd his sight,
That to Damascus led, he there
>   Might fix in prayer.

Three days he fasted, and was blind,
With an illuminated mind;
On Jesus' Voice he only mused,
>   With tears infused.

Sweet Jesus' wrongs his spirit gored,
He them with bitter grief deplored;
To cause God-man, his Saviour, smart,
    Quite broke his heart.

He God's benignity admired,
'Midst all his outrages untired,
Love penitential at that thought
    Was sweetly wrought.

His faith up to assurance grew,
Since he by glad experience knew
God-man; O none to that degree
    Could love, but he.

To ease His votary, well-nigh spent,
God Ananias to him sent,
Sight by his blessing was restored;
    Both God adored.

Then in the wave of his own tear
He was baptised, his guilt to clear,
Renounced the name of raging Saul,
    For milder Paul.

There with the saints awhile he stay'd,
For the divine assistance pray'd,
There God gave faith and love full height
    By rapturous flight.

In vision, or in soul he flew,
Of the third Heaven to take a view,

And the sublimities heard there,
>> Durst not declare.

Lest he thus rapt, with pride should swell,
God loosed a tempter, who from hell
Temptations thorny with him brought,
>> Which weakness taught.

But prayer procured sufficient grace
To quell the fiend, and self debase;
He seem'd improved by trial more,
>> Than flight before.

His faith and love, when thus refined,
In mutual actuations join'd,
Faith light imparted, and love heat,
>> In union sweet.

Of those bright graces when possess'd,
He with apostolate was bless'd,
All climates round the solar course,
>> Soon felt their force.

Firm was his faith, and lively hope,
Yet charity had greatest scope;
The last, though lovely all appear'd,
>> Was most endear'd.

No other knowledge he desired,
But what the Love of Jesus fired;
All worldly things he counted loss
>> For Jesus' Cross.

To the great God of Love he pray'd,
And never fail'd of gracious aid;
He sweetly felt that Love constrain
              To love again.

He lived by faith, but more by love,
Had foretastes of the bliss above,
Not to be thought by human mind,
              For love design'd.

The boundless length, breadth, depth and height
Of Jesus' Love, was his delight;
In every track he strove to tread,
              Where Jesus led.

He of past sins kept humble sense,
A conscience void of all offence:
No wrongs his love, when storm'd by foes,
              Could discompose.

He own'd himself of sinners chief;
Yet ignorance and unbelief,
When on God's gracious balance weigh'd,
              His guilt allay'd.

He flesh subdued by prayer, tear, fast,
Of votaries deem'd himself the last;
Though super-effluently graced,
              Was most debased.

Ills, when God's lovers here sustain'd,
He knew were for their good ordain'd;

Love which on him the Spirit shed,
              Was void of dread.

He single seem'd a martyr'd host,
Could more than all apostles boast;
Not in himself, but in the height
              Of heavenly might.

Stripes, labours, prisons, stonings, blows,
Deaths frequent, confluential woes,
Thieves, Pagans, the apostate crew,
              And spiteful Jew.

Fatigues, and shipwrecks on the deep,
Cold, nakedness, and want of sleep,
Thirst, hunger, all the grievous ills,
              Which hell instils.

All these, whose number, crowd, and weight,
'Tis hard to their full pitch to rate,
For lustres seven the Saint endured,
              To pains inured.

He of all churches bore the care,
In all saints' sorrows felt a share;
For lapse of all who truth believed,
              Was deeply grieved.

'Midst perpetuity of woe,
Joy would his heart co-overflow,
Hymns in the stocks he would recite
              In dead of night.

To all the saints he hymns enjoin'd,
In sufferings not to be declined,
Love to the Cross his soul impulsed,
        And griefs adulced.[1]

A long fierce fight his love maintain'd
Against the world, and conquest gain'd,
And to hell-powers, which souls invade,
        This challenge made :—

Forge all the terrors which you can,
To damp my love of great God-man,
Your darts shall unsuccessful fall,
        I'll stand them all.

Should tribulation, or distress,
Dire persecution, nakedness,
Sword, famine, peril, me assail,
        Love shall prevail.

My Jesus, out of love to Thee,
I all day long would murder'd be,
Die deaths more than a numerous fold,
        For slaughter sold.

My love shall to a higher name
Than conqueror advance my aim,
I'll triumph, in God's love exult,
        And hell insult.

---

[1] *Adulced*, softened, sweetened.

ST. PAUL.

Nor death, life, tyrants, devils' might,
No depths of woe, no honour's height,
No prefent, nor no future ftate,
    Shall love abate.

Oft thus he Jefus' Love revolved,
And fweetly long'd to be diffolved;
Yet his fweet longings would refign
    To Will Divine.

At laft the God of Love was pleafed
His aged lover fhould be eafed;
And nobler to atteft his creed,
    At Rome fhould bleed.

By Nero doom'd, he loft that head
Which o'er the world falvation fpread;
His foul had all he wifh'd before,
    And long'd no more.

God gracious wonders by him wrought,
Whatever touch'd him, virtue caught,
To heal the fick, fiends difpoffefs,
    And eafe diftrefs.

The world his diocefe was ftyled,
He conquer'd nations fierce and wild;
And ready was more worlds to crave,
    Which he might fave.

All praife to God for bleffed Paul,
For his grace, gifts, converfion, call,

Example, labours, wonders, pains,
                Religious gains.

The Holy Spirit be adored,
Who him with revelations ſtored,
That light to us he might tranſmit
                In Sacred Writ.

May I from his own writings learn
His love, and ſaving truths diſcern,
Till thirſting for the joys on high,
                I long to die.

PURIFICATION OF ST. MARY THE VIRGIN.

OF all the ſolemn days,
    Devoted to God's praiſe,
This day, methinks, the Church miſnamed,
It might have juſter title claim'd;
    No ear can well endure
Purification of a Mother pure.

The womb which Jeſus choſe,
    His Godhead to encloſe,
From wilful ſin we gueſs was free,
Fit for the God of purity;
    And might have rites declined,
Which for impure conceptions were deſign'd.

But her Great Infant few
  Immaculate then knew,
 She might the region ſcandalize,
 If judged law ſacred to deſpiſe;
  And meekly ſhe thought fit
In charity and wiſdom to ſubmit.

  She with like humble thought,
  Her Babe to Temple brought,
 The ſtated ranſom down to lay,
 Which Jews for their firſt-born ſhould pay.
  The Mighty Child ſhe knew,
To all God's laws would yield ſubmiſſion due.

  The holy Virgin nought
  But two young pigeons brought,
 An offering of the meaneſt rate,
 To ſhow her humble, poor eſtate;
  She the vain world denied,
She perfect contradiction lived to pride.

  Herſelf and Son ſhe there
  Devoted to God's care;
 She knew the dire predicted woe
 Her Son for man ſhould undergo;
  And though to tear inclined,
All her ſoft yearnings to God's Will reſign'd.

  It was the Infant's aim
  When He to Temple came,

To God Himself entire to give,
In constant sacrifice to live,
  And on the Cross to bleed,
To work that good His Father had decreed.

  Saints to the house of prayer
  Wont daily to repair,
The glory of God-man beheld
In splendour which the ark excell'd;
  They saw the truth foretold,
The second Temple now out-shined the old.

  Simeon, devout and just,
  Purged from terrestrial gust,[1]
Had waited with a longing eye,
To see Messias from on high;
  And Heaven ere he expired
Had promised him the bliss so much desired.

  The Spirit, ever bless'd,
  By force of Love impress'd,
Was to God's House the lover's Guide,
Where God Incarnate he descried,
  At his first heavenly view,
He Israel's wish'd-for consolation knew.

  The saint at that glad sight,
  Raised to ecstatic height,

[1] *Gust*, taste, appetite.

With love the whole assembly fired,
Embraced the Babe, to Heaven aspired,
　　Could earth no more endure,
And into hymn brake out, for Heaven mature.

　　God-man has bless'd my eye,
　　In peace, Lord, let me die,
　　I the Redeemer now behold,
　Whose Love even Gentiles shall enfold,
　　Be the world's glorious Light,
And shed o'er Israel rays benign and bright

　　Next he the parents bless'd,
　　And prophecy express'd,
　That when the Babe commenced His reign
　　Many should fall and rise again,
　　Many should be averse,
And sword-like grief should the dear Mother pierce.

　　Then the Babe's blessing he
　　Imploring on his knee,
　The Infant gave him his release,
　And in sweet beam a kiss of peace,
　　His spirit burst its clay,
And flew to hymn God-man in endless day.

　　Prophetic aged Anne
　　Came next to see God-man,
　Her life she in the Temple spent,
　On prayer and fast entirely bent,

She sang a song of praise,
Soon as she Jesus saw in gracious rays.

　　　All who cursed sin bemoan'd,
　　　And for a Saviour groan'd,
　　She warn'd on Jesus to rely,
　　And rapt at His endearing Eye,
　　　Could life no more abide,
But in sweet, amorous liquefaction died.

　　　Home went, when rites were done,
　　　The parents with their Son;
　　At Nazareth abode they made,
　　Lived in obscure, and humble shade,
　　　From the vain world estranged,
And loves with their sweet Infant interchanged.

　　　O all ye worldlings, see
　　　How happy souls may be
　　Without wealth, pomp, which you admire,
　　And madly to your bane desire;
　　　The happiest of mankind,
The humblest are to Jesus' view confined.

　　　Jesu, I Thee adore,
　　　Who sinners to restore,
　　Wouldst no humiliations scorn,
　　Thou Godhead's co-immense First-born,
　　　Wouldst have Thy ransom paid,
Who wast Thyself the world's great Ransom made.

May I in Thee delight,
Keep Thee in ghostly sight;
Like Thy bless'd parents Thee enjoy,
On Thy sole Love myself employ;
And from the world retired,
See nothing but Thyself to be desired.

May I in prayer and fast,
Still mindful of my last,
Like Anna on Thy house attend,
All solemn hours devoutly spend;
There my dear Jesus meet,
And of Heaven's joys have prelibations sweet.

May I, in this lapsed state,
For Thy salvation wait,
By faith, like Simeon, Thee embrace,
Make my own heart Thy dwelling-place,
On Thy dear Love rely,
And sing my own glad requiem when I die.

ST. MATTHIAS'S DAY.

NEXT to the name of devil, none
Than Judas we more odious own,
It seems song sacred to pollute,
And best may with invective suit.

But I, since I Matthias sing,
And story little aid can bring,
In his cursed character immerse,
To draw the Saint by his reverse.

The Gospel which our pastors chose
Seems the Saint's likeness to enclose,
And while my song his draught designs,
May furnish supplemental lines.

Both seem'd in grace alike to share,
Devoted to bless'd Jesus' care,
And both that call propitious heard,
Which souls to Jesus most endear'd.

Come all who sink with load and toil,
I'll you from pressures disembroil;
I'm meek and lowly, learn of Me,
Take My light yoke, 'twill set you free.

To take Christ's yoke they both profess'd,
To him 'twas pain, to this 'twas rest.
He eyed the Man, and this the God,
Both in antarctic footsteps trod.

He Jesus' easy yoke forsook,
And sins much heavier on him took;
Without this yoke of his, ne'er stept,
Which lighter grew, the longer kept.

He more retainer might be deem'd,
This a true votary esteem'd;

ST. MATTHIAS'S DAY.   341

He fought to be enrich'd by stealth,
This to renounce pomp, pleasure, wealth.

He of disciple had but paint,
This was sincere and real saint;
He for great favours was ingrate,
This highly would the meanest rate.

His call he to bless'd Jesus owed,
On this God call by lot bestow'd;
Yet when we both their calls review,
His seems the happier of the two.

He was apostle to the Light
While in the flesh, and lived by sight;
This walk'd by Faith, and call obtain'd,
While Jesus absent Heaven regain'd.

He truth drew from the Heavenly Source,
But closed his heart against its force;
This from the rills instruction drew,
And practised all the truths he knew.

Both to height apostolic reach'd,
Both mysteries evangelic preach'd;
He with a coldness, this with zeal,
Which seem'd the truths he taught, to feel.

Hell into him dire thoughts instill'd,
His heart was with cursed Satan fill'd;
Illapses of the gracious Dove
Fill'd this with a victorious love.

He Jesus with a kiss betray'd,
This faithful duty to Him pay'd;
He thirsted Jesus' Blood to shed,
While this for Jesus would have bled.

Both to repentances inclined,
His made him worse, this grew refined;
His drave him to a fierce despair,
This pardon gain'd by tear and prayer.

He felt anticipated hell,
At last the devil's martyr fell,
Was his own hangman, burst in twain,
By furies dragg'd to endless pain.

A life of love and joy this led,
And martyr's crown adorn'd his head;
Had foretastes of eternal bliss,
And gladly could his soul dismiss.

His crime predicted was of old,
His name, in Book of Life enroll'd,
Was by bless'd Jesus quite erased,
And in infernal records placed.

This all his life, abroad when sent,
In charitable labours spent;
This wonders wrought, this hell controll'd,
This added flocks to Jesus' fold.

This with fierce Pagan lands conversed,
Salvation far and wide dispersed,

Had his name wrote in beams, and shines
Indelible in heavenly lines.

Soon as the Saint to Heaven took flight,
All the inhabitants of light
Gave him of peace the rapturous kiss,
And sung God's praises for his bliss.

Soon as he had his glorious crown,
He on his radiant throne sat down,
Assessor to God-man ordain'd,
When the twelve tribes shall be arraign'd.

That throne for Judas once design'd,
Ere from his duty he declined,
To bless'd Matthias was ensured,
Reward for woes he had endured.

Cursed Judas at last day shall see
Matthias, who his judge shall be,
And hear his doom at that bright throne,
Which once he might have styled his own.

In hell, the heavenly throne and call
Eternally his soul will gall;
The greater grace he here received,
The more he will below be grieved.

With a feign'd saintship for awhile
Cursed traitors may the world beguile;
But death will counterfeits expose,
And damn to undissembled woes.

ST. MATTHIAS'S DAY.

O Gracious God! how apt are we
To prove like Judas falſe to Thee,
We call Thee Lord, but little mind
Obedience to Thy laws enjoin'd.

Falſe Judas, Lord, when Thee he ſold,
Had thirty pieces to him told;
His gain he but ten hours poſſeſs'd,
Diſturb'd with horrors in his breaſt.

We ſell Thy favour every day
For trifles which ſoon fade away;
Which freſh vexations ſtill create,
And which provoke Thy boundleſs hate.

The traitor grudged the ointment ſhed
By humble Mary on Thy Head;
We on our luſts profuſe, repine
To give Thee tenths of what is Thine.

If Judas, when apoſtle made,
His Lord and his own ſoul betray'd,
We from our proneneſs to backſlide,
Self-jealous, ſhould in Thee confide.

All praiſe to Thee, Who didſt aſſume
Matthias in the traitor's room,
An envoy after God's own mind,
Whoſe preference God Himſelf deſign'd.

May I, Lord, like Matthias ſtrive,
From Thee my copy to derive;

O may the world me never fway,
My God, like Judas, to betray.

All praife to Thee, Who didft extract
Good from the traitor's fouleft act,
His kifs Thy paffion introduced,
And all the joys of Heaven unfluiced.

ANNUNCIATION OF THE BLESSED VIRGIN MARY.

WHEN God the radiant Gabriel chofe,
His will to Zechary to difclofe,
The faints and angels all agreed
There was fome gracious thing decreed,
God, fuper-effluently bright,
Gave them additional delight.

But when fix moons were gone about,
And Gabriel was again call'd out,
They then beheld the glorious Trine
In brighter rays than ever, fhine,
Which with benignities immenfe
Caufed joys unfpeakably intenfe.

His robe was of a glory made,
Like that was on the ark difplay'd,

His wings of gradual beams were wove,
And as with them he ether clove,
Heaven stood in infinite amaze,
And overflow'd in songs of praise.

The morning stars in memory bore,
The rays God at creation wore,
When pleased He all His works survey'd,
And they in song first homage paid.
These inconceivably excell'd
The splendour which they then beheld.

Paternal God to blissful sight
Appear'd in full propitious might,
The gracious Dove, with Wings outspread,
Stood ready on the world to shed
Of sweet enlivening influence more
Than e'er the chaos had before.

The angels by God Filial taught,
His chariot of salvation brought,
By horses of salvation drawn,
Along the beatific lawn;
Unlock'd was the celestial gate,
That down He might descend in state.

Meanwhile bright Gabriel swiftly flew,
Till Nazareth open'd to his view,
He smell'd of prayer the odorous fume,
And traced it to the homely room,

Where he a Virgin had in fight,
Who feem'd to blifs juft taking flight.

Such heavenly air he in her eyed,
Which with his own angelic vied,
Towards God fhe with fuch ardours foar'd,
With fuch devotion God adored,
That till he mark'd her well, he guefs'd
'Twas feraph in a female veft.

He then began, with afpect fweet,
What God enjoin'd him to repeat:
Hail, Mary, beft of mortal race!
Hail, highly favour'd, full of Grace!
The Lord will temple in thy heart,
Thou happieft of all women art.

The humble Maid was in furprife,
At the bright envoy in her eyes,
He mildly adds, Surprife forbear,
You in God's Love have greateft fhare,
You fhall conceive a wondrous Child,
Who fhall, when born, be Jefus ftyled.

He fhall be great, by all revered,
God's only Son, to God endear'd;
God will His father David's throne
On Him beftow, He'll reign alone
O'er Ifrael, and a fceptre fway,
A kingdom which fhall ne'er decay.

How can this be, the Saint replied,
Since I a virgin will abide?
The Holy Ghoſt, he then rejoin'd,
Shall make illapſe upon thy mind,
God's gracious power on thee ſhall ſtream,
And crown thee with enamouring beam.

The Babe who in thy womb ſhall lie,
Shall be the Son of God moſt High,
When thrice the moon its courſe ſhall run,
Eliza old ſhall have a ſon.
Thought nothing can too hard conceive
For power unbounded to achieve.

God's handmaid, cried ſhe, here behold,
May all ſucceed thou haſt foretold.
Then humbly Gabriel bade adieu,
And while he to his hymns re-flew,
In Heaven below ſhe acquieſced,
Benignly deluging her breaſt.

Her thought on dear Meſſias dwelt,
To languor ſhe began to melt,
While God from Heaven a viſit made;
Fulfilling what His envoy ſaid,
The Father, Son, and Holy Dove,
Diffuſed on her Triunal Love.

Down to the Virgin, Filial God
With chariots of ſalvation rode,

Of her heart blood by Love enflamed,
He for Himself a temple framed;
Debasement was His sole intent,
To Heaven His chariot empty went.

Her soul to dear Messias cleaved,
In a sweet rapture she conceived,
Just in the moment God design'd,
To be in her pure womb enshrined,
And as He entrance made, began
The union of great God with man.

While God was in her womb contain'd,
In constant rapture she remain'd;
Should all the denizens of light
Their joys and loves in one unite,
Of God inwomb'd one gracious ray
Would all their quintessence outweigh.

Yet like her humble Son, that she
His Mother dear might humble be,
She lived in silence and retired,
Love blazed not, though by Godhead fired,
Her joys, her graces she conceal'd,
Till Gabriel them in part reveal'd.

He Mary God's high favourite named,
He full of grace her soul proclaim'd,
Heaven when such titles it bestows,
A sanctity transcendent shows;

We know she had the full extent
Of all which by that style is meant.

A love aspiring towards immense,
A charity to all propense;
A soul from sensual gust refined,
Benign, meek, lowly, and resign'd;
A blissful joy, a zeal devout,
All powers towards God still flowing out.

For these, Lord, and unnumber'd more,
With which Thou didst Thy Mother store;
We offer up our hymn this day,
And beg that all our lives we may
Tread in Thy Mother's steps divine,
As she devoutly trod in Thine.

The Virgin hastes the happy news
Into Eliza to infuse;
Her joy she with the news imparts,
They mutually transpired their hearts,
The Holy Ghost Eliza fill'd,
And gratulations sweet instill'd.

O happy Virgin undefiled,
Bless'd Mother of a Blessed Child,
Who deigns to honour my poor cell,
Soon as your bliss I heard you tell,
Your Babe inspired my unborn boy,
Who danced within my womb for joy.

Fresh joys the Virgin then possess,
Such which hymn only could express.
My soul God's praises shall recite,
And in my Saviour take delight,
Who on His handmaid deigns to rest,
And future times shall call me Blest.

The Mighty works for me great things,
His Holy Name my spirit sings;
His mercy on each age descends,
Which Him with filial fear attends.
His sovereign Arm brings down the proud,
And dissipates their boastings loud.

He sinks to nought the worldly great,
Exalts the humble to their seat:
The hungry with good things sustains,
And sends the rich away with empty veins;
He to good Abraham's faithful race,
Shews to the full all promised grace.

The Virgin then to Nazareth went,
Her ecstasies in hymn to vent;
As in her womb God took repose,
O may my heart my God enclose.
In Heaven shall centre my desire,
And in perpetual hymn aspire.

ST. MARK'S DAY.

FOR your conversion, holy Mark,
  Though story leaves us in the dark,
    Yet humbly we conclude,
    When Heaven your soul subdued,
    The light celestial shined
In full meridian splendour on your mind.

  You by Levitical descent
  Your age on legal shadows spent.
    Priests long to shadows train'd,
    Pure, solid truth disdain'd,
    And when they faith profess'd,
Were with convictions super-effluent bless'd.

  God His apostle Peter chose,
  Who should your heart to truth dispose;
    His ghostly net he threw,
    And up your spirit drew;
    God moved his hand, that he
From the tempestuous world should set you free.

  He, when his Master he denied,
  By Jesus was benignly eyed;
    By that Attractive dear
    Was melted into tear,
    Was taught your soul to treat
With zeal obliging, and compassion sweet.

Of all the converts which he gain'd
You moſt his tender paſſion drain'd;
   You his beloved child
   Endearingly he ſtyled,
   You he companion made,
And coadjutor, where he truth diſplay'd.

To Rome, you with your patron ſteer'd,
That Jeſus there might be revered;
   By your unwearied care
   You reap'd glad harveſt there,
   Then ſpread the truth divine
O'er all the wide Suburbicarian line.

By Roman converts you beſought,
The heavenly truths which Peter taught,
   And you from him imbibed,
   You from your heart tranſcribed;
   Your goſpel he peruſed,
And recognized the truth he had infuſed.

When Rome with Proſelytes was fill'd,
Egyptian fields remain'd untill'd,
   God there your zeal decreed,
   Should ſow ſupernal feed,
   And by your gracious toil,
You more than Nile ſoon fertiliſed the ſoil.

You all great Alexandria o'er
Made infidels God-man adore;

Your zeal no limits knew,
It o'er rude countries flew,
  Marmorica it tamed,
And out of Lybian chaos churches framed.

You, men than savage beasts more wild,
Could sweeten to a temper mild;
  No monsters Afric bred,
  No brutes which venom shed,
  No scorching heats you fear'd,
Zeal to save souls, all you sustain'd, endear'd.

Your miracles, example, zeal,
Salvific mysteries to reveal,
  O'er multitudes prevail'd,
  They all their sins bewail'd,
  Abjured cursed Satan's reign,
When in the hallow'd laver born again.

Back to your Alexandrian seat
You from your travels made retreat,
  Saints who with hymn o'erflow'd,
  For aids on you bestow'd,
  Your pastoral chair revered
Placed in the Mother-Church which there you
    rear'd.

Of all the thrones for learning famed,
Your city the precedence claim'd,
  All scientific light
  There reach'd its utmost height;

Yet when your rays they felt,
They found they in Egyptian darkneſs dwelt.

The joyful day when Jeſus roſe,
Began its luſtre to diſcloſe,
  Saints riſing God adored,
  Their riſe from ſin implored,
  And with immortal bread
Were by your bleſſing at the Altar fed.

Curſed Satan made a fierce eſſay,
To deſecrate that ſacred day,
  The Pagans he convened,
  From hell the rabble glean'd;
  Serapis up they cried,
And you, high Heaven's ambaſſador, defied.

The ſpiteful fiend above the reſt,
Who the foul idol long poſſeſs'd,
  The infidels enraged,
  And in your death engaged,
  Leſt you ſhould him expel,
And from his temple drive him back to hell.

Your body o'er the ſtreets they dragg'd,
Where every flint your muſcles jagg'd,
  Your confluential wound
  With blood bedew'd the ground,
  Till into priſon thrown,
To ſpend the night in agonizing moan.

But gracious God foft pity took,
He never His dear Saint forfook,
   He in that dolorous night
   Gave you of blifs a fight,
   That fight your fpirit cheer'd,
And all the torment you fuftain'd endear'd.

Their rage renew'd at morning dawn,
You o'er the ftreets again were drawn,
   And praying for your foes,
   Opprefs'd with numerous woes,
   You fetch'd your dying groan,
By angels wafted to your heavenly throne.

Of life the furies you deprived,
Their madnefs yet your fate furvived;
   Your corpfe to flame they doom'd,
   To afhes ftraight confumed,
   Your afhes, though difperfed,
Omnifcience counts, till to their fites reverfed.

For you, blefs'd Saint, be God adored,
Who you with gifts and graces ftored;
   May I your volume read,
   My life like you to lead,
   As of Incarnate God
You in the imitable footfteps trod.

ST. PHILIP AND ST. JAMES'S DAY.

WHEN Solomon the Temple rear'd,
   Where 'twixt the cherubs God appear'd,
  At entrance he two pillars placed,
  Which the fair porch upheld and graced,
Renown'd for their diameter and length,
Jachin and Boaz, stablishment and strength.

  Thus Jesus, when His Church He form'd,
  Which should by hell in vain be storm'd,
  Two saints for sacred pillars chose,
  Who hell's first onsets should oppose,
Philip and James, stability and might,
With zeal to raise, and keep salvific light.

  With apostolic call first bles'd,
  Philip gave pattern to the rest;
  James the first bishop they decreed,
  The Heavenly Bishop to succeed,
With force endearing Philip truth display'd,
James fix'd the Church on sure foundations laid.

  His heavenly might first Philip tried
  When to Nathaniel he was guide,
  He saw the Israelite sincere,
  To Jesus at first view adhere;
He gave to God for that great convert praise,
And in conversions vow'd to spend his days.

When Gentiles led by Jesus' fame,
To visit Him at Salem came,
To Philip they themselves address'd,
To make to Jesus their request;
His zeal for converts was illustrious grown,
That all with him their Saviour's Love might own.

When Jesus of His Father spake,
To Whom He an ascent would make,
Shew us the Father, Philip cried,
That Faith and Love may firm abide;
Great God was 'twixt the cherubs wont to shine,
Vouchsafe us of His Presence now a sign.

Our Lord replied, In seeing Me,
You my co-glorious Father see,
He with His co-eternal Son,
Is an Indivisible One;
And Godhead brighter shines in flesh enclosed,
Than when the glory on the ark reposed.

Bless'd Philip, when the gracious Dove
Rain'd down full showers of Light and Love,
In Phrygia settled his abode,
Which he with seeds immortal sow'd,
There in short time he for the realm of peace
Of converts reap'd a thousand-fold increase.

When spent with toil, by Heaven's decrees,
Hell ere aware procured his ease,

Fiends which he from their temples drave,
  Conspired to lodge him in the grave,
The Pagan ruler by their rage possess'd,
Sent the old martyr to his wish'd-for rest.

As Philip, Pagans to convert,
  Was wont his vigour to exert,
  Bless'd James, the brother of God-man,
  Of Church establish'd drew the plan
At Salem, when committed to his care,
He raised his pastoral and ideal chair.

James on the Cross saw Jesus dead,
  And made a vow to taste no bread
  Till Jesus risen he beheld,
  And when our Lord death-shades dispell'd,
To His disciple early He appear'd,
Dissolved his vow, and His sad votary cheer'd.

Bless'd Peter, by an angel freed,
  Dispatch'd a messenger with speed,
  Who should to holy James relate
  The opening of the iron gate;
He to the Mother-Church due deference taught,
And the first news was to the bishop brought.

In the first synod James alone,
  Who sat in the Archshepherd's throne,
  The last decisive vote express'd,
  In which the saints all acquiesced.

'Twas Jesus' chair, not Peter's, which then sway'd,
And Peter to bless'd James submission made.

   You happy Saint in Jesus' chair,
   Of Jesus' grace had liberal share;
   You from bless'd Jesus borrow'd light,
   And shined in an example bright,
Even envious Jews your sanctity would own,
You by the name of James the Just were known.

   You every day took up your cross,
   Esteem'd this world but dung and dross;
   From wine and flesh you still abstain'd,
   You all your appetites restrain'd;
You on mere necessaries taught to live,
And the superfluous to the poor to give.

   You lived in a quotidian fast,
   In lively prospect of your last;
   Your flock had your paternal care,
   Your business was perpetual prayer;
Your forehead and your knees were callous grown
With long prostrations at the heavenly throne.

   When at the Paschal feast your eye
   Could the whole Jewish race descry,
   You on the Temple took your stand,
   You Jesus preach'd to all the land;
Till, by a rude and hell-directed blow,
You were forced headlong to the ground below

ST. JAMES'S DAY.

Bruiſed by the fall as down you fell,
Your ſtoning was contrived by hell,
And while the flints were at you aim'd,
With Chriſt-like charity inflamed,
For ſelf and foes, with like devout effort,
You begg'd their pardon, and your own ſupport.

You, bruiſe and pain and wound all o'er,
Kneel'd, agonizing in your gore,
While a wretch, cruel in intent,
Deterr'd by Heaven to kind event,
Daſh'd out your brains, and you flew up in ſtate,
Convey'd by angels to the bliſsful gate.

Bleſs'd James and Philip on one day,
When martyr'd, met upon the way;
In ether, as they ſoar'd to bliſs,
They join'd in mutual, holy kiſs;
The bleſt received them in embraces dear,
And joy was doubled o'er the heavenly ſphere.

We double praiſes, Lord, this day,
To Thee for Thy two pillars pay,
For ſtrength the faith in Aſia gain'd,
When Philip ſaving-truth explain'd;
For James by ſaints moſt worthy judged to be
Firſt biſhop of the firſt eſtabliſh'd ſee.

In preaching Philip ſpent his might,
And little leiſure had to write;

James a divine epistle penn'd,
Both had the same salvific end.
May we, like them, Thy sacred truth embrace,
With strength of faith, and stablishment in grace.

ST. BARNABAS THE APOSTLE.

ALL who to Jesus came,
 And felt the force of that dear Name,
 The more they Jesus knew,
The more enamour'd still they grew,
 Each grace which in Him shined,
With zeal they copied in their mind.

 Each grace though they revered,
Yet some one grace was more endear'd;
 As in a sinner's breast,
The darling sin o'erpowers the rest;
 Thus in the saints we trace
Indulgence of a darling grace.

 Our Lord, benign and mild,
Was Israel's Consolation styled;
 And Joses, o'er whose soul
Loved Jesus had entire control,
 Revolved with most delight
Our Lord's consolatory might.

The Saint of temper sweet,
Wont souls endearingly to treat,
With sympathising heart,
Would gladly the supports impart,
From Jesus' Love received,
Whene'er he felt his spirit grieved.

Saints him for sweetness famed,
The Son of Consolation named;
They Barnabas decreed
The name of Joses to succeed;
And ever since by none
But that sweet name the Saint is known.

When Holy Church first rose,
To triumph o'er infernal foes,
Bless'd Barnabas for gold
His plentiful possessions sold,
And the vast sum complete
Laid down at the Apostles' feet.

Thus eased of clogs terrene,
With conscience from pollution clean,
Himself he daily spent,
Of saints the number to augment;
With holy Paul he join'd,
To God alike both co-inclined.

In missions, dangers, cares,
And sufferings, they went equal shares;

  Vaſt regions they ſurvey'd,
Foundations there of churches laid,
  With alms their wants ſupplied,
Confirm'd them, leſt they ſhould backſlide.

  From union with bleſs'd Paul,
The ſaint had apoſtolic call;
  Paul, when they Lyſtra taught,
A cure miraculouſly wrought,
  A cripple he reſtored,
And Lyſtra would have both adored.

  Both gods to Pagans ſeem'd,
Paul, Mercury they all eſteem'd;
  But Barnabas they took
For Jove, when they obſerved his look;
  In him was mixture rare,
Benign, majeſtic, graceful air.

  Soon as they gods were thought,
The Pagans ſacrifices brought;
  But both their veſtures rent,
The profanation to prevent;
  Took item from falſe zeal,
True God their Maker to reveal.

  No ſaints were better pair'd,
When truths ſalvific they declared;
  Paul with a ſacred heat
Would down the realm of Satan beat,

But Barnabas in meek
And gentle style would all bespeak.

He the foundation clear'd,
And of the Church the fabric rear'd;
This would the frame secure,
That all rude shocks it might endure,
He saving faith inspired,
This with soft Love believers fired.

Within this vale of tears
Temptations, sorrows, frailties, fears,
The faithful soul infest,
Raise agonies in human breast,
And a fierce, stormy ill
None but a Barnabas can still.

Should we the topics guess
On which he laid prevailing stress,
Yet how he them enforced,
With what sweet energy discoursed,
And troubled hearts composed,
Can never fully be disclosed.

Dear soul, he oft would cry,
While tears ran down from either eye,
Your deep afflictive moan,
By sympathy becomes my own,
I know your painful sore,
And by God's aid will you restore.

No grief can you surprise,
But comes from God, just, powerful, wise;
　　As just and wise, in vain
He ne'er inflicts a causeless pain,
　　His power controls its source,
Its progress, and confines its course.

　　God sends instructive woes,
That they for Heaven may souls dispose,
　　All aiming at our good,
When their design is understood;
　　And when a heart is broke,
Paternal pity gives the stroke.

　　That pity gives relief,
It joins a comfort with each grief;
　　You have in all distress,
To Love immense a free access;
　　That Love to cure your wound,
By promise, and by oath is bound.

　　Your strength love nicely weighs,
And load too heavy never lays;
　　All woes are short and light,
When joys eternal are in sight;
　　And when God's word you read,
You sovereign cordial never need.

　　All the co-glorious Three
In consolations sweet agree;

You God in every groan,
Comforter, Father, Saviour, own,
 O then your will refign
To that co-amiable Trine.

God-man our miferies felt,
When He on earth afflicted dwelt;
 By woes which He fuftain'd,
He pities every faint when pain'd;
 With fuch fupports as thefe,
We guefs our Saint gave fpirits eafe.

When he and Paul agreed
They from each other would recede,
 Blefs'd Barnabas took fail
For Cyprus with a profperous gale,
 There to his native clime
To confecrate his care and time.

Till now, that fertile ifle
Men could not juftly happy ftyle,
 Luft there appear'd barefaced,
Laws were promulged againft the chafte,
 'Till God employ'd the Saint,
To keep the devils in reftraint.

Among the fiends of hell,
Unclean are hardeft to expel;
 With inbred luft they fide,
And poifon in foul pleafure hide;

ST. BARNABAS.

The Saint soon clear'd the coasts,
And drave to hell reluctant ghosts.

His light we guess was spread
Beyond the isle where he was bred;
But his congenial air
Remain'd the centre of his care;
And thither he return'd,
In his birth-place to be inurn'd.

Though the foul devils fail'd,
When fiercely they the Saint assail'd;
Yet into harden'd Jews,
When truth he labour'd to infuse,
They murder'd him with stone,
Kind spite advanced him to his throne.

All praise to God above,
For our soft Saint's condoling love;
May we our passions chain,
Strive his sweet temper to obtain,
And on the Christian race
Shed like consolatory grace.

ST. JOHN BAPTIST'S DAY.

GABRIEL to Daniel, when at prayer,
Was sent Messias to declare,
And then to Heaven reflown,
Attended at the Throne,
Till seventy annual weeks ran out,
In hymn devout
He never ceased; yet in that blest employ
He could no tedium feel, but unsuccessive joy.

Again, God call'd him from on high
With evangelic news to fly;
To Zachary he appear'd,
A priest to God endear'd;
As with the fume of incense fired,
His prayer aspired,
To promise him from Heaven a sacred son,
Who the so-long-desired Messias should fore-run.

O wondrous boy! by Heaven foretold,
Of parents childless, barren, old,
Who had by dumbness seal'd
The happy news reveal'd,
Whose birth restored his father's voice,
Made saints rejoice
With dear Eliza, while with loosen'd tongue,
Blest Zachary of his babe a hymn prophetic sung.

ST. JOHN BAPTIST'S DAY.

O wondrous Child! by Heaven decreed
The world's Redeemer to precede,
   Elias to outſhine
   In gifts and grace Divine;
Of prophets chief of all mankind,
       The moſt refined!
When embryo you Incarnate God fore-ran,
And leaping in the womb, your prophecy began.

When Herod Bethlehem infants ſlew,
None 'ſcaped but Infant-God and you;
   In deſert you ſecured,
   Were in a cave immured,
Your parents by kind Heaven inſpired,
       With you retired,
They of God's law gave you ſweet early taſte,
Which to the Love Divine kept your affection
   chaſte.

The aged ſaints taught you God's Will
With reſignation to fulfil,
   Each imitable grace
   In the angelic race;
To love great God with utmoſt might,
       In God delight,
In meditation to employ your days,
In miniſtering to ſouls, and in inceſſant praiſe.

They taught on Heaven to fix your aim,
This world evanid to diſclaim,

ST. JOHN BAPTIST'S DAY.

  Your flesh subdued to keep,
   In clothes, food, pleasures, sleep,
  Devout, pure, humble, in retreat
     With God to meet,
Zeal void of dread, habitual fast and prayer,
All virtues for God-man fit entrance to prepare.

  Your habitation from a child,
  Was 'mongst the beasts, fierce, ravenous, wild,
   You them familiar made,
   They all your voice obey'd.
  What changes should by you be wrought,
     God early taught,
That you should men from brutish sins reclaim,
A labour much more hard than savage beast to tame.

  You, ere your parents bliss obtain'd,
  The height of heavenly wisdom gain'd,
   You to repentance then
   Were call'd to waken men,
  An active life God you enjoin'd,
     But yet design'd
No power to you of miracles to give,
Fore-seeing you yourself a miracle would live.

  In vest of camel's hair array'd,
  With leather girt, you entrance made,
   The humble garb you chose,
   This world's denial shews:

ST. JOHN BAPTIST'S DAY.

You locusts and wild-honey eat
   For daily meat.
The less you on external aids relied,
The more you aid Divine unrivall'd glorified.

 You God's great harbinger were sent,
 To move all sinners to repent,
  With future wrath to scare
  Hard hearts to humble prayer,
And gleams of cheerful hope to shed,
   To mix with dread;
You taught God's gracious kingdom drawing nigh,
In which none lived, but they, who to the world would die.

 You suited rules to all degrees,
 To set all consciences at ease,
  To beg of Heaven recruits,
  And bring forth heavenly fruits,
You crowds baptized in tear and wave,
   Their souls to save;
You shew'd yourself to all where'er you came,
A shining, burning light, to lighten and enflame.

 You great God-man baptized, and eyed
 The Empyreum opening wide,
  Saw the supernal quire
  In lofty hymn conspire;

The heavenly Dove His Wings outſpread
O'er Jeſus' Head,
You heard a voice deſcend from bliſsful height,
This is My Son beloved, in Whom I take delight.

To Jeſus you oft witneſs gave,
The Lamb of God, Who came to ſave;
Fierce Herod, you revered,
Your warnings gladly heard;
And he from various ſins abſtain'd,
By you reſtrain'd,
Till his adulterous inceſt you reproved,
Which to fierce female ſpite his lewd adultreſs
moved.

You ſhew'd that ſaints may martyrs bleed,
For moral truths, as well as creed;
The ſword your ſoul ſet free
That glorious ſtate to ſee,
Of which you oft to liſtening Jews
Gave lively views,
You in both realms had the ſame honour'd place,
Fore-runner of God-man in bliſs as well as grace.

All praiſe to God, Whoſe tender care
The way for Jeſus to prepare,
Sent John all guilt to clear,
By penitential tear,
To raiſe of Jeſus' Love immenſe
A previous ſenſe.

All, who for sin excited were to grieve,
With open arms and hearts a Saviour would
receive.

Teach me, my God, by Thy dear Saint,
To keep my passions in restraint,
By penitential moan,
To break my heart of stone,
Thy Love will make it whole again,
And ease my pain;
Thou for Thy mansion wilt my heart endure,
When made for Thee by tear preparatory, pure.

May I, with a devotion due,
Fix on the Lamb of God my view;
That lovely, gracious sight
Will cast enamouring light,
My soul will love for Love return,
Will shine and burn.
Like John, this world I'd trample under feet,
And but for doing good, ne'er leave devout retreat.

ST. PETER'S DAY.

OUR Lord, when Simon to Him came,
To Cephas changed his name,
In His all-comprehending view,
He hell's assaults foreknew.

And of a fisher form'd a rock,
    To stand infernal shock.

To raise a realm o'er humankind,
    When, Lord, Thou hadst design'd,
Sure such a high heroic deed
    Should some great monarch need,
Whose conduct, wealth, and numerous hosts,
    Should clear the adverse coasts.

But God, to baffle human might,
    And raise to Him our sight,
The powerful, rich, wise, noble, brave,
    Was wholly pleased to waive,
He mean, unarm'd, illiterate chose,
    The scorn of all His foes.

His foes, who saw the weak repel,
    The force of world and hell,
How God in weakness power display'd,
    Power so notorious made,
Which with beams universal shined,
    Too bright to be declined.

When near the Galilean Lake
    Our Lord truth heavenly spake,
That He from crowd might sit remote,
    He enter'd Simon's boat,
And soon as it was launch'd in wave,
    From thence instructions gave.

Our Lord to miracle inclined,
    To fix each doubting mind,
Bade Simon to caſt down his net,
    Who nought all night could get;
He and his brother ſtood amazed,
    When on the draught they gazed.

Depart from me, Lord, Simon cried,
    Since ſinful I abide:
Ot God offended, the ſad thought,
    Deep ſelf-debaſement wrought,
He from humility took flight
    To apoſtolic height.

Our Lord to both ſpake, Follow Me,
    Of men you'll fiſhers be,
Both at His gracious Look and Voice,
    Made His ſole Will their choice,
And with ſupernal power endow'd,
    Thence fiſh'd among the crowd.

Our Lord, the future ſtate to ſhew
    His Church ſhould undergo,
Enjoin'd His votaries to embark,
    And in the diſmal dark,
The ſhip was by the billows toſt,
    In danger to be loſt.

In the fourth watch Incarnate God
    On the rude billows trod;

To meet him Simon only dared,
  But cried, by tempeſt ſcared,
Lord ſave me; Jeſus him ſuſtain'd,
  Till both the veſſel gain'd.

Our Lord, whom wind and ſea obey'd,
  The tempeſt ſoon allay'd:
Church militant, the veſſel paints,
  And Simon, all the ſaints;
In ſtorms which Church or ſouls endure,
  Our Lord will them ſecure.

To unbelievers Peter's ray
  Made truth as clear as day,
While Simon taught each faithful ſoul
  How we towards frailty roll,
To humble, yet ſupport mankind,
  God grace and weakneſs join'd.

Even Peter, though a rock ordain'd,
  Yet Simon ſtill remain'd,
The man was with apoſtle link'd,
  Yet both were ſtill diſtinct,
Curſed Satan Simon had betray'd,
  Had not loved Jeſus pray'd.

In Jeſus, Peter faith profeſs'd,
  And was by Jeſus bleſs'd;
His Church he would on Peter rear,
  No force of hell to fear,

The keys to Peter He consign'd,
    With power to Loose and Bind.

But Simon, when our Lord declared,
    The Cross for Him prepared;
From the dire Cross which him dismay'd,
    Tried Jesus to dissuade;
But Jesus, warm'd with sacred ire,
    Bad Satan straight retire.

His fall to Simon was foretold,
    When scatter'd was the fold;
But Peter vow'd he'd rather die,
    Than his dear Lord deny;
Yet Simon, ere the cock crow'd twice,
    Denied his Master thrice.

But Jesus Who sweet pity took,
    On Simon cast His look,
The cock his second crow began,
    Apostle chid the man,
Unutterably Simon grieved,
    And Peter soon retrieved.

Our Lord, when risen, He appear'd,
    And His sad votaries cheer'd;
To Peter, pain'd with broken heart,
    A visit made apart,
His mournful tears he clear'd away,
    By sweet absolving ray.

Thrice Simon's love bless'd Jesus tried,
    Since he had thrice denied;
Thrice Simon had express'd his flame,
    And Peter thence became;
Our Lord re-loved him, and decreed
    He sheep and lambs should feed.

When Jesus charge to votaries gave,
    The world to teach and save;
And then ascending, from above
    Sent down the gracious Dove,
Bless'd Peter, not supreme, but prime,
    Shared in the gifts sublime.

He then, rock Peter, persevered,
    The Church was on him rear'd;
He the first powerful sermon preach'd,
    Which various nations reach'd,
And full three thousand whom he taught,
    At but one draught he caught.

His net straight took two thousand more,
    Of souls he gain'd such store,
That in our Lord's late little fold,
    Were multitudes enroll'd,
Loved John, with Peter, bore a part,
    But Peter had the start.

He truth with wonder first assured,
    When he the cripple cured;

His voice ſtruck Ananias dead,
    And the whole Church with dread;
And at his ſhadow paſſing by,
    Diſeaſe away would fly.

He Simon, the magician, quell'd,
    And helliſh charms diſpell'd;
All quarters of the land he view'd,
    And ſouls to Heaven ſubdued;
Raiſed weak Eneas from his bed,
    And Dorcas from the dead.

By viſion God to him reveal'd
    High truths, till then conceal'd,
That Gentiles ſhould in God believe,
    The Holy Ghoſt receive;
Fulfill'd he ſaw it in event,
    When to Cornelius ſent.

He, when a priſoner doom'd to bleed,
    Was by an angel freed;
His treble love ſpread Love Divine,
    Of the co-lovely Trine;
He o'er all Abraham's numerous race
    Shower'd apoſtolic grace.

To Rome at laſt he viſit made,
    The Gentiles' guide to aid,
Both numerous flocks to Jeſus gain'd,
    To love of Jeſus train'd,

There to the crofs by Nero doom'd,
    He was to blifs affumed.

With previous fcourgings he was lafh'd,
    And as his joints they gafh'd,
He humbly to hang downwards pray'd,
    Reverfe to Jefus made;
He deem'd it honour much too high
    Upwards, like Him, to die.

His confort had her daily fhares
    In all his woes and cares;
When fhe to martyrdom was drawn,
    He faw her glory dawn,
And fweetly put his Saint in mind
    Of joys for her defign'd.

When he eclipfed, left heavenly light
    Should not continue bright,
He lodged in writings what he taught,
    To ftore devoted thought,
Which ftill fweet, powerful influence fhed,
    When with devotion read.

For Peter, God be ever praifed,
    On whom the Church was raifed,
Who ghoftly nets for finners caft,
    And drew up numbers vaft,
Who left to faints in heavenly lines,
    Of truth two wealthy mines.

The faint each day his fall review'd,
   His cell with tears bedew'd;
Like him, we daily Christ deny,
   When we His laws defy;
May we, like him, to love and tears
   Devote residuous years.

ST. JAMES THE APOSTLE.

WHEN God in flesh would be enshrined,
   He took a form the meanest of mankind,
And meanest instruments He chose
The world to conquer, and hell-powers oppose,
   The foolish to confound the wise,
The weak to humble haughty scornful eyes,
   To teach antipathy to pride,
In aid Divine, not human, to confide.

   From a mean toil, and land infame,
Bless'd Jesus fishers call'd to spread His Name,
   James, Andrew, Simon, John, all four
Inhabitants of the Tiberian shore,
   In grace all partners, as in trade,
All saw God-man's omnipotence display'd;
   When they in vain all night had wrought,
Unnumber'd shoals at Jesus' word they caught

   They, call'd by Him, their ships forsook,
Charm'd by His gracious power, and Heavenly
   Look,

As when dry bones the vale beſtrow'd,
Out the four winds, call'd by the Prophet, flow'd,
　　With vital breathings to reſtore
Skin, life, fleſh, ſinews, which they had before;
　　God-man on Jews in ſin long dead,
Thus call'd out four, enlivening truths to ſhed.

　　James and his brother John inclined
To Jeſus, left their aged ſire behind,
　　They early, if God call'd them, knew
To natural ties they were to bid adieu;
　　Yet parents had their filial prayer,
Both ſtrove for Heaven their father to prepare,
　　Their mother Salome both revered,
Who lived a ſaint, by their direction ſteer'd.

　　Though John was the beloved declared,
With him and Peter, James in favour ſhared,
　　All three, bleſs'd Jeſus with Him led,
When He raiſed Jairus' daughter from the dead.
　　All three aſcending Tabor's height,
Beheld Him ſhine in beatific light,
　　All three as deareſt friends He choſe,
Who ſhould atteſt His agonizing woes.

　　Both James and John with zeal inflamed,
By Jeſus were the Sons of Thunder named,
　　Zeal would to indignation riſe,
When they ſaw ſinners, Love immenſe deſpiſe;
　　For God they jealous rage tranſpired,
And wiſh'd by Heaven a ſtubborn village fired;

But Jesus taught, that His sweet power
Sent fire to melt mankind, but not devour.

    Their mother, Lord, pray'd that they might
Sit in Thy realm, enthroned on Left and Right.
    Ambitious love the thought inspired,
Which to be nearest Thy dear Love desired;
    Ambition was by Thee restrain'd;
The Love Divine its vigorous force retain'd;
    Both vow'd the dolorous cup to drink,
And neither, when 'twas offer'd them, would
      shrink.

    James oft would with loved John contend,
Which of their loves the other should transcend;
    God's lovers never jealous are,
When they together loves divine compare;
    They to each other yield contest,
A humble love still thinks another's best;
    Their loves in strength were equal deem'd,
John's of the two, the tenderest was esteem'd.

    Bless'd James around the Jewish line,
Disseminated Truth and Love Divine,
    While Jesus here on earth conversed,
His apostolic mission Light dispersed;
    When Jesus, re-enthroned on high,
His Spirit sent, His Presence to supply,
    James, then with wondrous gifts endued,
His labours with a treble force renew'd.

Like fire, within his bowels pent,
His arduous zeal for Jesus forced a vent;
　　He threaten'd Jews with vengeance dread,
For precious Blood of God Incarnate shed;
　　Pronounced all damn'd for boundless guilt,
Unless wash'd clean in that dear Blood they spilt;
　　To mournful penitents he taught
Grace, pardon, bliss, by Jesus' sufferings bought.

　　His miracles, endearing force,
Admired example, and Divine discourse,
　　Made numerous souls their sins deplore,
And God, Whom they had crucified, adore.
　　To truth he votaries daily gain'd,
Confounded Jews, infernal powers restrain'd,
　　Till faithless men, and fiends of night,
His life assaulted with confederate spite.

　　To king Agrippa both address'd,
They storm'd his ear, and these enraged his breast;
　　Cries and injections never ceased,
His hate of Jesus hourly they increased;
　　Bless'd James he into prison cast,
And final sentence on the guiltless pass'd;
　　And he had emptied Peter's veins,
Had not high Heaven the tyrant kept in chains.

　　As to the scaffold James was led,
The first Apostle who for Jesus bled,
　　A Pagan soldier, who the Saint
Had guarded during his severe restraint,

    And with Heaven-brighten'd eyes had seen
His patient, humble, gracious, heavenly mien,
    While in the way, fell at his feet,
With tears the martyr's pardon to entreat.

    The Saint with joy the soldier rear'd,
The penitent with Jesus' merits cheer'd,
    Gave him spiritual release,
Embraced him with a tender kiss of peace;
    He deeply all past sins bemoan'd,
Himself a Christian publicly he own'd,
    Till his last fatal doom was read,
And he, with James co-martyr'd, lost his head.

    The Saint beheld the brandish'd blade,
And in ecstatic joy his exit made,
    To think that at the scaffold he
A convert gain'd, as Jesus on the Tree;
    At parting, he renew'd his kiss,
Assuring him they both should meet in bliss;
    The soldier promised life despised,
And gasp'd for Heaven, in his own blood baptized.

    Heaven sent the convert, guardian aid,
Just at the moment when he wept and pray'd,
    His angel watch'd, away to chase
All tempters who would storm his infant grace;
    When Satan shot a fiery dart,
'Twas quench'd and blunted, ere it reach'd his
        heart.

Of martyrs' love, one minute may
Ten luſtres ſpent in penance overweigh.

Death to their ſouls full freedom gave,
Both with their guardians ſhot ethereal wave;
With angels' ſpeed they upwards dived,
All heaven with joy received them, when arrived;
James his apoſtle's throne poſſeſs'd;
Both had a martyr's radiant crown and veſt;
Heaven Jeſus hymn'd, in lofty ſtrain,
By whom ſaints triumph over death and pain.

High praiſe to God for all the woes
Bleſs'd James ſuſtain'd, ſalvation to diſcloſe,
We Thy triumphant grace adore,
For ſaints baptized in their own purple gore;
May I, like James, ſpread ſaving light,
And to the love of Jeſus ſouls invite:
With joy I death-pangs ſhall endure,
If but one ſoul I can for Heaven ſecure.

ST. BARTHOLOMEW THE APOSTLE.

THIS morn, bleſs'd Saint, our zeal devout
    May ſeem encumber'd with a doubt;
But we through cloud diſcover day,
When probabilities we weigh;

ST. BARTHOLOMEW

We juſtly gueſs, though under double name,
Nathanael is with Barthol'mew the ſame.

 Bleſs'd Philip, in Divine Record,
 Brought dear Nathanael to our Lord,
 Who ſtill by Barthol'mew is meant,
 When he to preach abroad is ſent:
Say then, bleſs'd Saint, why choſe you to be known
More by your father's name, than by your own?

 To three evangeliſts we fly,
 And they all paſs Nathanael by;
 Loved John of good Nathanael wrote,
 And Barthol'mew ſeems there forgot;
Say, holy Church, how may the doubt be ſolved,
In which your ſons have been ſo long involved?

 Of all who near to Jeſus drew,
 None was ſo happy at firſt view,
 To come to the Phyſician whole,
 Who came to ſave the ſickly ſoul,
As bleſs'd Nathanael, who a ſaint appear'd,
And was by Jeſus honour'd and endear'd.

 Bleſs'd Jeſus, whoſe all-ſeeing eye
 Could ſecrets of the heart deſcry,
 Seem'd at firſt ſight to canonize
 Nathanael with a ſweet ſurpriſe;
Behold, ſaid He, an Iſraelite indeed,
Whoſe peaceful ſoul from wilful guile is freed.

The Saint by Jesus thus renown'd,
In a humility profound,
Men's admiration to decline
Should they have known that Voice Divine,
The splendour of his sanctity to cloud,
In Barthol'mew Nathanael strove to shroud.

Though story then gives no supplies,
When this Saint's life we supervise,
Since him God-man was pleased to style,
An Israelite exempt from guile,
He lives eternally characterised,
More than if volumes had his acts comprised.

I then Nathanael's life will sing,
Before he came to Israel's King:
Great God of men requires the heart,
With which but few will freely part;
When they a heart acceptable present,
It must be broken, soft, contrite, and rent.

Nathanael with o'erflowing eyes,
And ardent penitential cries,
Which mercy for his sins besought,
His heart to God for offering brought;
It humbly panting at God's footstool lay,
And God shined on it in a gracious ray.

The gracious ray his sorrow cheer'd,
His heart he on the Altar rear'd:

And in the temple, as bright flame,
From Heaven upon the victim came:
Thus Love Divine set Barthol'mew on fire,
And made him fume towards Heaven in warm
   desire.

  His phylacteries to recite,
  With fervent zeal, was his delight;
  There to love God we are enjoin'd
  With all the heart, soul, strength, and mind.
Command for love, he thought God well might
   spare,
None who God truly know, can love forbear.

  Such love, such heart, bless'd Jesus knew
  Lodged in this evangelic Jew;
  The force he of the promised seed
  Had felt, in Jesus pre-decreed;
But when he bless'd Messias had in sight,
His love aspired to a much nobler height.

  By Jesus' Love, Nathanael fired,
  In love reciprocal transpired,
  Thou art the Son of God, he cried,
  By all God's lovers glorified,
Thou art the King of Israel, and to Thee,
All, who Thy subjects are, must bow the knee.

  If such a height Nathanael gain'd
  When first by Jesus entertain'd,

Who can his elevations guess,
When daily he had free access;
But on the Cross when great God-man expired,
His love a martyr's altitude acquired.

But well he weigh'd that God disclaim'd
A sacrifice deform'd or maim'd;
With that he search'd his heart anew,
And God, who best the traitor knew,
He humbly importuned to guide his eye,
That no one sin might undiscover'd lie.

When he had full discoveries made,
And every labyrinth survey'd,
Had no known sin left unbemoan'd,
And with fresh tears had God atoned,
Tears which from pardoning Love were now
 derived,
Which, as they sweetly dropp'd, his heart revived;

His heart from sin and guile refined,
He then for holocaust design'd,
Which, while 'twas on the Altar raised,
And all with Love celestial blazed,
Himself, the priest, fell prostrate on the floor,
And thus began acceptance to implore.

O gracious God, I at Thy Throne
Devote my all, which is Thy own,

My mind Thy holy Word to heed,
And relish every truth I read;
Thought, which to meditation I'll enure,
And memory, known duties to secure.

Purified fancy, to exclude
The ills and errors which intrude,
My senses, duly to be drain'd
From filth, and from excess restrain'd;
Will, which to Thee entirely shall propend,
And passions, on my will to co-attend.

I, all I am, to Thee resign,
Thou art my God, I, Lord, am Thine,
My love with constant, filial awe,
Shall pay regard to all Thy law,
And live in languor till my bliss commence,
That it may be unchangeably intense.

'Tis all I have, that all, accept,
O may that all by Thee be kept;
In my own keeping should it stay,
'Twill tempted be to go astray.
The holocaust had no reserve of ill,
God ne'er rejects a consecrated will.

When from His grave bless'd Jesus rear'd,
To His dear Israelite appear'd,
And he, with eyes on Heaven intent,
Spectator stood of His ascent,

His love to humble, full assurance rose,
And long'd for Heaven all others to dispose.

 In story though we little read,
 Told of the Israelite indeed,
 Yet learn, that he the Indians taught,
 St. Matthew's gospel thither brought,
And left with them that evangelic code,
To guide them, whensoe'er he changed abode.

 Towards Phrygia then he journey made,
 Till at Hierapolis he stay'd,
 Nathanael there dear Philip join'd,
 Was overjoy'd his friend to find;
But both by Pagans soon were doom'd to die,
Both pleased they should to Heaven together fly.

 Bless'd Philip, welcoming his fate,
 Soon enter'd the supernal gate;
 Nathanael on the cross was laid,
 But Pagans, of God's wrath afraid
For guiltless blood they had profusely shed,
Spared him, not out of love, but present dread.

 The devils next to hell he chased,
 In Lycaonian temples placed;
 His course then to Albania steer'd,
 Where cursed idols domineer'd;
There on the cross, his love surmounting pang,
He cheer'd the saints, and his own requiem sang.

All praiſe to God for this great Saint,
Whoſe heart, of guile abhorr'd the taint;
May we by his example train'd,
Keep hearts by wilful guilt unſtain'd:
At the great day, when all their dooms ſhall hear,
None on the Right ſhall ſtand but the ſincere.

ST. MATTHEW THE APOSTLE.

THOUGH votaries, whom our Lord deſign'd
To preach ſalvation to mankind,
    Might in the world's eſteem
    But deſpicable ſeem,
Yet none was hated and infame,
Till Matthew had enroll'd his name.

Our Lord, when waiving worldly wiſe,
He call'd illiterate men to riſe
    To apoſtolic height,
    In weakneſs ſhew'd His Might;
But boundleſs mercy He diſcloſed,
When Matthew He for Heaven diſpoſed.

The Publicans deep gored the ſoul
Of every Jew, in gathering toll,
    By their curſed avarice ſway'd,
    They on their country prey'd;

The Jews themselves from them estranged,
With sinners, harlots, heathens ranged.

Such Matthew was before his call,
When set in his extorting stall,
    While Jesus passing by,
    Upon him cast His Eye;
Soon as He, Follow Me, had said,
He rose, and leaving all, obey'd.

Strange Voice! which more Divine appear'd
Than that which once dead Lazarus rear'd,
    He in the grave enclosed,
    Ne'er Jesus' call opposed,
While Matthew's masters, wealth, account,
Its force contended to surmount.

But when Almighty Love essays
A soul from ghostly death to raise,
    It in reluctant wills
    Propension sweet instils,
Its calls have a creative force,
Which is of life and love the source.

Such was the call, which at first thought
The wondrous change in Matthew wrought;
    From earth he turn'd his view,
    To wealth antarctic grew,
His Pagan masters he disclaim'd,
Stark cold before, was now inflamed.

He to the Romans paid their due,
And satisfied each injured Jew,
    Then choice sedate to shew,
    Ere he would all forego,
For friends he made a farewell treat,
Where Jesus deign'd to take His seat.

The Pharisees, who thither came,
Began our Gracious Lord to blame,
    That He with Him to sit
    Should Publicans permit;
Sure Heaven that day their tongues controll'd,
That Jesus thus might Love unfold.

Physicians needless to the whole,
Are used by the unhealthy soul.
    Sin is the foul disease,
    Wont on mankind to seize;
I sinners to repentance call,
But none can rise, who never fall.

Come sinners, who incur the hate
Of God and man, avert your fate;
    Our Jesus for your sakes,
    His Passion undertakes;
He calls, O come, He'll give you rest,
You'll live, like Matthew, ever blest.

From worldly clogs, bless'd Matthew loose,
Devoted all to sacred use,

That, Follow Me, his ear
Seem'd every day to hear,
His utmoſt zeal he ſtrove to bend,
Towards Jeſus' likeneſs, to aſcend.

His zeal firſt in Judæa reign'd,
Then Ethiopian conqueſts gain'd,
Made warlike Parthian race
The peaceful truth embrace;
Turn'd Perſians from their idol flame,
To worſhip the Triunal Name.

Whether with Pagan rage oppreſs'd,
By martyrdom he flew to reſt,
No certainties we find,
But from his will reſign'd,
We know, though he might ſcape the fire,
He lived a martyr in deſire.

His body daily down he beat,
He ſenſual turn'd to heavenly heat,
On herbs, roots, berries fed,
Of carnal ſelf in dread;
And He a martyr's death ſupplied,
By living ſtill ſelf-crucified.

When from Judæa he retired,
He wrote his book, by Heaven inſpired,
That ſaints the truth they knew
Might keep in lively view;

The Church has there celestial stores,
And still for Matthew, God adores.

When other saints him Matthew style,
In his own sight he humbly vile,
    To keep of his offence
    True penitential sense,
And boundless mercy to proclaim,
Of Publican retains the name.

What mighty turns recorded be,
When Jesus utter'd, Follow Me!
    The same He still repeats,
    Still Wisdom walks the streets,
Where'er we go, she's in our eyes,
Though few attend her gracious cries.

God by His word, priests, holy rites,
And inward movements, souls excites,
    By promise and by threat,
    By woes which them beset,
By patience, which their doom delays,
By numberless endearing rays.

God sweetly calls us every day,
Why should we then our bliss delay?
    He calls to endless light,
    Why should we love the night?
Should we one call but duly heed,
It would to joys eternal lead.

How God's converting calls conspire
With our free-wills? fond men inquire;
    By taste, we know their force
    Much more than by discourse;
Each call to beatific sight,
Conveys a corresponding might.

Let Pagans then our Saint upbraid,
That he a folly rash betray'd,
    That moment to forsake
    His all, as Jesus spake,
Ah! had they heard that heavenly Voice,
They would have made like heavenly choice.

All praise to God for Matthew's care,
Truth evangelic to declare;
    When on his sacred book,
    I fix my heedful look,
By Jesus' copy, which he drew,
May I my faded soul renew.

Praise, Lord, to Thee, for Matthew's call,
At which he left his wealthy all;
    At Thy next call may I
    Myself and world deny;
Thou, Lord, even now art calling me,
I'll now leave all, and follow Thee.

SAINT MICHAEL AND ALL ANGELS.

BLESS'D angels, whether you on high
    Adore the great Tri-unity,
  Or here on saints below
  Your guardian cares bestow;
We keep this day, to take review
Of all the blessings we receive by you.

  Your stations in the heavenly sphere,
  Your spirits from dull matter clear,
    Your beatific sight,
    Your intellectuals bright,
  Your wills to central God inclined,
Your love from mutability refined;

  Your zeal devout, which never tires,
  Your concerts on celestial lyres,
    Your conversations sweet,
    When you each other greet;
  Your hymns to glorify God's Name,
Which while you spend them, re-enforce your
    flame.

  Your glorious conquests o'er damn'd ghosts,
  Who durst defy your loyal hosts,
    Rays supplemental gain'd,
    When you the rebels chain'd,

ALL ANGELS.

With all that God to you imparts,
We now congratulate with joyful hearts.

With grateful reverence we own
Your love to God Incarnate shewn,
    You to the Virgin bless'd,
    The wondrous news express'd,
You bright'ning Bethlehemitic plains,
Proclaim'd His birth in hymn to humble swains.

You in the waste to Him appear'd,
You Him, when agonizing, cheer'd;
    You worship to Him paid;
    He in your arms was stay'd;
Twelve legions on the heavenly line,
Drew up to aid Him, had He made the sign.

You kept the grave where He reposed,
His glorious Rising you disclosed;
    You to the mountain went,
    Attending His Ascent,
You shall the trump to judgment sound,
And with obsequious wings the Judge surround.

You on the heirs of Heaven attend,
To comfort, counsel, warn, defend,
    You in their infant age,
    To tender them engage,
You quicken saints who grow remiss,
And you at death transport their souls to bliss.

You Abraham of a son assured,
You Lot from Sodom's flames secured,
   You bless'd Elijah fed,
   You circle a saint's bed,
To work our bliss, to guard from woe,
You the expanse pass hourly to and fro.

You in the furnace cool'd the saints,
You kept fierce lions in restraints;
   You Peter freed when chain'd,
   You Paul in storm sustain'd,
You God's high Will in dreams detect,
You pious souls to faithful guides direct.

You in God's house trisagions[1] sing,
You veil your rays with awful wing,
   Our temples you frequent,
   Devotion to foment,
God's boundless wisdom there to hear,
Mysterious truths to learn and to revere.

Your piercing eyes inspect our ways,
You sing for our conversion praise,
   You, all the saints you meet,
   Like fellow-servants treat,
At the great day, of all the just
You shall collect the dissipated dust.

The great usurper in the skies,
The murderer, the source of lies,

---

[1] *Trisagions*, a hymn in the Eastern Liturgy.

With all his legions dire,
   Which in our bane confpire,
 By force, injection, fnare or wile,
Souls to o'erpower, delude, pollute, beguile;

Would foon the Church in pieces rend,
 Did not you angels it befriend;
   You watchers ready ftand,
   To check the hellifh band,
 You their outrageous fpite confine,
To bounds permitted by the Will Divine.

In dragon's fhape, when Satan raved,
 And with his legions Michael braved,
   Seven-headed, and ten-horn'd,
   With glaring crowns adorn'd;
 Bright Michael's troops upon them fell,
And fpurn'd the monfter with his crew to hell.

You execute juft God's decrees,
 When He obdurate finners fees;
   You low proud Herod laid,
   Till worms upon him prey'd;
 You down the hoft Affyrian mow'd,
And Judah's plains with their dead foes beftrow'd.

Great God! for aid, and for defence,
 Which angels in our need difpenfe,
   For bleffings never known,
   Innumerable grown,

Our hymn we to Thy Altar bring,
O had we angels' tongues, Thy praiſe to ſing!

Bleſs'd Jeſus! 'tis Thy Will that we
In duty ſhould like angels be;
   They always Thee behold,
   They ne'er in hymn grow cold;
They all Thy attributes admire,
Their loves towards an infinity aſpire.

They live in an immenſe delight,
At Thy command take ſpeedy flight;
   O may we grace derive
   From Thee, my God, to ſtrive,
That we ſincere, like angels may
Contemplate, hymn, admire, love, joy, obey.

You moſt my love, bleſs'd ſpirits, gain,
By your adoring the Lamb ſlain;
   Dear Jeſus' dolorous ſmart
   Lies ever next my heart;
When to your conſort I aſcend,
On Jeſus' Love, eternity I'll ſpend.

The Lamb for you ne'er ſhed His Gore;
Yet the Lamb ſlain you all adore,
   Rapt with a juſt eſteem
   Of that endearing theme,
Our indevotion you upbraid,
Who mind ſo little ſuch a ranſom paid.

You sons of God, like us, are styled,
We rise above the rank of child,
   Great Godhead condescends
   To call the faithful, friends!
More love from us to God is due,
Since we are more immensely loved than you.

   Guardian, when chill my love shall grow,
   Up to fresh flame the embers blow;
      Chide warmly my neglect,
      And your own love traject;
   Or rather sing of the Lamb slain,
And love, though dying, will revive again.

ST. LUKE THE EVANGELIST.

FAIR Antioch, the rich, the great,
   Of learning the imperial seat,
      You readily inclined
      To light, which on you shined,
It soon shot up to a meridian flame,
You first baptized it with a Christian name.

   To keep your souls on truth intent,
   Saints of first magnitude were sent,
      When Barnabas and Saul
      Renew'd your heavenly call;

Luke rapt at Jesus' Love, who came to save,
Himself a holocaust to Jesus gave.

    Luke, superfluently fired,
    Straight from all worldly cares retired,
      To holy Paul adhered,
      Grew daily more endear'd;
He his new-birth to that apostle owed,
And filial love to his converter show'd.

    Luke in your academy train'd,
    A mighty stock of learning gain'd;
      Yet by his genius led,
      He chiefly Physic read;
He that one science as his business plied,
And all the rest as his diversions eyed.

    Oft have I heard injurious fame,
    For unbelief physicians blame;
      But they, of all mankind,
      If their own views they mind,
Meet, like bless'd Luke, such confluential woes,
As natively for serious thought dispose.

    Luke, who disease was wont to trace,
    Through hospitals of human race,
      Oft heard sad wretches cry,
      Yet could no help apply,
His art, he knew conjecture, at the best,
And with some ills no medicine could contest.

THE EVANGELIST.

Oft pierced with agonizing groan,
He studied topics to ease moan;
   Yet found them all in vain
   To quell insulting pain;
Men must, he thought, tyrannic fate endure,
Or by self-murder strive to work their cure.

Self-murder seem'd the readiest way,
But should there come a judgment-day,
   'Twere then no ease to die,
   'Twould dangerous be to try;
Thus Pagans rolling on a dolorous bed,
Felt Life a torment, and yet Death a dread.

Paul, fill'd with Wisdom from on high,
Which could the very thoughts descry,
   With such sweet timely force,
   Attemper'd his discourse,
That he, his catechumen to persuade,
His own experience, his conviction made.

You, son, said he, by visits know
The ills your patients undergo;
   With them you sympathise,
   When nought you can advise;
When a distemper baffles all your skill,
You never traced the fountain of the ill.

Then he began from man's pure state,
His deviation to relate,

ST. LUKE

  How soon as Adam fell,
  Cursed sin with death and hell,
O'erwhelm'd lapsed man with coetaneous rage,
And ever since to plague him co-engage.

  How Filial God came from His Throne,
  Paternal Godhead to atone,
   How He for sinners bled,
   Hung crucified and dead,
How rose again, how back to Heaven He flew,
Sin, death, and hell, on purpose to subdue.

  How misery, disease, and pain,
  The dire effects of sin remain,
   How, when for sin we grieve,
   Full pardon we receive
For Jesus' sake, how when we Jesus please,
He sweetens all our misery, pain, disease.

  Bless'd Jesus came to make us whole,
  He's the Physician of the soul,
   He cures a wounded heart,
   Beyond all human art,
And when He sweetly has their grief suppress'd,
Translates His patients to eternal rest.

  That Great Physician, Luke revered,
  Attently the Apostle heard,
   He in his heart enroll'd
   Each syllable He told;

Oft begg'd He that dear ſtory would repeat,
His evangelic volume to complete.

    When Luke that Bleſs'd Phyſician knew,
    Hippocrates away he threw,
        He learn'd ſick ſouls to ſave,
        He ghoſtly phyſic gave;
And joy'd when he one ſoul recover'd, more
Than in a thouſand ſick he cured before.

    In danger, trouble, priſon, toil,
    Luke never would from Paul recoil,
        He, loved phyſician ſtyled,
        Through regions vaſt and wild,
As fellow-labourer, ſpent with him his days,
And in the Goſpel has immortal praiſe.

    He prayed for Paul, when kneeling down
    To loſe his head and gain a crown;
        He ſaw his chariot fly,
        Up to his throne on high,
Which made through the expanſe a wake more
        bright,
Than that Elias left along his flight.

    Since that, bleſs'd Saint, how long, and where,
    You ſpent your charitable care,
        Whether you martyr fell,
        No certain ſtories tell;
Yet this we know, though none your acts atteſt,
Your zeal for ſaving ſouls could never reſt.

The force of that unwearied zeal
The saints still in your gospel feel;
   There Jesus' wonders stand,
   Recorded by your hand;
From that original all souls devout
Have ever since their Saviour copied out.

Next, to the life you strove to paint
Your apostolic martyr'd saint,
   And to all future view
   The Church in landscape drew,
How when the Heavenly Dove His effluence shed,
In a short time the Light celestial spread.

Though you your sacred books design'd
For all who things supernal mind,
   Yet one above the rest
   Lay nearest to your breast,
Theophilus, for rare example famed,
Whom justly you most excellent have named.

Some Antiochian, rich and great,
With style of excellent, you treat,
   Theophilus implies
   One who for Heaven is wise,
Who from evanid things withdraws his love,
To fix it on its centre, God above.

Bless'd Union! where are reconciled,
The saint, and noble, great and mild,

Where rich to trace incline,
　　Benignity divine;
Wealth when an idol made, hell-flame enſures,
When ſacrifice, it heavenly bliſs procures.

All praiſe to God, Who Luke refined,
To turn phyſician of the mind,
　　To picture in true light,
　　Bleſs'd Jeſus to our ſight;
May truth medicinal, which he ſupplies,
Our ſouls reſtore, our love immortalize.

ST. SIMON AND ST. JUDE, APOSTLES.

O HOLY Church, whom we reſpect,
　As Mother of all ſouls elect,
　Even angels, who repair
　To your reſorts of prayer,
To turn your catechumens, all combine,
And learn the wiſdom of the gracious Trine.

Two Saints this feſtival are join'd,
For meditation both deſign'd;
　Such unions to our eyes,
　Some leſſons ſignalize;
What is that leſſon, bleſſed Mother, ſay,
Which ſhould employ our ſolemn day?

Gift, miracle, example, grace,
In each apoſtle, we can trace;
   You ſomething elſe intend,
   When two you recommend;
And when the Sacred Hiſtory I read,
I gueſs what you deſign your ſons ſhould heed.

Curſed heretics of old you knew,
From Pagan ſchools who poiſon drew,
   While they indulge their luſt,
   To marriage were unjuſt;
You married Jude, with Virgin Simon join,
To ſhew both ſtates may ſhare in Love Divine.

Bleſs'd Jude his conſort with him led,
Both undefiled preſerved their bed;
   Both all exceſſes fear'd,
   Each other both revered;
Celeſtial Love entirely both enflamed,
Both co-harmonious at God's glory aim'd.

No wilful ſin they could endure,
Both kept for God His temples pure;
   Both the vain world forſook,
   Both fix'd on Heaven their look,
And like the ſaints in beatific light,
Both would each other to God's praiſe excite.

With co-united hearts they pray'd,
They two a congregation made,

Assured from what God spake,
That He the third would make;
When sacred hunger seized them, they both fed,
With heavenly pleasure on Immortal Bread.

Both would to short recess consent,
To be in prayer and fasting spent;
    The oftener they withdrew,
    Still easier parting grew;
Though death awhile their union might untie,
It would indissoluble be on high.

Both joy'd in children God had sent,
Which would the quire above augment;
    The virtues they possess'd,
    They on their line impress'd,
And in short time two of their hallow'd race
Of martyrdom received the glorious grace.

Bless'd Jude in the inspired record
Is styled the brother of our Lord,
    He Jesus copied out,
    To do good went about,
O'er the Judæan and Samarian lands,
O'er Syrian, Lybian, and Arabian sands.

His consort to his side adhered,
No danger, hardship, trouble fear'd,
    They to each other paid
    Sweet mutual comfort, aid,

She as a common, tender nurſe, relieved
All who were ſick, pain'd, naked, hungry, grieved.

  To Perſia Jude at laſt removed,
  Their rites idolatrous reproved,
    Till they his death decreed,
    For Jeſus glad to bleed,
And if his deareſt conſort him ſurvived,
She joy'd that he at bliſs was firſt arrived.

  Since, then, the apoſtolic ſtate
  Suits with a matrimonial mate,
    Why ſhould we prieſts decry,
    Engaged in ſacred tie,
In innocence 'twas bleſs'd, by none reviled,
But thoſe who with foul luſt, chaſte love defiled.

  Good Simon honour'd that dear pair,
  Knew ſuch examples were but rare,
    Saw few of womankind
    From vanity refined:
He fear'd the avocations of a wife,
And ſacrificed to God a Virgin life.

  He ſtill the angels kept in mind,
  To their ſimilitude inclined,
    Whene'er they of the fair
    Aſſumed the guardian care,
They with no ſenſual tendencies were fired,
And Simon to like purity aſpired.

The angels who this earth frequent,
Are still on God above intent,
   Their Heaven they cannot miss,
   God's pleasure is their bliss;
mon, led by illuminations bright,
ay'd more for will resign'd than blissful sight.

His angel for his friend he chose,
Who should for God his friend dispose,
   In saints their nuptial knots
   Are soil'd with venial spots,
)r were that passion, like angelic Love,
ints married here, re-marry would above.

The angels who no offspring have,
Delight in every soul they save,
   And with harmonious voice
   Their brethren co-rejoice:
efs'd Simon's children were the souls he gain'd,
)r whom he guardian tenderness retain'd.

The angels freed from earthly weights,
No clog their speed to Heaven abates,
   Simon with treatment rude
   His body had subdued,
hat he his flesh might immaterialize,
nd it to Heaven might unobstructed rise.

No worldly cares the angels know,
On God they all their powers bestow,

They love, sing hymns, obey,
Thus spend eternal day;
And Simon from usurping passions clear,
Loved, hymn'd, obey'd, alacrious and sincere.

The angels sent from God on high,
Unwearied o'er all regions fly,
    Simon no toil declined,
    For mission when design'd,
To savage Africans he truth declared,
With holy Jude in Persian conquest shared.

From thence he took remoter flight,
Disseminating heavenly Light,
    Till he from martyr's fate,
    Rose to his Throne of State;
And various lands lay to his relics claim,
Beyond rich mummies all embalm his name.

Seven lamps were by two branches fill'd
With oil which from them both distill'd,
    The apostolic two
    Thus shed celestial dew;
They lamps, which in their churches shined, supplied,
That saving truth should ever bright abide.

Jude wondering why our Lord His ray
Should not to all the world display,
    Bless'd Jesus waived the thought,
    And Love celestial taught,

That Love would into glad obedience melt,
And God Triune in every lover dwelt.

   From the same Source of Love immense
   Bless'd Simon drew a love intense,
      He justly Zealot named
      With love more vigorous flamed,
Such as bless'd Jesus in God's House devour'd,
When He profaners with His whip o'erpower'd.

   For Jesus, Jude true zeal express'd,
   Which made him heretics detest;
      But a compassion sweet
      Attemper'd still his heat,
He pitied all whom in the fire he saw,
And out with gentle hand would sinners draw.

   Bless'd Simon's indignation rose
   To see vile mortals God oppose,
      To jealousy propense,
      At every bold offence,
The name of Jealous, God Himself assumed,
And Simon's love with hallow'd anger fumed.

   With love his sacred writings Jude
   Took care to preface and conclude;
      He Jesus' Love adored,
      Which had fall'n man restored,
He to that Love himself and saints resign'd
In which God overflow'd to lost mankind.

Simon, when Jesus' Love he weigh'd,
His sacred anger was allay'd,
  His heart for sinners bled,
  Soft tears for them he shed,
When he in penitential tears was drench'd,
His indignation was that moment quench'd.

On the same day both breathed their last,
To Heaven they with their angels past,
  They, crown'd with treble rays,
  Began high songs of praise;
The saint, apostle, martyr, in both shined,
Each title had peculiar joys assign'd.

We treble praise, Lord, sing below,
For joys which those bright saints o'erflow;
  May we, like that bless'd two,
  Give Thee all honour due,
Though martyr and apostle are too high,
O may we learn like saints to live and die.

ALL SAINTS DAY.

YE Spirits ever-bless'd,
  Of joys supernal now possess'd,
  To whatsoe'er degree
  Of bliss you elevated be,

ALL SAINTS DAY.

    Whether you there display
 A lunar, solar, starry ray,
You from the saints who died this Vigil know,
We now begin your festival below.

    Whether you have your post
 In splendid vests among the host,
    Which milky steeds bestrides,
 And whom the Word Eternal guides,
    Or you the train compose
 Which join the Lamb where'er He goes,
Or in His blood have wash'd your mantles white,
Or in your fronts are seal'd with glories bright;

    Whether, since life's sweet close,
 In Abraham's bosom you repose,
    In the third Heaven remain,
 Or happy Paradise regain,
    In outward court abide,
 Or in the temple-walls reside,
Or near the Throne enjoy the blissful sight,
Or in the quire with seraphims unite;

    This day all God's first-born,
 With their assembly must adorn,
    All Jesus' heavenly fold,
 In register of life enroll'd,
    All spirits of the just,
 Who have shook off their mortal dust,
Triumphant Church with militant must join,
To make an offering at the Throne Divine.

ALL SAINTS DAY.

  You blessed saints on high
Have always Jesus in your eye,
  You see His Love to those
Who His unbounded Love oppose,
  You with a zeal devout
Strive that pure Love to copy out,
And you no sooner take to Heaven your flight,
But charity attains perfection's height.

  You in the happy sphere
Cannot forget this vale of tear,
  You know the conflicts well
We have with flesh, the world and hell,
  You safe the gulf have shot,
Eternal glory is your lot,
You on the dangers think, yourselves have felt,
And for our state with dear compassion melt.

  Bless'd souls, with fervour strong,
Under the Altar cry, How long!
  And if you never cease,
When in the realm of love and peace,
  God's vengeance to implore
On tyrants drunk with martyrs' gore,
Much rather you for faithful brethren pray,
Since charity with you has sovereign sway.

  Though in your bounded sphere
You cannot single votaries hear,
  And we in no distress
To single saints make our address;

ALL SAINTS DAY.

    Yet if, like you, we heed
  The saints' communion in our creed,
We of each others' state have general view,
You pray for us, and we give thanks for you.

    To your assistance, all
  The ministerial angels call,
    That they may ready stand,
  Each with his censer in his hand,
    Search heavenly spheres around,
  Till the gold vials all are found;
Them and your censers fill till they o'erflow
With your sweet, odorous prayers, for us below.

    Your love we to repay,
  Will for your consummation pray,
    For hastening the last doom,
  That you your flesh may reassume,
    For which you groanings have,
  Till it gets freedom from the grave,
That death may vanquish'd lie beneath your feet,
And bliss in Christ-like bodies be complete.

    In praise, as well as prayer,
  We all desire with you to share;
    Your joys in blissful light
  To everlasting hymn excite;
    From you we borrow fire,
  And to your pitch of hymn aspire;
For single songs since you're too numerous grown,
We bring our universal to the throne.

ALL SAINTS DAY.

  The God of Love be praised
For all the saints to glory raised;
  For patriarchs, who mankind
From their congenial dross refined;
  For prophets, who of old
Glad tidings to the world foretold;
For bless'd apostles, who convey'd the sound
Of saving-truth to the terraqueous bound.

  For all, who wealth profuse
Employ'd on charitable use;
  For saints' firm faith and hope,
Their courage with hell powers to cope;
  Their patience, will resign'd,
Their ardent love, and heavenly mind,
Their temper humble, sweet, benign, and mild,
For all characteristics of God's child.

  For all, who virgins died,
And sensual appetites denied;
  For martyrs, who at stake
Devoted lives for Jesus' sake;
  For confessors, who stood
Heaven's candidates to shed their blood;
For holy pastors, whose unwearied aim
Was souls from sin and error to reclaim.

  For every gift and grace
Of the Christ-imitating race,
  Their writings or discourse,
Their gracious wonder-working force,

ALL SAINTS DAY.

Their toils, griefs, various needs,
In sowing evangelic seeds,
Their prayers, example, and intrepid zeal,
And horrid tortures on the rack and wheel.

For these, and all their store
Of virtues, Lord, we Thee adore;
To Thee is glory due,
From Thee they ghostly vigour drew,
They on this mortal stage
Lived blessings to all future age:
O while their bright ideas we revive,
May we to emulate their virtues strive.

Bless'd spirits, you and we
Make one celestial family;
One Father we revere,
To one Fraternal Love adhere,
You are in happy state,
Our bliss is only inchoate:
O may we strangers here, this world repel,
And with our heavenly brethren chiefly dwell.

Of all the places here
None pictures the celestial sphere
More than God's House of Prayer,
When faithful souls sing praises there;
When Heaven and earth conspire
In one harmonious hymning quire:
O may we, free from wilful, sensual taints,
Live in communion with supernal saints.

When souls to you take wing,
You in a hymn their welcome sing;
 And we, in humble lays,
Congratulate your heavenly rays,
 One sacred hymn, like you,
We here incessantly renew,
And all our powers to utmost vigour strain,
To sing the Lamb of God, for sinners slain.

 Should Heav'n its doors unfold,
I then, like John, might bliss behold,
 Where saints on thrones sit down,
In Christ-like robe, and radiant crown,
 High favours, never known
To angels, but to saints alone;
Even angels, on throned, robed, crown'd saints
  attend,
And ne'er to joys which Jesus bought, ascend.

 Saints there new anthems sing,
Drink at the pure, immortal Spring,
 Make their approaches free
To the life-giving, loaded Tree;
 They crop, unstinted shares
In the twelve pleasant fruits it bears;
In all-sufficient God they acquiesce,
They cannot wish for more, or sink to less.

 O would some happy friend
A harp celestial to me lend,

To the harmonious ſtring,
Like you, bleſs'd ſaints, I'd ſtrive to ſing,
But as I muſt deſpair
To reach on earth your heavenly air,
O I ſhall languiſh till with you above,
I at your height ſhall harp, ſing, joy and love.

HOLY BAPTISM.

BLESS'D hour! when I was born again,
And cleanſed from either guilt or ſtain;
I then, adorn'd with Chriſt's dear Name,
To Chriſt-like bliſs had Chriſt-like claim;
Myſelf in the baptiſmal wave
A holocauſt to God I gave.

The Heaven-born Love which me then fired
Should have to native Heaven aſpired,
But woe is me my pondus turn'd,
And with ſtrange fire my offering burn'd,
A ſenſual miſt eclipſed my mind,
My will from God to ſin declined.

I when at font a new-born child,
Great God, my God, my Father ſtyled;
But ſoon as filial love and dread
From my degenerate ſoul were fled,
I felt my ſins' companion, ſhame,
I durſt not uſe that gracious name:

While shame yet in my soul remain'd,
Tears soon might have my steps regain'd;
Shame for preservative decreed,
That Christians might from filth be freed,
Hell is of souls but half possess'd,
While shame lurks in the sinner's breast.

But when my spirit, shame erased,
And harden'd was to sin barefaced,
'Tis from that moment I must date
My provocation of God's hate;
I conscience damp'd, my heart grew stone,
And Satan claim'd me for his own.

My vow of duty which I made,
I to God's adversary paid,
And a vile slavery endured,
To hell, world, lust, which I abjured;
Renouncing joys of heavenly bliss,
For torments in the dark abyss.

An indeliberate thought arose
Of death and everlasting woes,
Can I at Judgment day appear,
And, "Go, ye cursed," fearless hear?
I fain would have the thought suppress'd,
But still it stirr'd, and gave no rest.

Since pure Philanthropy Divine
Did not to duty me incline,

It pleaſed God horrors to inſtil,
Which ſhould deter my ſoul from ill;
Yet from ſoft Love thoſe terrors came,
At once to frighten and enflame.

From holy fear, love filial grew,
Made me baptiſmal vow renew:
Let Heaven and earth my vow atteſt,
And hymn God's Love which me thus bleſs'd;
Lord, keep alive my Chriſtian flame,
With Chriſt-like love, and Chriſt-like aim.

CONFIRMATION.

UNCTION, the Chriſtian name implies,
In that, a Chriſtian's ſafety lies:
The Holy Ghoſt on Jeſus' Head
Unmeaſurable graces ſhed;
His Unction's influential force
Of all His actions ſteer'd the courſe.

Chriſtians, who Chriſt's anointed are,
In His celeſtial Unction ſhare;
The Spirit templing in their hearts,
His all-ſufficient aid imparts,
The Chriſtian feels no wants, no fears,
By Unction, who to Chriſt adheres.

Persons and things, to God applied,
Were by anointing sanctified;
To turn them to a worldly use
Was sacrilegious abuse.
Christians, when they to sin decline,
Lose Unction, and their name divine.

When Pagan tyrants sceptres sway'd,
The Christian name a crime was made;
But Christians gloried in that style,
They heard the infidels revile;
Christians, in tortures' dire effort,
Felt from their name strong sweet support.

As odorous ointment pour'd on sores
Diffuses kindly through the pores,
Enlivens, supples, heals, and cheers,
By gentle force the cure endears;
The Christians thus their Unction find
Cures all diseases of the mind.

O may I, with a faith unfeign'd,
Preserve my Christian name unstain'd!
To copy Christ, O may I strive,
From Whom I that dear name derive!
And die, when death shall me arrest,
A Christian with Christ's Unction blest.

THE EUCHARIST.

JESU, I in Thy Gospel read
   That ere Thou didst for sinners bleed,
Thou didst the Eucharist ordain,
                Souls to sustain.

From the bless'd Table Thou didst go
To Thy strong agonizing woe,
   Thence humble, meek, resign'd, sedate,
                Thy death await.

Thy soul Thou at Thy dolorous end
Didst to Paternal God commend,
And of pure Love to Thy great Sire,
                Martyr expire.

Adoring Him with filial dread,
Thou on the Cross didst bow Thy Head,
Didst die, a Victim to fulfil
                His gracious Will.

Saints whom death threaten'd to invade,
Thy Altar still their refuge made,
Humbly assured they best could there
                For death prepare

Thy death was pictured in that rite,
Thy dolours there were in their sight,

Dolours which all who did behold
                With tears condoled.

Thee they not only pictured saw,
But thence were virtue wont to draw,
Virtue which cured all ills,
                And gain'd their wills.

Not only virtue they possess'd,
They with Thy Flesh and Blood were bless'd,
They Food in that mysterious treat
                Immortal eat.

Immortal Food they felt excite
A super-human Christ-like might;
Like Thee to die in love enflamed,
                They chiefly aim'd.

They of dire torture had no dread,
By the Viaticum when fed;
They to that Heavenly Food inured,
                The Cross endured.

The Source of Life was in their breast,
By death they could not be distress'd;
Death gave them of their Saviour dear
                The vision clear.

Death both illumined and refined
By that Inflammative the mind,
Love watch its most exalted height
                At Jesus' sight.

THE EUCHARIST.

Bless'd age, when saints were daily fed
With Jesus their life-giving Bread,
Which gave them vigour strong and sweet,
    Grim death to meet.

Souls now stand trembling at death's sight,
We want true Eucharistic might,
Of Heavenly Food we them deprive,
    Scarce half alive.

The prophet's cakes twice twenty days
Secured his vigour from decays,
Twice twenty years God manna rain'd,
    Which Jews sustain'd.

Nor cakes nor manna them sufficed,
Their hunger them again surprised;
But souls who Food Immortal taste
    Shall never waste.

After an abstinence severe,
Jonathan from his pointed spear
Suck'd honey drops, and his eyesight
    Grew quick and bright.

When saints, of all their sins released,
On Jesus mystically feast,
They relish with immense delight
    Love infinite.

Jesu, when death approach shall make,
May I of Thy dear Self partake,

That with a will refign'd I may
    Thy call obey.

May I like Thee my death-pangs bear,
Refting on God's paternal care,
Spreading my wings to take my flight
    To blifsful fight.

May I, like Thee, the world defpife,
And languifh till to Thee I rife;
In hymning Jefus, O may I
    To Jefus fly!

ABSOLUTION.

THERE is a vale of tears which mountains
  bound,
And from terreftrial profpect wall it round,
Where only Heaven is open to the fight,
Where happy fouls to blifs commence their flight;
There in a land, to the loofe world unknown,
The awful houfe of mourning ftands alone;
Phylthreno, angel of repentance ftyled,
Of afpect gracious, and of language mild,
Stands at the gates, and with obliging air,
Opens to all who to the place repair;
Blefs'd Jefus thither guides returning ftrays,
And thither his new convert, John conveys:

Phylthreno, who the loved difciple eyed,
And his Hymnotheo penfive by his fide,
Into a charitable tranfport breaks,
His welcome in a hallelujah fpeaks;
Down in his foft embrace the youth he takes,
Who ftraight into the houfe his entrance makes,
While John to his Ephefian flock re-flies,
For all fpiritual needs to bring fupplies.

 The building was quadrangular, and plain
And humble, like the fouls which there remain,
It folemn yet moft uniform appear'd,
The pile was all of blackeft marble rear'd,
Which fhed inceffant tears at every pore,
As if 'twould its inhabitants deplore;
'Twas cloifter-wife contrived with arches ftrong,
Its area a fabbatic journey long,
That all the mourners might apart abide,
In little cells, which the whole pile divide;
A bible, kneeling defk, and books of prayer,
The furniture in each apartment were;
Phylthreno firft into the ftorehoufe ftept,
Which for the mourners' tears receivers kept;
That for the youth, Phylacter one might choofe,
Which when retired he in his cell might ufe;
And a ftrict charge he to the guardian gave,
That he in that Hymnotheo's tears fhould fave;
For angels, who their cryftal vials fill
With tears, which from their penitents diftil,
To Heaven with their dear burdens joyful fly,

Grateful peace-offerings at the throne on high!
Phylthreno, Salvian paffing by, defcried,
A tender, wife, experienced, ghoftly guide,
Who of the vale poffefs'd the paftoral chair,
Straight he refigns Hymnotheo to his care;
Salvian his charge with benedictions meets,
The youth with lowly reverence Salvian treats:
With that Phylthreno to the gate withdrew,
While Salvian leads the youth the place to view;
He there conducts him to each vacant cell,
To fay in which he moft defired to dwell:
In this, faid he, king David was inclofed,
And his feven penitential pfalms compofed;
Jeremy made his lamentations here,
And wrote them down in overflowing tear;
This Peter chofe his lapfes to recall,
And wept at each cock-crowing for his fall;
Magdalen's tears there from her eyes diftill'd,
And her lachrymatory daily fill'd:
Thefe and all other vacant cells he fhows,
The youth the cell of mournful David chofe,
Where his fweet harp, to which his pfalms he fung,
Which the harmonious youth well fkill'd, was hung.

Each mourner there lives filent and alone,
No noife is heard but a deep figh or groan;
Some on their knees abide, fome proftrate lie,
Some various, painful, felf-revenges try;
One wrings his hands, another fmites his breaft,

Some their paſt ſins implacably deteſt;
Some death and hell contemplate, to raiſe fear,
Others with hopes of Heaven their ſpirits cheer;
Some at the thoughts of the laſt judgment quake,
Backſlidings make the hearts of others ache;
Their troubled ſpirits ſome by weeping eaſe,
The pangs of ghoſtly birth on others ſeize;
This bluſhes when his eyes he heavenward rears,
In that ſhame and confuſion domineers;
This ſpirit's wounded, and that heart is broke,
All with ſtrong cries God's tenderneſs invoke;
There evil ſpirits at a diſtance ſtand,
Kept from the cells by God's propitious hand;
Should they the penitents' confeſſions hear,
Where all the ſecrets of their hearts appear,
Temptations they would form, ſize, ſuit, adulce,
Too ſtrong for man to conquer or repulſe.

    A garden in the arches lay encloſed,
Which at firſt view for ſerious thought diſpoſed;
Sepulchral cypreſs, laurel, pine, and bays,
Yew, and all trees, whoſe verdure ne'er decays,
Are planted in long rows where mourners walk,
And of their inward griefs condoling talk;
While others into grots obſcure retire,
And, unobſerved, to Heaven in ſighs aſpire;
Tall weeping trees in every quarter ſtand,
And water with continual tears the land;
Such as in torrid iſlands men deſcry,   [ſupply:
Whoſe dropping boughs the want of ſhowers

Arbours are there of close and solemn shade,
For recollection and retirement made;
There solitary sparrows sit alone,
Complaining pelicans themselves bemoan;
Soft doves vent their compassionating note,
All creatures there are heard which grief pro-
    mote;
No beauteous flowers there spring, no pleasant
    fruits,
Rue, carduus, wormwood, various bitter roots,
And every herb unpalatable grows,
Wont the old paschal salad to compose;
Their vests are hair or sackcloth, dust their bed,
Wash'd with the overflowing tears they shed;
Their drink from ever-dropping trees is rain'd,
Like Marah's streams, of which the tribes com-
    plain'd;
And as with bitter draughts they quench their
    thirst,
Into the cup their briny torrents burst;
The coarsest meal for daily bread they use,
Moisten'd with tears their mournful eyes infuse;
The heavenly sun there daily wont to rise,
Cheers with his healing wings the mourners' eyes,
From his propitious throne each moment sheds
Encouraging mild rays upon their heads;
In Adam's sons the Son of God delights,
And mournful sinners to His Arms invites;
His love is wont immensely to rejoice,
Whene'er a humble convert hears His Voice;

His precious Blood for sinful man He lost,
And loves the purchase for the Price it cost.

   Salvian, the youth then to the wardrobe guides,
Where hair and sackcloth vests hung round the
      sides;
The youth a girdle chose and coat of hair,
Such as great penitents are wont to wear;
Having put on his penitential weeds,
Salvian the youth next to the chapel leads.

   There stands just in the middle of the square,
Circled with cedar trees, a House of Prayer;
Architects there strove their best skill to show,
'Tis built of polish'd marble, white as snow;
Mourners who in their cells affect black night,
Appear at church as candidates of light:
It is a pile magnificent and large,
Of which collegiate pastors have the charge;
Their prelate Salvian over them presides,
To penitents they are sagacious guides;
Confessions private at their Chairs are made,
Which they to souls command not, but persuade,
In scandals chiefly, or distress of mind,
But all are to confess to God enjoin'd;
The mourners, who the penitent espied,
An universal miserere cried;
And soon as he far off the temple view'd
His self-humiliations he renew'd;
His feet unworthy he esteem'd to tread

The very path which to God's presence led;
And at a distance, in the outward court,
His humble spirit spent its first effort;
Jacob, who heard God speak, and angels saw,
Felt not at Bethel a more solemn awe,
With downcast looks ashamed to be erect,
When on offended Heaven his thoughts reflect;
With tears, and sighs, and groans, together mix'd,
Sent from a breaking heart by guilt transfix'd;
He smiting oft his self-upbraiding breast,
His guilt he like the publican confest;
All-gracious God, for lovely Jesus' sake,
On vile Hymnotheo tenderest pity take:
The prayer was short, but of eternal force,
And took to Heaven an instantaneous course.

In the great portico there night and day
A lazaret of wounded spirits lay;
None daring to approach the sacred door,
While they the prayers of entering saints implore;
Kissing their feet, bathing themselves in tears,
A breaking heart through every look appears;
Notorious and flagitious sinners there,
With long sharp Penances their souls repair;
As the sick man lay to Bethesda nigh,
And on the pool still kept his longing eye,
Wishing that some kind hand would him befriend,
To move him when the angel should descend;
Thus they, with eyes fix'd on the holy gate,
Their ghostly angel's benediction wait;

Within the hallow'd door on either hand,
The Penitents advanced to Hearers' ſtand,
Who after a due Penance are thought fit
Their duty to re-learn from ſacred writ;
The Proſtrates near the ſacred deſk are placed,
By ſelf-humiliations more debaſed,
They in humility proficients grow,
Are raiſed the more the more themſelves they know;
Confiſtents, who by penitential moan
Are ripe for prieſtly Abſolution grown,
Above the Proſtrate ſtand, and join in prayer,
With faithful ſouls, who next the Altar are.
The Faithful who retrieve baptiſmal flame,
Re-ſeal'd for bliſs with the Triunal name;
They inward joys of Abſolution feel,
And glory in their re-imprinted ſeal:
They have ſubdued concupiſcential ſtrife;
They at the Altar eat the Bread of Life:
They Heaven foretaſte, they God their Father call,
Jeſus their Love, and fear no future fall.

THE VISITATION OF THE SICK.

'SEE, ſee, my fleſh, death with his dart,
  You and my ſpirit now muſt part:
I dolorous ſtruggles feel of vital force,
And all my powers diſpoſing for divorce.

My stomach fails, I can no more
  With fresh recruits my strength restore,
My feet begin to freeze, my flaccid nerves
Have for their craving drains no brisk reserves.

My pulse scarce beats, my heart grows chill,
  Can scarce with blood my arteries fill;
My arteries unreplenish'd starve my veins,
But little circulation now remains.

My eyes grow dim, I scarce can speak,
  Strong pangs in twain my fibres break,
Small aid my tendons to my muscles lend,
My joints grow stiff, with difficulty bend.

The channels to my heart grow dry,
  My spirits wanting due supply,
But little vigour to my brain convey,
I colder grow, my motion faints away.

My mournful friends stand all aghast,
  And think each breath will be my last,
The world an universal blank appears,
And a mere cypher all foregoing years.

My will is seal'd, and with my heir
  The poor proportionably share,
I pardon, and ask pardon of mankind,
And leave no dues unsatisfied behind:

All human succours now are flown,
  And I await my dying groan;

OF THE SICK.

My soul is parting from this earthly vale,
Into the state invisible to sail.

 I my Viaticum received,
  And that my ghostly strength retrieved;
'Tis by repentance only I am eased,
And Jesus' Love, who angry God appeased.

 To God I have my will resign'd,
  To God I elevate my mind,
My ghostly guide has me Absolved, and I
Have nought to do, but pray, and love, and die.

 Good God me from delirium frees,
  My soul grows healthy by disease,
Towards independency I feel it spring,
And my own requiem now prepare to sing.

 My Jesus treats me as His friend,
  I long till I to Him ascend,
Though death stares on me frightful, pale, and grim,
My soul shall entertain him with a hymn.

 My God, my Love this soul sustains,
  And sweetens all my dying pains.
Thou, Lord, didst bitter death endure for me,
And hast from all death's terrors set me free.

 Sin only death had dreadful made,
  But since Thou hast our ransom paid,

Thou of his deadly sting dost death disarm,
He may my soul unloose, but cannot harm:

   Jesus when dead yet rose again,
     And from the grave began His reign,
His Soul and Body re-united were,
And flew to Heaven triumphant through the air.

   As the first fruits God's hallow'd due,
     To God were offer'd by the Jew;
Which in God's sight the priest was wont to wave,
And God to all the crop His blessing gave.

   Thus Jesus risen from the dead,
     On all men vital influence shed;
Death can no faithful souls of life deprive,
But by our First Fruit's rising shall revive.

   You, my dear flesh, till the great day
     Must to the worms become a prey,
This debt you to the lapse primeval owe,
Must humbly with submission undergo.

   You shall return to human ore,
     But God will you to life restore,
He'll register each atom of your dust,
And sort it at the rising of the just.

   As grain lies buried in the grave,
     Till it a resurrection have,
Then from the ground its lofty head uprears,
And with an hundred-fold increase appears.

Thus you'll to priſtine clay return,
  Till God remands you from your urn,
You'll the bright Form with rapture then behold,
To which God ſhall your ſcatter'd duſt remould.

Worms ſhall no more your limbs devour,
  In weakneſs ſown, you'll riſe in power;
From mortal you ſhall to immortal paſs,
To incorruption from corrupted maſs.

Your clay by the laſt fire calcined,
  Shall to ſpiritual be refined,
And like Bleſs'd Jeſus' glorious Body, bright,
Will fitted be to enter bliſsful light.

O'er death you'll then full conqueſt gain,
  And hymn the Love of the Lamb ſlain,
You'll, paſt all ſtorms, reach the celeſtial ſhore,
Your body glorified can die no more.

Were there no joys, in that high ſphere,
  Freedom from ſin would death endear;
God's lovers here their days in ſorrow ſpend,
While tempted boundleſs Goodneſs to offend.

To the laſt ſpark of vital flame,
  My lips ſhall gaſp out Jeſus' Name.

HOLY ORDER.

LOVE is the badge which Jesus' lovers wear,
Cemented daily by their mutual prayer;
To all who from our first-form'd sire descend,
Our loves, like God's, soft mercies should extend;
But saints to saints by heav'nly Love allied,
Are to a nobler love more strictly tied;
The Church like one sole family appear'd,
The young, like fathers aged saints revered,
Old saints, of Jesus' lambs took tender care,
Equals, like brethren might in love compare;
For public sins they weekly stations kept,
They fasted, pray'd, gave liberal alms, and wept;
What one enjoy'd was common to the rest,
One purse, one house, one table they possess'd;
One spirit seem'd to actuate the frame,
One faith, one love, one joy, one heav'nly aim;
All stranger saints found home where'er they went,
All would with tears the lapse of one lament;
They nursed the sick, they ev'ry want relieved,
Condoled and comforted the souls who grieved;
With charitable kisses seal'd their prayer,
The Rich, love-feasts would for the Poor prepare;
Even infidels their mutual love confess'd,
While they the grace which they admired oppress'd;
They visited the gaols and mines, where saints

Felt loathsome and calamitous restraints;
Warm prayers they made for martyrs, kiss'd their
   chains,
Brought ghostly cordials to allay their pains;
Meek martyrs, whom no outrage would provoke,
And for the villains pray'd who gave the stroke;
Saints dress'd the martyrs' wounds, and cleansed
   the gore,
Honour'd the marks of Jesus which they wore;
They fearless them attended to the stake,
Of their dear reliques sacred care to take;
With spices to embalm their hallow'd clay,
And to their graves with rev'rence to convey;
Of death saints lived in view, but not in dread,
Bless'd Jesus' Body was their Daily Bread;
They who the same both Faith and Love profess'd
Lived in dear sweet communion like the bless'd;
To praise, adore, love, hymn the Love divine,
Like saints in glory, was their chief design;
Heresies, Faith which Love excites, confound,
Schism, discords, raised love's harmony to drown'd,
But Jesus in His realm vice-gerents placed
To keep Faith uncorrupted, and Love chaste;
Who should of Jesus' pastoral Love partake,
And feed His flock beloved for Love's sake;
Who should from Him alone commissions hold,
And be successive pastors to His fold.

   By Jesus' rules, His substitutes select,
   The hierarchy determined to erect;

They all inspired by universal vote,
Our Lord's own kinsman to the chair promote,
The humble James o'er Salem to preside,
And for that flock celestial food provide;
God to His Israel one High-priest assign'd
While to one nation He the Church confined;
With Priests, the temple who in course supplied,
And Levites, to more servile stations tied;
Of all the Church o'er Palestina spread,
Their great High-priest was God's vicarious head;
His hallow'd unction influenced the land,
And of their union was the sacred band;
All the united members thrice a year
Commanded were before him to appear;
He was their oracle, and he alone
Deputed was God's anger to atone;
One temple, priest, and altar, God ordain'd,
Which unity of faith and love maintain'd;
God-man, whose Love in gracious oceans stream'd,
Which had no shores, but the whole world redeem'd;
Our great, our sole archetypal High-priest,
When from the grave His Body was released,
Made through the vail supernal His ascent,
His Blood and Intercession to present;
A numerous high-priesthood then decreed,
For ever should His sovereign one succeed;
In great resorts to fix a pastoral chair,
To which the flock might for due aids repair;
The Spirit He on the first mission breathed,

To the whole race, His Truth, Peace, Love,
    bequeathed;
They in the Mother Church the fabric rear'd,
James firſt at helm the Church Judaic ſteer'd;
Parochial Prieſts were fix'd in every vill,
Who under him ſhould ſaving truth inſtil;
Deacons next choſen were on prieſts to tend,
And on the poor their pious labours ſpend;
All were obliged their Paſtor to revere,
The ſole intelligence who roll'd their ſphere;
And while with him in union they remain'd,
Their faith, peace, love, were ſteady and un-
    ſtain'd.

With the primeval Church thus Salem bleſs'd,
The lovely model gave to all the reſt;
Soon o'er the empire, and in lands remote,
High-prieſts were fix'd in all reſorts of note;
And while all ſouls to their high-prieſt adhered,
Sweet mutual love their ſpirits co-endear'd;
Each biſhop had bleſs'd Jeſus' keys, to lock,
Or open the Church entrance to his flock;
He faithful care of catechumens took,
Their growth in faith and love to overlook;
And when he thought them for Cummunion fit,
Would to the font, Love's candidates admit;
He, that their faith and love might grow adult,
Though luſt, the world, and hell, ſhould them
    inſult,
Impower'd by Jeſus, to their ſouls convey'd,

By Confirmation, supplemental aid;
He lovers to the Altar would invite,
To raise their love to a triumphant height;
Their love, by that Immortal Banquet fed,
To torture and to martyrdom was bred.
When wanton souls, who brake baptismal pact,
Would leagues with sin, the world, and hell contract;
The prelate the adulteress would call,
Then meekly mind her of her dangerous fall;
And warn'd, the spouse of Jesus would abjure,
And mourn for her adulteries impure;
He Penances restorative enjoin'd,
To mortify the sin, and purge the mind;
True lovers with their tears her lapse bewail'd,
And for her pardon humbly Heaven assail'd;
When all her satisfactions were complete,
She begg'd her Absolution at his feet;
All lovers seeing her rekindled love,
Joy'd for her here, as angels joy'd above;
But when bold sinners wholly Love disclaim'd,
Gave public scandals and the truth defamed,
Defied all sacred powers, and would endure
No one restorative to work their cure;
He, the apostates, jealous for his God,
Devoted to the sin-avenging rod;
Against their entrance shut the temple door,
And to infernal fury gave them o'er;
Just doom of souls to Heavenly Love unchaste,
Down to the diabolic state debased.

Each paſtor, that in his large flock he might
Raiſe and augment celeſtial Love and Light,
Choice under-ſhepherds carefully ordain'd,
Their chief and they the burden co-ſuſtain'd;
They ſheep and lambs with ſacred doctrine fed,
They nouriſh'd them with Euchariſtic Bread;
They in aſſemblies offer'd prayer and praiſe,
In ſtudying holy writ ſpent all their days;
They bright examples of true lovers gave,
They ſtrove all others to enflame and ſave;
They, as they ſaw the tempers of their ſheep,
Would comfort, warm, reprove, pray, joy, or
  weep;
The ſtate of every ſoul they juſtly weigh'd,
And to their wants due applications made;
Wont tenderly ſaints dying to frequent,
Their love, by their own fervours, to foment;
Saints' tears were by their Abſolution dried,
And lovers in their arms reſignedly died;
They of each ſoul committed to their truſt,
Gave their high prieſt accounts minute and juſt.

 Each biſhop rules took care, to his own tribe,
For decency and order to preſcribe;
And of his prieſts a council oft to hold,
The endleſs bliſs conſulting of his fold;
All might adviſe, his voice ſuperior ſway'd,
All to his negative due deference paid;
When needful, he would ſolemn faſts indict,

Religiously observed in his district;
Of all the hallow'd treasure he stood charged,
Which by their weekly offering saints enlarged;
The priests, church, poor, due portions from him
    gain'd,
Himself he to just competence restrain'd;
What lovers gave on lovers he bestow'd;
But alms to lovers in distress o'erflow'd;
Pride, avarice, pomp, ambition, then were fled,
Wealth never was a prelate's aim, but dread.

    Good prelates shall Love Catholic maintain,
In aristocracy spiritual reign;
Till the Church east and west asunder start,
And into various subdivisions part;
Baptismal faith shall yet be kept entire,
Though all hell-powers to ruin it conspire;
Some pastors their commissions may exceed,
Unnecessary things may be decreed;
Men's minds may differ, yet in faith agree,
From damning error, not from frailty free;
Two sister churches may have different rite,
While in Love Catholic they both unite;
The saints primeval the idea are,
By them the Church must all her practice square;
They came together, for God's guidance pray'd,
Choice of Matthias for cursed Judas made;
And pastors, when they saw a vacant chair,
A lover for successor chose by prayer;
And if a bishop faith or love betray'd,

True bishops met, the Judas to degrade;
All vacancies with lovers they supplied,
Who the loved flock with tender zeal should guide.
Apostles, though inspired, when doubts arose,
A council summon'd difference to compose;
Conducted by the Spirit they implored,
Faith, Peace, and Love, they to the Church re-
   stored;
The future Church shall the same method use,
When error shall its pestilence diffuse;
And should inferior councils strive in vain,
Bold errors to suppress or to restrain,
The Synods Catholic where all convene,
Shall still the storm, and keep the Church serene;
For order's sake one primacy may claim,
But none at a supremacy must aim;
All like vice-gerents of bless'd Jesus are,
And in fraternal love have equal share;
From Jesus, bishops equal keys derive,
And Jesus-like, must not for empire strive.

MATRIMONY.

(*Prince Edmund seeks council of S. Hubert.*)

O FATHER; you can unperplex my mind,
  My realm are for my marriage all inclined;
I love, but know not who she is, or where,
And to discover either, I despair;

Defpairing, I in celibate would live,
Since I my heart can to no other give;
I feel too great a load in cares of ftate,
Cares conjugal may much increafe the weight;
More hours I fain would in my clofet fpend,
Pure Virgins beft, the affairs of Heaven attend.

 Son, faid the faint, if you both lives compare,
Both different ways may in God's favour fhare;
Prayers, meditations, and intentions pure,
A heart which no temptations can allure;
Self-abnegation, and a confcience clear,
Enduring no one luft to domineer;
All graces which Incarnate God enjoin'd,
The married equally with Virgins bind.

 Contemplatives have eafy loads to bear,
Freer from trouble and diftracting care,
Loofe from the world, and difembroil'd from fenfe
Their prayers may longer be, and more intenfe:
To no relations Virgins have a tie
To pluck them back, but unmolefted die;
A Virgin Prieft the Altar beft attends,
Our Lord that ftate commands not, but com-
  mends.
Saints in both ftates have purity retain'd,
Both dear to God, have the like glory gain'd:
The man whom God for bufinefs has defign'd,
In bufinefs may keep folitude of mind;
Retirement and converfe may interchafe,

That, will repair what this, may oft deface.
He when on public of his time profuse,
May in his oratory turn recluse;
Converse and business God's appointments are,
They, well conducted, please as well as prayer;
If business should the length of prayer abate,
A warm devotion makes it up in weight;
High education and command of time,
A liberal soul with wealth and power sublime,
Work charitable wonders far and near,
And wrought by none who in public disappear.

 Both solitude and business open lie
To Satan's spite, both must keep watchful eye:
In this, the world a thousand various snares,
For every passion, every sense prepares,
Ill maxims, customs, company there sway,
Pride, vanity and lust our souls betray:
That, often is exposed to Satan's wiles,
Who the imagination oft defiles,
Sloth, tedium, and self-love, if there they meet,
They form a prison rather than retreat:
This Martha chose, with a too anxious heart;
In that, calm Mary chose the better part;
Had they both interchangeably combined,
By composition both had been refined;
In Jesus co-harmoniously both join,
And form th' idea of a life divine;
Whole nights alone His soul to Heaven aspired,
He to the desert forty days retired;

For prayer would unfrequented mountains climb,
In solitude devout oft spent His time;
And yet from doing good He ne'er refrain'd,
But a converse promiscuous entertain'd.
Thus in the world we must the world exile,
And to the world our closet reconcile.
Great saints, like Jesus, in the world may dwell,
The timorous rather shelter in a cell:
Both must co-equally on God rely,
Who only can proportion'd aids supply.

God the chaste, social, happy life ordain'd,
In innocence, when man was yet unstain'd;
Even Paradise was but a lonely place
Till God sent Eve to Adam's dear embrace:
Heaven by virginity would empty stand,
'Tis marriage peoples all the blissful land;
Prescribed as gentle med'cine to the just,
To allay the calentures of baneful lust:
God His first blessing on that state bestow'd,
That blessing down to all successions flow'd;
In pairs on the dread ark the cherubs wait,
In pairs the seraphs tend God's Throne of State;
We from their Temple-union humbly guess,
That they like friendships now in Heaven possess;
Both charity and friendship are at height
In married saints, who in chaste love unite.

APPENDIX.

First Version of the Three Hymns, by the Author of the Manual of Prayers for the Use of the Scholars of Winchester College. From the edition of 1700.

A MORNING HYMN.

AWAKE, my soul, and with the sun
Thy daily stage of duty run;
Shake off dull sloth, and early rise
To pay thy morning sacrifice.

Redeem thy mispent time that's past,
Live this day, as if 'twere thy last:
To improve thy talent take due care,
'Gainst the great Day thyself prepare.

Let all thy converse be sincere,
Thy conscience as the noonday clear;
Think how all-seeing God thy ways
And all thy secret thoughts surveys.

Influenced by the Light Divine,
Let thy own light in good works shine:
Reflect all Heaven's propitious ways
In ardent love and cheerful praise.

Wake and lift up thyself, my heart,
And with the angels bear thy part,
Who all night long unwearied sing
Glory to the Eternal King.

I wake, I wake, ye heavenly choir,
May your devotion me inspire,
That I like you my age may spend,
Like you may on my God attend.

May I like you in God delight,
Have all day long my God in sight,
Perform like you my Maker's Will,
O may I never more do ill.

Had I your wings, to Heaven I'd fly,
But God shall that defect supply,
And my soul, wing'd with warm desire,
Shall all day long to Heaven aspire.

Glory to Thee, Who safe hast kept
And hast refresh'd me whilst I slept;
Grant, Lord, when I from death shall wake
I may of endless Light partake.

I would not wake, nor rise again,
Even Heaven itself I would disdain,
Wert not Thou there to be enjoy'd,
And I in hymns to be employ'd.

Heaven is, dear Lord, where'er Thou art,
O never then from me depart;

For to my foul 'tis hell to be
But for one moment without Thee.

Lord, I my vows to Thee renew,
Scatter my fins as morning dew,
Guard my firft fprings of thought and will,
And with Thyfelf my fpirit fill.

Direct, control, fuggeft this day
All I defign, or do, or fay;
That all my powers, with all their might,
In Thy fole glory may unite.

Praife God, from Whom all bleffings flow,
Praife Him all creatures here below,
Praife Him above, ye angelic hoft,
Praife Father, Son, and Holy Ghoft.

AN EVENING HYMN.

GLORY to Thee, my God, this night,
For all the bleffings of the light;
Keep me, O keep me, King of kings,
Under Thy own Almighty Wings.

Forgive me, Lord, for Thy dear Son,
The ill that I this day have done,
That with the world, myfelf and Thee,
I, ere I fleep, at peace may be.

Teach me to live, that I may dread
The grave as little as my bed;
Teach me to die, that so I may
Triumphing rise at the last day.

O may my soul on Thee repose,
And with sweet sleep mine eyelids close;
Sleep that may me more vigorous make
To serve my God when I awake.

When in the night I sleepless lie,
My soul with heavenly thoughts supply,
Let no ill dreams disturb my rest,
No powers of darkness, me molest.

Dull sleep, of sense me to deprive,
I am but half my days alive;
Thy faithful lovers, Lord, are grieved
To lie so long, of Thee bereaved.

But though sleep o'er my frailty reigns,
Let it not hold me long in chains,
And now and then let loose my heart
Till it an Hallelujah dart.

The faster sleep the sense does bind
The more unfetter'd is the mind;
O may my soul, from matter free,
Thy unveil'd Goodness waking see!

O when shall I in endless day
For ever chase dark sleep away,

And endleſs praiſe with the Heavenly choir
Inceſſant ſing, and never tire?

You, my bleſt Guardian, whilſt I ſleep,
Cloſe to my bed your vigils keep,
Divine Love into me inſtil,
Stop all the avenues of ill.

Thought to thought with my ſoul converſe,
Celeſtial joys to me rehearſe,
And in my ſtead all the night long
Sing to my God a grateful ſong.

Praiſe God, from Whom all bleſſings flow,
Praiſe Him all creatures here below,
Praiſe Him above, ye angelic hoſt,
Praiſe Father, Son, and Holy Ghoſt.

A MIDNIGHT HYMN.

LORD, now my ſleep does me forſake,
The ſole poſſeſſion of me take,
Let no vain fancy me illude,
No one impure deſire intrude.

Bleſt angels! while we ſilent lie,
Your hallelujahs ſing on high,

You, ever wakeful near the Throne
Proſtrate, adore the Three in One.

I now awake, do with you join,
To praiſe our God in hymns divine:
With you in Heaven I hope to dwell,
And bid the night and world farewell.

My ſoul, when I ſhake off this duſt,
Lord, in Thy Arms, I will entruſt;
O make me Thy peculiar care,
Some heavenly manſion me prepare.

Give me a place at Thy ſaints' feet,
Or ſome fall'n angel's vacant ſeat,
I'll ſtrive to ſing as loud as they
Who ſit above in brighter day.

O may I always ready ſtand
With my lamp burning in my hand,
May I in ſight of Heaven rejoice,
Whene'er I hear the Bridegroom's voice.

Glory to Thee in light array'd,
Who light Thy dwelling-place haſt made,
An immenſe ocean of bright beams
From Thy all-glorious Godhead ſtreams.

The ſun in its meridian height,
Is very darkneſs in Thy ſight:
My ſoul O lighten and inflame
With thought and love of Thy great Name.

A MIDNIGHT HYMN.

Bleſt Jeſu, Thou on Heaven intent,
Whole nights haſt in devotion ſpent;
But I, frail creature, ſoon am tired,
And all my zeal is ſoon expired.

My ſoul, how canſt thou weary grow
Of antedating Heaven below,
In ſacred hymns and Divine Love,
Which will eternal be above?

Shine on me, Lord, new life impart,
Freſh ardours kindle in my heart;
One ray of Thy all-quickening Light
Diſpels the ſloth and clouds of night.

Lord, leſt the tempter me ſurpriſe,
Watch over Thine own ſacrifice,
All looſe, all idle thoughts caſt out,
And make my very dreams devout.

Praiſe God, from Whom all bleſſings flow,
Praiſe Him all creatures here below,
Praiſe Him above, ye angelic hoſt,
Praiſe Father, Son, and Holy Ghoſt.

INDEX OF FIRST LINES.

	PAGE
ALL praise to Thee, great God, we owe	83
All praise to Thee, my God, this night	3
All who to Jesus came	362
A Song of Jesus I design	152
As to myself, to be to others kind	65
As when a visit emperors intend	16
Awake, my soul, and with the sun	1
Awake, my soul, and with the sun	455
Bless'd Andrew! in your call we trace	318
Bless'd angels, whether you on high	400
Bless'd hour! when I was born again	425
Bless'd Jesus from His radiant cloud descends	188
Bless'd Jesus, on the Cross in boundless pain	179
Bless'd Jesus, Thy propitious Heart	276
Bless'd Jesus, who didst wondrous grief sustain	120
Bless'd Spirit, aid me, while I sing	314
Blest Spirit, who the woman's Offspring led	92
Blest Spirit, who on Jesus' sacred Head	104
Celestial harps prepare	17
Ere the intelligence, from nothing rear'd	112
Eternal Dove, by Jesus sent	195

INDEX OF FIRST LINES.

	PAGE
Fair Antioch, the rich, the great	405
Faith, hope, and fear within my breaſt	28
Falſe world, I'll you no more endure	295
For your converſion, holy Mark	352
Friend, for my pain your moan forbear	82
From Adam all, to thoſe who ſtay	218
Gabriel to Daniel, when at prayer	369
Glory to Thee, my God, this night	457
God a command upon me lays	7
God-man, Who on the dolorous Tree	163
God, Who is pleaſed bright Angels down to ſend	58
Great Day! to mortals kept unknown	13
Great God Triune, enthroned above	227
Hark, O my ſoul, the trumpet blows	86
How Godhead to our human fleſh was join'd	149
In univerſal dread I waked	75
I ſing, my God, the Saint this day	22
Jeſu, I in Thy Goſpel read	429
Jeſu, Who, man in bliſs to re-inſtate	127
Let others ſail the world about	254
Lord, now my ſleep does me forſake	459
Lord 'tis not in Thy Church alone	73
Love is the badge which Jeſus' lovers wear	444
Melt me all o'er, eternal, gracious Dove	138
More bleſs'd to give than to receive	259
Moſes on high twice twenty days	271
My faith and hope, your powers unite	199
My God, now I from ſleep awake	5
My God, ſince I in exile here	244
My God, Thy wiſe, propitious Will	117

INDEX OF FIRST LINES.

	PAGE
My God, 'tis by Thy sweet supports	69
My Jesus, since Thy Love Divine	251
My Jesus, Thou all lovely art	264
My prayers for Love to Heaven directly fly	305
Next to the name of devil, none	339
Nor eye, ear, thought, can take the height	311
Of all the conquests which Thy grace	326
Of all the gifts which Heaven design'd	299
Of all the monsters which appear'd	297
Of all the solemn days	334
Of all who e'er with heart unfeign'd	101
O Father; you can unperplex my mind	451
Of Jesus' brethren to take care	198
O foolish heart, which often strays	257
O Fountain of all Grace Divine	211
Oft has my mind took flight	291
O Great God-man! my grovelling spirit raise	47
Oh, I shall ne'er forget the happy hour	222
O holy Church, whom we respect	411
O Jesu! with Thy Spirit fill my breast	279
O Life, what art thou? oft I try	247
Our Lord, when Simon to Him came	374
Say, blessed angels, say	165
See, see, my flesh, death with his dart	439
See there a Jew from th' hallow'd town	274
Soon as great God in flesh enshrined	34
Soul, when your flesh dissolves to dust	67
The king who with just title reigns	194
The loved disciple, full of Love Divine	237
There is a vale of tears which mountains bound	432
This morn, bless'd Saint, our zeal devout	387
Those days I often call to mind	287

	PAGE
Though votaries, whom our Lord defign'd	394
Thrice happy man whofe foul is ftaid	303
Thy Juftice, Lord, my fong excites	78
'Tis, Lord, Thy Will that all mankind	39
Unction the Chriftian name implies	427
Upon the octave of Thy birth	43
We, like the fly, muft from the world retreat	99
When Adam finn'd, and all his line	267
Whene'er my voice of Jefus fings	191
When God from Heaven came down	53
When God in flefh would be enfhrined	382
When God the radiant Gabriel chofe	345
When Jefus notice gave	322
When Jefus truth celeftial taught	173
When our redemption was complete	208
When Solomon the Temple rear'd	357
When the Archangel's trump fhall found	11
Whether I will or no, I find	308
Ye fpirits ever-blefs'd	418
You bleffed angels at the Throne	242
You Friend of God, for God's dear fake	233

CHISWICK PRESS:—PRINTED BY WHITTINGHAM AND WILKINS, TOOKS COURT, CHANCERY LANE.

www.ingramcontent.com/pod-product-compliance
Lightning Source LLC
Chambersburg PA
CBHW051857300426
44117CB00006B/430